Constructing Identity

TRANSATLANTIC STUDIES
IN BRITISH AND
NORTH AMERICAN CULTURE

Edited by Marek Wilczyński

VOLUME 18

PETER LANG
EDITION

Agatha Handley

Constructing Identity

Continuity, Otherness and Revolt in the Poetry of Tony Harrison

PETER LANG
EDITION

Bibliographic Information published by the Deutsche Nationalbibliothek
The Deutsche Nationalbibliothek lists this publication in the Deutsche Nationalbibliografie; detailed bibliographic data is available in the internet at http://dnb.d-nb.de.
Library of Congress Cataloging-in-Publication Data
Names: Handley, Agata, 1979- author.
Title: Constructing identity : continuity, otherness and revolt in the poetry of Tony Harrison / Agata Handley.
Description: Frankfurt am Main ; New York : Peter Lang, 2016. | Series: Transatlantic studies in British and North American culture ; 18 | Includes bibliographical references.
Identifiers: LCCN 2016033981 | ISBN 9783631658819
Subjects: LCSH: Harrison, Tony, 1937---Criticism and interpretation.
Classification: LCC PR6058.A6943 Z65 2016 | DDC 821/.914--dc23 LC record available at https://lccn.loc.gov/2016033981

The publication was supported by the University of Łódź.
Cover image: © Paweł Kwiatkowski
Technical editor: Karolina Goławska
Reviewer: Dorota Filipczak

ISSN 2364-2882
ISBN 978-3-631-65881-9 (Print)
E-ISBN 978-3-653-05198-8 (E-Book)
E-ISBN 978-3-631-69659-0 (EPUB)
E-ISBN 978-3-631-69660-6 (MOBI)
DOI 10.3726/978-3-653-05198-8

Peter Lang – Frankfurt am Main · Bern · Bruxelles · New York · Oxford · Warszawa · Wien

This publication has been peer reviewed.

www.peterlang.com

For Grażyna, Robert and Paweł

The author would like to give special thanks to:
Prof. Jerzy Jarniewicz, Prof. Joanna Jabłkowska, Prof. Dorota Filipczak,
Prof. Jacek Gutorow, Ed Lowczowski, Andrew Tomlinson

Contents

Introduction

"The whole view North" 11

Chapter One

"Correct your maps: Newcastle is Peru!" Continuity of Exploration and Exploitation in *The Loiners* 33

Chapter Two

"Wherever did you get your talent from?" Continuity of Poetic Heritage in *The School of Eloquence* 67

Chapter Three

"The still too living dead." Continuity of Mourning in the Selected Elegies from *The School of Eloquence* 101

Chapter Four

"Half versus half, the enemies within." Changing Patterns of Revolt in *v.* 133

Chapter Five

"This frightening mask." Continuity of Poetic Gaze in Selected War Poems 163

Conclusion

"How have you been useful for the polis?" 187

Bibliography 195

Introduction

"The whole view North"

Born in 1937, Tony Harrison is a poet who crossed the boundary dividing the English working and middle classes. He was one of those children who, due to educational reform,[1] received state scholarships and went to grammar schools, and as a result, had the opportunity to become the students representing the first generation of the working class of the North at university level. Reading Harrison's poetry, it seems justifiable to say that his poetic path started not when he published his first poem but much earlier, in 1948, when, as a "scholarship boy," he crossed the threshold of Leeds Grammar School, finding himself from that moment onwards "at the friction point of two cultures,"[2] as Richard Hoggart put it (2005: 239). This was a crucial moment, a triggering point that changed the trajectory of Harrison's

---

1 Joanna Bourke comments on the British education system in "Working-Class Cultures in Britain 1890–1960" providing a useful background for understanding the situation in which children like Harrison found themselves:

> By the 1940s, it was clear … that the education system was in crisis and radical reforms were needed. The Education Act of 1944 was advertised as 'Free Secondary Education for All'. Based on the principle that every child should be educated 'according to his age, aptitude and ability', Butler's Act [1944] abolished tuition fees at state maintained schools, raised the leaving age to 15 years, and introduced the tripartite system of secondary schools (grammar, modern and technical), which in the 1950s became bipartite (grammar via the 11-plus, and secondary modern)…. Despite these attempts to promote greater social equality in access to education, class differentials persisted…. Educational policy ignored some of the fundamental reasons for the under-representation of working-class children in higher education. Scholarships relieved only a portion of the educational burden…. Schools within working-class areas were underfunded. (1994: 117–120)

2 "Until the 1970s, it was largely agreed that the working class was characterised by distinctive cultural values and practices which stood outside and in opposition to those of the middle and upper classes. A series of landmark studies of working-class culture, especially those carried out between the 1950s and the late 1970s … emphasised the distinctive values and solidarities seen as characteristic of working-class life. Examples include studies such as Thompson's *The Making of the English Working Class* (1963), Hoggart's *The Uses of Literacy* (1957), Williams's *The Long Revolution* (1961), Dennis et al.'s *Coal is Our Life* (1956), Goldthrope et al.'s *The Affluent Worker* (1968) and Willis's *Learning to Labour* (1977)." (Savage et al. 2005: 97)

life, opening doors to the world of eloquence and simultaneously depriving him of a clear identification with the place he grew out of, and one to which he will be returning again and again in his verse, continually "Facing North," as one of his titles asserts. In this poem, Harrison describes "the act of poetic composition" as "luminous O of … light, itself illuminating" (Byrne 1998: 177) darkness.

> God knows why of all rooms I'd to choose
> the dark one facing North for me to write,
> ….
> The window's open to the winter's chill,
> to air, to breezes and strong gusts that blow
> my paper lantern nothing will keep still
> and let me make things happen in its O.
> ….
> Now when the wind flays my wild garden of its green
> ….
> and starts the lightbulb swinging to and fro,
> and keeps it swinging, switched off, back and forth,
> I feel the writing room I'm leaving grow,
> dark, and then darker with the whole view North. (Facing North 1–2, 17–20, 41, 45–48)

Harrison's description of the act of creation can be explained in relation to the words of Barbara Skarga, who in her book *Tożsamość i Różnica*, comments on Emmanule Levinas' thought:

> 'Light'—writes Levinas—'is what makes a given thing different from what I am, and in the same time as if it came from me.' An illuminated object is *something we encounter* but precisely because it is illuminated, we simultaneously encounter it *as if it came from us* … Therefore seeing, capturing something in the light is identical not only with … *understanding of it* but also with *exerting control over it*.[3] To see is—to make something one's own, to include it in the realm of our *knowledge* and our *power*, it is to lose the awareness of otherness.[4] (Skarga 2009: 172–173)

3 Emphasis added by the author of this book.

4 My translation of:
'Światło'—pisze Levinas—'jest tym, przez co rzecz jakaś jest inna niż Ja, a jednocześnie jakby pochodziła ze mnie.' … Przedmiot oświetlony jest zarazem czymś, co napotykamy, lecz właśnie dlatego, że jest oświetlony, spotyka się go, jak gdyby pochodził od nas … Widzenie bowiem, a więc uchwytywanie czegoś w świetle, jest tożsame nie tylko z jego rozumieniem … lecz także z panowaniem nad nim. Widzieć—to uczynić swoim, to włączyć w obszar własnej wiedzy i własnej władzy, to zatracić świadomość inności. (Skarga 2009: 172–173)

In the poem, light actually illuminates lines of text—something familiar as it quite literally comes from the speaker but also from something other than the Self, something that must be encountered and confronted by the one who wants to read it. "The act of poetic composition," (Byrne 1998: 177) whose metaphorical rendering in the poem is based on the opposition between light and darkness, is, first of all, the act of seeing. The idea refers to the broader concept which recurs in Harrison's work, namely that the poet's unflinching gaze, maintained even in the face of the atrocities of history, and a continuous observation of reality are necessary elements of literary craft. Other necessary elements are mastering eloquence and *exerting control* over a language which quite literally, Harrison says, serves as a tool of power, since a "tongueless man gets his land took" (Harrison National Trust 17) and loses influence over his own fate.

In the third stanza of the poem, the northern wind swings the lamp, the circle of light loses its shape, chaos replaces cosmos, and suddenly, in a fashion that brings to mind the metaphysical imagery of John Donne and Andrew Marvell, the room grows into a universe with "planets hurled/… off their courses" where "there is no gravity to hold the world" (Facing North 26–28). Luke Spencer comments on this sudden change of perspective, suggesting that in the poem, the North gains a broader, more universal meaning:

> In the meditation/lucubration … the North is extended beyond its typical English association—of dourness, ugliness, lack of compromise—to encompass an older, more archetypal image of all that has immemorially threatened human comfort, not to say complacency. 'The whole view North,' with its darker perspective on both past and present is an essential element in Harrison's vision. His continuing exposure to the chilling but bracing challenge reinforces his artistic survival skills. The unlit, draughty writing-room … is a metonymy for his continuing—intermittent but unbreakable—commitment to facing the puzzlement and anguish by which humanity has always been beset. (Spencer 1994: 100)

The circle of light shed by a lamp hanging over the poet's desk in his writing room, which opens to the dark and cold North, marks the boundaries within which his writing takes place. The source of light enables the speaker to "make things happen in its O" (Facing North 20) but it is the surrounding darkness that gives definition to the glowing shape. Harrison's writing acquires much of its form from the pressure exerted by his past, or, to use his own words, by the "background material"[5] extracted like coal from the history of the working-class North, which slowly sinks into oblivion. Darkness is the North and the North is darkness, and facing it means not only being always alert to its presence, but also taking on the

5 "Background Material" is the title of one of his poems from *The School of Eloquence.*

challenge of accepting a northern heritage, however impenetrable and oblique it may seem. As Byrne suggests, "the poem evokes not just a landscape but a psychological terrain" (1998: 177) which is stressed by the choice of the epigraph, the words of Louis MacNeice[6] "The North begins inside" (1937: 250). MacNeice's statement "emphasizes Northerness as a state of mind and feeling rather than a simple physical origin or location" (Spencer 1994: 100) and turns the act of facing North into a self-exploratory journey.

The starting point of the analysis is the book proposed by Helga Geyer-Ryan, a researcher of Harrison's poetry, which holds that the mature Harrison is a poet endowed with "differential identity" because he acquires his raw poetic material from culturally and politically different spheres[7] (1988: 210). Joanna Bourke writes that "working-class scholars found themselves in danger of being estranged from relatives, neighbours, and friends"[8] (1994: 120) and to support her statement, quotes Valerie Walkerdine, a working-class girl who, like the young Tony Harrison, received a scholarship and went to grammar school. Her recollections reveal that the idea of becoming a stranger to the working-class community was very closely connected with acquiring new pronunciation. Speaking the language which belonged to "them" was perceived as form of a betrayal of working-class values:

> They held out a dream. Come, they told me. It is yours. You are chosen. They didn't tell me, however, that for years I would no longer feel any sense of belonging, nor any sense of safety. That I didn't belong in the new place, any more than I now belong in the old. So around every corner of apparent choice lurked doubt and uncertainty. My mother described its pejorative connotations as typified by a change of accent which she referred to as 'lasting and pasting'. The fear in this working-class morality of putting on airs and graces was the fear of being found to be an impostor. The terror was not a simple matter

6 The quotation comes from Louis MacNeice's 'Epilogue for W.H. Auden' which appeared in *Letters from Iceland* published by Faber & Faber in 1937. The book comprises different texts written by Auden and MacNeice during their journey to Iceland which they made in 1936.

7 "An example of this may be Harrison's tendency to combine simplicity of utterance characteristic for everyday speech of the working-class community of Leeds with refined forms which respect all the rules of traditional poetics" 'Przykładem może być tutaj częste u Harrisona łączenie prostoty wypowiedzi charakterystycznej dla mowy potocznej robotniczego środowiska Leeds z wyrafinowaniem formy respektującej wszelkie rygory tradycyjnej poetyki'. (Zadura: 2009 My translation)

8 The process of entering a different class as a result of having access to education, becoming "unfixed, mobile, in-between" (Medhurst 2000: 20) proves to be an important topic for numerous cultural-studies scholars (P. Mahony and C. Zmroczek, D. Reay, B. Skeggs, C. Steedman), many of them coming from a working class background.

> of working-class pride. It was all right to talk like that if you had a right to belong to that class. (qtd in Bourke 1994: 120)

Although the story of Harrison's alienation was to a certain extent similar[9], since the "*rite de passage* by which he became a scholar-poet" (Roberts 2007: 217) introduced him into a new language, his writing has nevertheless remained in accordance with Ted Hughes's belief that "whatever other speech you grow into … your dialect stays alive in a sort of inner freedom" (Hughes 1980: 202). What Harrison adds to this statement is that this freedom can never be taken for granted but must be continually earned and protected with "elbow grease,/ deep thought, long practice and much sweat" (Facing North 33–34). Not fate, nor chance, but "years of struggle" (Harrison "Facing North" 25) formed Harrison's mature poetry. As Geyer-Ryan emphasizes, although eloquence and erudition as well as the knowledge of Greek and Latin[10] alienated Harrison from the working community of Leeds, they did not have the power to drive the language of periphery out of his poetry (1988: 207–217). On the contrary, in his poetry, Greek and Latin co-exist

---

9 See for example an autobiographical poem entitled "Me Tarzan": "Outside the whistled gang-call, *Twelfth Street Rag* /…./ He shoves the frosted attic skylight, shouts: / *Ah bloody can't ah've gorra Latin prose.* / His bodiless head that's poking out's / like patriarchal Cissy-bleeding-ro's" (1, 13–16). The poem focuses on the alienation of a scholarship boy from his peers, a social phenomenon described by Brian Jackson and Dennis Marsden in a relatively early publication on the education of working-class children (*Education and the Working Class* was first published 1962) where the path to eloquence is presented as a process marked by a dramatic, either-or choice:

> The children who lasted the full grammar school course …. where those who …. accepted the new school with its different values …. new manners, new friends, new accents, new knowledge …. it had meant a rejection … of the life of the 'neighbourhood' …. A minority of the survivors came from those children who had declared for the neighbourhood and against the grammar school. (1986: 171–172)

10 In Leeds Harrison studied classical languages and he always stresses the importance of Greek heritage as a source of inspiration, values and ideas. As Neil Astley writes in "The Wizard of [uz]," the reason why "Homer and the Greek tragedians have been so important to him" is because "they gave … [him] a means of confronting horrors which have silenced other twentieth-century writers" (Astley 12: 1991). Harrison gives an insight into this idea in a radio broadcast called "The Memory of Troy":

> The ancient Greek plays were about the primacy of language, how language was able to express *everything*, grapple with *all* the worst things that we can imagine … Language which is rhythmical and spellbinding can draw people's imagination *further* into horror and take them on that journey, make them *see* everything but make them feel that it's impossible to survive what they've witnessed.
> (BBC Radio 4, 24 August 1988)

with the Northern dialect, which advances from barbarian speech to the level of poetic discourse, traditionally conducted in Great Britain in Received Pronunciation, a version of English universally understood as a language norm, a standard.[11] The term Received Pronunciation is used here intentionally instead of a more general term, i.e., Standard English, since Harrison's poetry refers persistently both formally and thematically to the spoken language (Barker 1991: 46). According to Barker, like William Wordsworth,

> Harrison intends his poems to be read aloud … Harrison's speech, for all its considered art, also aims to communicate very directly and with all the urgency of W. H. Auden's thirties statement: 'All I have is voice / To undo the folded lie.' (Barker 1991: 46)

The lie which must be exposed is manufactured by the advocates of RP, who consider it to be the only version of English pronunciation worthy of respect.[12] In

---

11 Mugglestone gives a definition of a standard given by William Enfield in *A Familiar Treatise on Rhetoric* in 1809, which, despite its age, is still relevant in the context of speech appropriateness: "A standard is that by which we ascertain the value of things of the same kind; so a standard weight is that by which we try the justness of all other weights" (1809: 5). As Mugglestone asserts, the importance of being able to adhere to the standard stretches far beyond the mere issue of clear communication:

> In popular (as well as prescriptive) beliefs, a standard variety—of pronunciation as much as anything else—was similarly to incorporate evaluative mechanisms of this order though the relevant values were, in connotative terms, rarely to be those of language alone. Extralinguistic images of 'elegance', 'propriety', 'politeness', and 'refinement' are regularly accorded to its use as well as extended to its users. Images of 'class', and 'status', 'vulgarity' or 'incorrectness', frequently surround the act of speech. Evaluation, in contexts such as these, tends to take on the nature of social response, fusing with the prejudices and preconceptions of society in its own notions of what is 'good' and 'bad', 'right' or 'wrong' (2007: 50).

12 For further discussion on the status of dialect vs. standard, see a book by John Edwards entitled *Language and Identity*. Harrison's approach to the issue is consistent with the opinion expressed by Edwards who writes:

> As with languages, dialects cannot be seen, linguistically, in terms of better or worse. However, while there may be (relatively) few people who would argue that French is better than English, the idea that Oxford English is better than Cockney remains a prejudice of broader appeal. 'Dialect' has long been used, of course, to denote a substandard deviation from some prestigious variety or more 'standard' form. Dictionary definitions have supported this view, with even the Oxford English Dictionary noting that dialect is 'one of the subordinate' forms or varieties of a language arising from 'local peculiarities'. In a sense this is correct to assume—as the definition would imply to many—that this 'subordinate' status has any inherent linguistic basis. (2009: 65)

such poems as "Them and [uz]" RP functions as an indicator of the social position of the speaker, a norm imposed by the institutions representing the class which is economically and culturally superior. What enrages Harrison is the widespread tendency to present RP as synonymous with such notions as English literature and English tradition, which according to some scholars can be rendered only in a "non-localized accent" (Mugglestone 2007: 4). According to Mugglestone, the author of *Talking Proper*, "how one speaks has ... almost always been bound up with conceptions of social identity" (2007: 7). She notes, too, that the major change in perception of regional dialects took place in the nineteenth century (2007: 4). In the mid-18th century, there was still considerable tolerance towards local vernacular, and so "even if the metropolitan accent of the court possessed evident (and higher) prestige it had been seen as no disadvantage for either upper or under class to speak in a way influenced by their regional location" (2007: 4). This was, however, about to change. As Mugglestone states:

> Notions of an accent free from regional markers (and assimilation to this) had come to act as a dominant social symbol throughout the nation, forming the salient element in what the phonetician Henry Sweet was to define as '*class dialect*[13] more than a local dialect ... the *language of the educated*[14] all over Britain'. As he added, 'the best speakers of standard English are those whose pronunciation, and language generally, least *betray their locality*.'[15] As many writers stressed for the ostensible benefit of their readers, a 'provincial' accent was to be seen as incompatible with any ambitions for social acceptability, as well as with any pretensions to either 'culture' or 'cultivation.' (2007: 4)

What Geyer-Ryan describes as a "language schism in Harrison's life," (1988: 210) which manifests itself in a multi-layer conflict between the languages of the working class and the language of so called "high culture," is undoubtedly a source of unquestionable dynamics in the author's works. As Zadura states in Harrison's poetry, childhood memories are neighboured by contemporary, social and political events (Zadura: 2009) and thus on the autobiographical level, Harrison's poetic "I" is constantly facing a sense of language alienation from both social class spheres in which it functions, as a result, it reveals a broader, political issue of the supremacy of the privileged class. Harrison's poetic identity is "identity in process," never in "stability for it is a result of surprising compositions of elements that belong to socially and linguistically mutually exclusive worlds" (Geyer-Ryan 1988: 210). In Harrison's poems, the identity of the speaker is never an attribute,

13 This seems to be in accordance with the way in which Harrison understands Received Pronunciation.

14 Emphasis added by the author of this book.

15 Emphasis added by the author of this book.

nor a fixed state in which the poetic "I" remains. In other words, it is not "something given" but it constitutes "a task to be fulfilled in the … cultural domain" (Burzyńska 2006: 523)[16]. Zygmunt Bauman addresses the question of why the issue of identity is central to Harrison's poetry:

> [I]ssues are not noticed …., are not subject to debate of how they are to be correctly defined till they start to trouble us.… We start to notice phenomena when they become problems, when they attract our attention and require our conscious effort and when we know or think that the facts if they at all exist and how they look like depend on that effort. The perception of a phenomenon follows its prior formulation; the problem itself reflects the task that we set. (Bauman 1993: 7)[17]

This book does not claim that constructing identity is the only task that Harrison—a poet—undertakes throughout his poetry, nor does it claim that it is the only pertinent issue he tackles in his work. The book states, however, that the process of identity construction while passing from one social class to another has had a significant impact on the content and form of his poetry, its simultaneous locality, and universality, and that the issue of constructing identity is a central, multilayered and multidimensional theme pervading the body of Harrison's work.

It should be stated at this point that Harrison's poetry, so deeply rooted in the social realities of the English working class and defined by numerous critics as politically engaged and subject specific, has its own powerful, universal dimension, which can manifest itself among others in a concern with the problem of identity construction. As Misztal claims, the concept of identity, having been defined and redefined by many scholars, "advanced from what was once a peripheral term to a central and autonomous concept which plays a crucial role in explaining processes of modern times"[18] (2000: 143). Harrison's poetry, sensitive to the dynamics of the constantly changing social and political context, constitutes another voice in the polemic; it portrays the condition of a contemporary man trying to

---

16 My translation of: czymś danym … zadaniem do wykonania w sferze kultury. (Burzyńska 2006: 523)

17 My translation of: zjawisk nie zauważa się…., nie podejmuje się sporu o ich poprawne określenie—póki nie przysparzają one kłopotu …. Postrzegamy zjawiska, gdy stają się dla nas problemem, gdy wymagają koncentracji uwagi i świadomego wysiłku i gdy wiemy lub sądzimy, że od tego wysiłku zależy czy i jakie będą. Postrzeżenie zjawiska następuje po sformułowaniu problemu, sam zaś problem jest odblaskiem zadania, jakie sobie stawiamy. (Bauman 1993: 7)

18 My translation of: z terminu niegdyś peryferyjnego … awansowało do centralnego dzisiaj i autonomicznego pojęcia, które odgrywa kluczową rolę w wyjaśnianiu procesów współczesności. (2000: 143)

define an identity in a society whose structure does not allow for easy identification. The speakers of Harrison's poems often face a situation defined by a lack of one specific place which could become an explicit source of identity; and they seem to be affected by the symptom of "homelessness of an individual" (M. Buber, N. Luhmann) characteristic of the final decades of the twentieth century. Neither Harrison the poet nor Harrison the poetic persona, nor the other protagonists populating the works discussed in subsequent chapters, can be "firmly located in one single subsystem of society, but rather must be regarded a priori as socially displaced" (Luhmann 1986: 15). Their condition may be illustrated by Bauman's statement, who in *Modernity and Ambivalence* comments upon Luhmann's argument. Bauman claims that in modern society:

> All individuals are displaced, and displaced permanently, existentially – wherever they find themselves at the moment and whatever they may happen to do. They are *strangers* everywhere and, their efforts to the contrary notwithstanding, at all places. There is no single place in society in which they are truly at home and which can bestow upon them natural identity. Individual identity becomes therefore something to be yet attained (and presumably to be created) by the individual involved and never secured and definitely possessed – as it is constantly challenged and must be ever anew negotiated. (1991: 201)

Identity is such a broad-ranging term that to establish its definite boundaries is a task for a separate book, but for the sake of the following analysis it is worth bringing forth certain elements of identity research and definitions of the term. First of all, it must be stated that exploring the issues of identity in Harrison's work is so difficult because of the multiplicity of contexts into which identity is being inscribed by the poet himself, and because of the vagueness of the term, whose numerous definitions are constantly being challenged and reconstructed by new generations of scholars. One approach to identity which seems to be an appropriate point of reference for Harrison's treatment of the subject is that of Anthony Giddens, an approach commented on by Chris Barker in *Cultural Studies: Theory and Practice*:

> For Giddens (1991), self-identity is constituted by the ability to sustain a narrative about the self. This includes the capacity to build up a consistent feeling of biographical continuity. Identity stories attempt to answer the critical questions: What to do? How to act? Who to be? The individual attempts to construct a coherent identity narrative by which 'the self forms a trajectory of development from the past to an anticipated future (Giddens 1991: 75). Thus, 'Self-identity is not a distinctive trait, or even a collection of traits, possessed by the individual. It is the self as reflexivity understood by the person in terms of her or his biography'. (Barker 2008: 219)

Since "Identity is not something we have, nor an entity or a thing to which we can point" (Barker 2008: 219), it must be something "we do" or consciously construct, a task, a project, which takes part in a specific social context. The stories we tell are never born in the void but are formed in culturally, politically, socially affected spaces and this is confirmed by Harrison's poetry. The problem with identity construction which requires a constant negotiation of different boundaries, appropriation of privileges, and occupation of culturally marked spaces, lies, according to Harrison, precisely in the fact that "the resources we are able to bring into an identity project are historically and culturally distinct. They depend on the *situational power*[19] from which we derive our cultural competencies within specific cultural context" (Barker 2008: 2018). If identity is, in Harrison's rendering, an unstable and shifting notion, an attempt to find a definition that will serve as a reference point for further discussion seems to be even more elusive.

The word Identity comes from the Latin "idem" meaning "the same", and was already in use by speakers of English in the sixteenth century, in reference first and foremost to algebra and logic; and "has been associated with the perennial mind—body problem in philosophy since the time of Locke" (Gleason 1983: 911). Gleason turns to Robert Langbaum, who suggests in *The Mysteries of Identity: A Theme in Modern Literature* (1977) that psychological connotations were made in relation to identity only after the belief in so-called "unity of the self" was undermined by empiricist philosophers (Gleason 1983: 911). As Langbaum observes, Locke and Hume "use the word Identity to cast doubt on the unity of the self" and so the "traditional Christian conception of the soul," which had been supporting the concept for centuries, ceased to suffice as its support (Langbaum 1977: 25). Much more could be said about the early "tradition of the usage" which is undoubtedly "important" for our understanding of the concept of identity (Gleason 1983: 911). Nevertheless, the book concentrates on the poetry written from the sixties onward and it is perhaps not surprising that twentieth century theoretical thought on identity creates the most useful analytical perspective.

Gleason comments on the first usage of the term in the social sciences, and an important shift in the approach to the subject of identity, which turned from a peripheral issue into one of the most widely discussed problems of the last century:

> It came into use as a popular social-science term only in the 1950s. The contrast between its handling in two standard reference works dramatizes its novelty. The *International Encyclopedia of the Social Sciences*, published in 1968, carries a substantial article on 'Identity, Psychosocial.' The original *Encyclopedia of the Social Sciences*, published in the early 1930s, carries no entry at all for identity, and the entry headed "Identification" deals with fingerprinting and other techniques of criminal investigation. (1983: 910)

---

19 Emphasis added by the author of this book.

For Gleason our contemporary usage of the word begins with Erik H. Erikson, the author of the term "identity crisis,"[20] known perhaps most widely for his "study of identity formation in adolescence" (Cote and Levine 2002: 14). Erikson might not have completed "the construction of a comprehensive, multidimensional theory of identity" but he definitely "left a basic foundation to do so" (Cote and Levine 2002: 17). It is the recognition that identity is multidimensional (psychological, social and personal) that makes him a progressive thinker among his contemporaries (Cote and Levine 2002: 14) and that makes Erikson's approach relevant for our subsequent discussion. He locates identity "in the core of the individual" and at the same time "in the core of his communal culture," (Gleason 1983: 914) and believes that identity "involves an interaction between the interior development of the individual personality" and "the growth of a sense of selfhood that arises from participating in society" (Gleason 1983: 914). The "interplay" which occurs between "the social and the psychic" lies at the heart of identity and its *stability*:[21]

> That is, a person requires a viable social identity of some sort, and when the person *develops* a workable social identity based on commitments integrating the person into a particular culture, the psychological sense of temporal-spatial continuity—ego identity—should be nurtured. Once a sense of ego-identity *is established*, people are *buffered and protected from the vicissitudes of social conflicts and tension.*[22] We [i.e. Cote and Levine] believe this position describes identity formation in all cultures .... According to Erikson, people of all cultures can develop a sense of ego identity based on role validation and community integration ... especially when there is a lack of ambiguity regarding cultural beliefs. (Cote and Levine 2002: 16)

The multidimensional character of identity and the resulting relationship between "the social and the psychic" are especially interesting in light of Harrison's persistently repeated opinion that social (outer) and individual (inner) aspects

---

20 It is important to understand that he "originally conceived of the notion of identity crisis when treating identity loss among war-trauma victims during the Second World War. The traumas they had experienced created severe symptoms of confusion and identity dissociation" (cf. Steinberg & Shnall, 2000). After the war, he spotted the trend toward:

> problematic identities among the general population of Americans, and he wrote extensively about the identity crises that he saw as a rising epidemic in modern societies. He later drew a parallel between identity disturbances and the experiences of 'severely conflicted young people whose sense of confusion is due to a war within themselves' (Erikson, 1968: 17). He also wrote about the identity problems of adulthood that he saw to be ... responses to the vicissitudes and alienation associated with modern, technological societies (Cote and Levine 2002: 16).

21 Emphasis added by the author of this book.

22 Emphasis added by the author of this book.

of human existence are inextricably linked and that poetry is born largely out of the tension which their constant interplay creates. What is more, "three forms of continuity" (Cote and Levine 2002: 16) of which Erikson speaks: "a sense of sameness of the self with itself, interrelationships between the self and the other; and functional integrations between other and other" (Cote and Levine 2002: 16) pertain to the theme of identity in Harrison's verse:

> The first type of continuity is what Erikson had in mind when he coined the term "ego identity" (i.e. a sense of self-sameness over time). The second type of continuity pertains to a person's relations with others that maintain the stability of personal and social identities .... the third type of continuity represents the stability of relations in a particular community or group. When these community relations are stable, people's personal and social identities are safeguarded. (Cote and Levine 2002: 16)

For Harrison, all the continuities are constantly being questioned; he describes them as vague possibilities, objects of longing or reminiscence, postulates not certainties. It can be argued that in his poetry "these three forms of identity continuity are ... experienced as problematic for ... western societies" (Cote and Levine 2002: 16) and are often described in terms of lack and absence. Problematic identity, is in Harrison's verse, an unquestionable fact of the human condition, a source of anxiety but also a source of artistic drive. Different personas in Harrison's poetry (including the poetic "I" Tony Harrison) are never "protected from the vicissitudes of social conflicts and tensions" (Cote and Levine 2002: 16), their lives being shaped by the changing forces of history, political storms and social upheavals. The influence of the social seems to be so pervasive that there can be no certainty that "inner sameness and continuity"[23] (Gleason 1983: 918) can be maintained and this is one reason why Harrison's poetry, although in itself a "continuity focused" project, treats identity as a process, a conflict, a task, a "strategy"[24] (Cote and Levine 2002: 34) and a source of anxiety rather than a prerequisite for ease and stability. Despite the fact that "research ... moved beyond Erikson," his role in developing identity

---

23 According to Gleason:

> For Erikson the elements of interiority and continuity are indispensable .... Working within the Freudian tradition, he affirms that identity is somehow "located" in the deep psychic structure of the individual. Identity is shaped and modified by interaction between the individual and the surrounding social milieu, but, change and crisis notwithstanding, it is at bottom an "accrued confidence" in the "inner sameness and continuity" of one's own being (1983: 918).

24 It can be argued that Harrison presents the process of constructing identity, especially identity of a "public poet" actively engaged in what is happening in the contemporary world as a strategy aimed against concrete, imposed political/social order.

studies cannot be dismissed (Cote and Levine 2002: 17) as salient for the development of sociological traditions.

Symbolic Interactionists, who appear on the scene in the 1940s, focus on social interaction and the way in which "social interaction mediated through shared symbolic systems, shape[s] the self-consciousness of the individual" (Gleason 1983: 917). They did not initially use the term "identity" in their writings but "the self," which remained privileged in their discourse till the 1960s (Gleason 1983: 917), by which time, the term "identity" came into use.[25] The first of two famous interactionist movements is the Chicago School of Symbolic Interactionism, for which the self is a product of different processes of communication during which humans create and recreate social reality by giving names and attaching meanings. The most notable representatives who have emerged from this scholarly tradition are George Herbert Mead, his student Herbert Blumer, Anselm Strauss and Erving Goffman. Mead is the author of *Mind, Self and Society* (1934), where he recognizes "three levels of analysis corresponding to personality (mind), interaction (self) and social structure (society) that provide a viable organizational framework for the comprehensive taxonomy of identity" (Cote and Levine 2002: 33). Strauss and Goffman take his thought further, Strauss in his influential *Mirrors and Masks: The Search for Identity* (1959), which focuses on the issues of self and identification[26], and Goffman in *Stigma: Notes on the Management of Spoiled Identities* (1963), and *The Presentation of Self in Everyday Life* (1959), a study "of the management of personal identities in day-to-day social encounters" (Cote and Levine 2002: 33).

The so called Iowa School of Symbolic Interactionism grows out of Meadian tradition and offers a variety of different approaches. Manfred Kuhn[27] agrees with Mead's opinion "that the organization of the self reflects the organization of society" (Weigert et al. 1986: 12) but the approach of Iowa School towards the self is seen by the scholars as opposite to the approach the Chicago School assumes, as the self is understood in their research rather

25 Mead does not use the term identity in *Mind, Self and Society* (1934) but Goffman in *Stigma: Notes on the Management of Spoiled Identities* (1963) already does. As Gleason writes; "By the mid-60s, the word identity was used so widely and so loosely that to determine its provenance in every context would be impossible" (1983: 918).

26 The problem of identification proves to be very significant for the understanding of the theme of identity in Harrison's poetry (see Chapter II of the book). The term has been "introduced by Sigmund Freud to designate the process by which the infant assimilates to itself external persons and objects" (Gleason 1983: 915) but later gained numerous definitions among them the one coined by Nelson N. Foote who sees it as "appropriation of and commitment to a particular identity or series of identities" (1951: 18).

27 The founder of the Iowa School (Cote and Levine 2002: 34).

> as “fixed, relatively stable … reliably measured as opposed to precarious, in need of continual reconstruction and open to introspection.” (Cote and Levine 2002: 33)

In the 1950s, the Iowa School conducted research which captured change in the way the younger generation understood identity, and which foreshadowed the postmodern perspective:

> A conclusion drawn from … research is that among college students since the 1950s, personal identities (defined in terms of styles of self-representation) seem to be increasing in importance, and social identities (understood as socially recognized roles) appear to be increasingly less important. Some 80% to 90% of college students now appear to favour reflective (personal) identities as their primary source of self-definition (compared to about 30% in the 1950; see Babbit & Burbach 1990), suggesting that the TST is a useful instrument for monitoring late modern or so-called “postmodern” trends in identity formation. (Cote and Levine 2002: 34)

Observing this change, Zurcher comes up with the idea of a “mutable self” as an “emerging identity strategy,” (Cote and Levine 2002: 34) which bears features of a later, postmodern self; its main characteristic being susceptibility to change:

> [It] is characterised by highly flexible and autonomous capacity to modify and control self-concepts and to experience various components of self in varying social contexts. Zurcher believed this versatile identity strategy is adaptive in the face of rapid social change and uncertainty. He also speculated that there is a loose developmental pattern associated with it, from the adoption of single identity modes transforming to an ability to switch identity modes as the situation demands. (Cote and Levine 2002: 34)

This line of thought is also followed by Turner (1976), who talks about an “institutional self” and an “impulsive self,” (each characteristic for a different type of individual); the former would be “attained, created or achieved,” the latter “discovered” through revolt against the imposed order, through “rejection of institutional constraints” (Cote and Levine 2002: 35). The Iowa school forges numerous other concepts of identity: McCall’s and Simmons’s “role-identity” (*Identities and Interactions* 1978), Styker’s “identity theory” (1968, 1987) and Tajfel’s “social identity theory of group relations” (Cote and Levine 2002: 35).

According to Cote and Levine, “the other three [modernist] sociological traditions have less developed theoretical and methodological orientations to identity, but deserve mention” (2002: 35). The School of Knowledge and Interpretative Sociology is associated with the work of Berger and Luckmann, (1966) the authors of *The Social Construction of Reality*, who see identities as “both objective and subjective: they are nominalist in the sense that they are derived from and negotiated within social constructions, but can have very real consequences for human welfare and survival” (Cote and Levine 2002: 35). The Structural—Functionalist

Tradition, is notable, according to Cote and Levine, for this attempt to explain how "societal differentiations can create widespread identity problems" (2002: 38). It notices the role of growing plurality and complexity of the contemporary world in the construction of identities:

> Social complexity presents a wide range of possible choices and subsequent cross-pressures once the individual makes a commitment to one or another set of positions and acquires the attendant identities .... The modern person is much more aware of the problem of identity than persons living in simpler, stabler societies. (Weigert et al. 1986: 19)

The last of the three, the Critical Theory School, deserves attention in the context of identity studies with respect to the work of Jurgen Habermas who "analyses the evolution of the way identity has been perceived through the centuries" and "describes ... [identity's] evolution from primitive mythic and kinship foundations to contemporary rational and communicative relationships" (Weigert et al. 1986: 25).

Postmodernism brings yet another new array of perspectives, forging the idea of identity as a shifting process which takes place in the "absence of any stable authoritative points of reference (universal truths, essences, centres)" (Dumitrescu 2001: 11) an absence that "decentres" the individual (Dumitrescu 2001: 11). As Barker confirms (2008: 220), such a condition is described by Stuart Hall in "The Question of cultural Identity," which presents three different conceptualisations of identity: The enlightenment subject, the sociological subject and the postmodern subject. Hall explains:

> [The enlightenment subject] was based on a conception of the human person as a fully centred, unified individual, endowed with the capacities of reason, consciousness and action, whose 'centre' consisted of an inner core .... The essential centre of the self was a person's identity .... The inner core of the [sociological] subject was not autonomous and self-sufficiant, but was formed in relation to 'significant' others, who mediated to the subject the values, meanings and symbols—the culture—of the worlds he/she inhabited .... The [postmodern] subject assumes different identities at different times, identities which are not unified around a coherent 'self.' Within us are contradictory identities, pulling in different directions. So that our identifications are continually being shifted about. If we feel that we have a unified identity from birth to death it is only because we construct a ... story or "narrative of the self"[28] about ourselves. (1992: 275–277)

---

28 The idea of constructing a "narrative of the self" corresponds to the third of the "four approaches to the study of self and identity" (Cote and Levine 2002: 40) developed by Gecas and Burke.

> 1. situational, which emphasizes ... maintenance of the self in situated (typically face-to-face) interactions. 2. social structural, which focuses on the self consequences of role relationships and other structural features of social groups. 3.

Despite Harrison's subversive linguistic strategies, his poetry cannot be called postmodern.[29] Some reasons for this are Harrison's belief in the importance of form, his persistent question about the power of language, his postulate of "public poetry" which has an important societal role, and his conviction (although not free from doubt) that words can describe the social and cultural context in which they are uttered. Nevertheless, certain tendencies of postmodern thought correspond to certain themes developed in Harrison's verse. The importance of self-narrative in identity construction mentioned by Hall is definitely one of them. It is unquestionably visible in the autobiographical character of familial sonnets from *The School of Eloquence*, where the heterogeneous, stratified identity of the poetic persona of Tony Harrison emerges from a maze of individual and communal histories, stories and memories of the poet's dead parents, whom the sequence commemorates.

It should be mentioned that the presentation of selected theoretical approaches undertaken in the Preface is by no means comprehensive. The decision to present the analyses developed by Gleason, Cote and Levine Weigert et al. and Dumitrescu was prompted by their focus on those elements of identity studies, which may be helpful when considering identity in the poetry of Tony Harrison. Firstly, they point to the twentieth century tendency of looking at identity as a process set amid a changing social and cultural environment, and this in turn, forces us to regard the private and the public sphere of human existence as closely related and mutually influential. Secondly, they stress the role of (dis)continuity and change in the process of constructing identity. Thirdly, they suggest the possibility that identity can be seen as a project, which stresses the importance of biography in

---

> biographical—historical, which focuses on the self as a cultural and historical construction. 4. interpersonal, focusing on processes within self and personality affecting behaviour. (1995: 42)

According to Cote and Levine biographical orientation is characteristic for the postmodern approach (2002: 40).

29 Mihaela Dumitrescu describes postmodern literature as follows:

> The language .... in its symbolic power and the free linguistic play takes precedence over discursive coherence and unity of form. The so-called self-reflective or metafictional novels of such authors as the American William Burroughs, John Barth, Donald Barthelme, Robert Coover, Thomas Pynchon and William Gass ... are based on the view of language as being explicitly and totally self-absorbed. Its self-referentiality is a subversive ... reaction against a civilisation that has turned out to be a ... fraud, and against its ... discourse that has ... proved to be an enormous mystification. The only reality is the text itself made up of words that bear no relation whatsoever to the world of objects .... The human subject becomes a mere verbal construct, as illusory and lacking in substance as the world around him. (2001: 12)

identity formation, and allows us to see revolt as one way in which individuals and groups establish their identities.

This book examines the issue of identity as present in Harrison's verse in reference to three dimensions: identity as a state or process, identity as continuity or change, and identity as a consequence of conformity or revolt. The three dimensions have been proposed by Zygmunt Bokszański in *Tożsamości zbiorowe* as a systematization of the ways in which identity can be interpreted and defined.

1. Identity—State or a Process

John Edwards explains that identity is usually understood in literature

> along a 'weak-strong' continuum anchored at one end by the idea that identity is a fixed asset and, at the other, by … conceptions of identity as a fluctuating, contingent and sometimes quite unstable phenomenon: a process, rather than an entity. It is obviously true than dynamism rather than stasis has always been the fact of human life. The simultaneous possession of many different social roles and masks is uncontroversial, identities are certainly in flux. (2009: 23)

Close reading of the body of Harrison's texts clearly shows that identity in his poetry should be understood as a *process* rather than a *state*[30], and as such, as undergoing a constant transformation. By assuming the approach that identity is a *state*,[31] in

---

30 Bokszański comments on these to approaches as follows:

> Inspiring sociological sources included in the works of classical representatives of symbolic interactionism strongly indicated a processual character in an approach to identity of an individual social actor …. The perspective was developed by the Chicago School, represented by researchers as distinguished as: Alfred Linde Smith, Everett C. Hughes, Herbert Blumer, Anselm L. Strauss, Howard Becker, Norman Denzin …. The point is, however, that … the concept of identity entered the mainstream sociology through the works of Erikson together with the approach which vividly defined identity as a stable system used for auto-definition of an individual, confirmed by a social environment. (Bokszański 2007: 33–34 My translation)
>
> Źródłowe socjologiczne inspiracje zawarte w pracach klasyków interakcjonizmu symbolicznego zdecydowanie wskazywały na procesualny charakter ujmowania tożsamości indywidualnego aktora społecznego …. Tę perspektywę podjęła i rozwijała szkoła chicagowska, grupująca badaczy tej miary co: Alfred Lindesmith, Everett C. Hughes, Herbert Blumer, Anselm L. Strauss, Howard Becker, Norman Denzin…. Rzecz w tym jednak, że … koncepcja tożsamości dotarła do głównego nurtu socjologii za pośrednictwem prac Eriksona. Zawarta w nich perspektywa wyraźnie definiowała tożsamość, jako stabilny układ autodefinicji jednostki, potwierdzony przez jej otoczenie społeczne. (Bokszański 2007: 33–34)

31 Emphasis added by the author of this book.

other words, a type of structure (Bokszański 2007: 24), as Aldona Jawłowska explains, "one asks the question what identity *is*. This question comprises an assumption, that identity is something an individual or group can 'possess,' with which it can or even should be 'equipped'"[32] (2001: 53). In the case of the second approach, i.e. identity seen as a *process*,[33] the question mentioned above loses its primary significance and when discussing the issue of identity in Harrison's verse, the main emphasis is to be put on analyzing the "main problems of identity development, inner and outer obstacles to the process, favourable or unfavourable circumstances, and … the direction the process assumes"[34] (Skarga 1997: 172).

The idea of seeing identity as a process rather than a state is also seen in the book with a similar understanding of class, as developed by John Frow, the author of *Cultural Studies and Cultural Value*:

> [Frow] argues that in a world where changes … have rendered older categorizations of class as outmoded, class can no longer be seen as some sort of economically determined essence, into which one is born and imprisoned. This does not mean that material privilege has ceased to exist or become irrelevant, but that in a contemporary climate it is more productive to think of 'processes of class formation … played out through particular institutional forms and balances of power … through desires, and fears, and fantasies' (1995: 111). Class for Frow, is not a pre-existing slot to which we are assigned, but a set of contestable relations; it is not a given but a process. (Medhurst 2000: 31)

Class as never "an objective entity" but always "a matter of history, a relationship with tradition, and a discourse of roots …. a question of identifications, perceptions and feelings" (Medhurst 2000: 20) can be inscribed into Harrison's discussion of identity construction, where a complicated situation of being in between classes, a position that requires constant re-definition and re-negotiation, is of crucial importance.

Considering the socio-political contexts which influence the poet's perception and act as an efficient building material for the imagery in his works, this book attempts to present and analyse the various complicated and often contradictory renderings of the theme of identity construction in Harrison's verse. The

32 My translation of: Poszukuje się więc odpowiedzi na pytanie, czym JEST tożsamość. W tak sformułowanym pytaniu zawiera się założenie, że tożsamość jest czymś, co jednostka lub grupa może 'posiadać,' w co może lub nawet powinna być 'wyposażona.' (Jawłowska 2001: 53)

33 Emphasis added by the author of this book.

34 My translation of: Zasadnicze problemy dotyczą warunków owego kształtowania, wewnętrznych i zewnętrznych przeszkód i sprzyjających okoliczności, a przede wszystkim kierunku, w jakim tworzenie [tożsamości] podąża. (Skarga 1997: 172)

analysis starts with his first critically acclaimed collection of lyrics *The Loiners* (1970), through subsequent works from his ongoing project *From The School of Eloquence* and *School of Eloquence Continuous* (1978, 1981, 1987), his most overly controversial elegiac poem *v.* (1985), up to his more recent poetry ("A Cold Coming" 1991, "Shrapnel," "Cornet and Cartridge"), engaged with the political issues of armed conflict and its representation.

2. Identity—Continuity or/and Otherness

This dimension of identity refers to the modes of identity creation. In reference to the above-mentioned concepts, i.e. continuity and otherness, the thesis refers to the approach presented by A. Jackobson-Widding in *Identity, Personal and Socio-Cultural*, where she suggests a differentiation between continuity/sameness and distinctiveness (1983: 13). John Edwards situates the notion of *continuity*[35] within the sphere of *identity*,[36] referring to the etymology of the term:

> The essence of *identity*[37] is similarity: things that are identical are the same, after all, and the word stems from the Latin *idem*. And this most basic sense is exactly what underpins the notion of identity as it applies to personality. It signifies the 'sameness' of an individual 'at all times or in all circumstances', as the dictionary tells us, the fact that a person is oneself and not someone else. It signifies a *continuity*,[38] in other words, that constitutes an unbroken thread running through the long and varied tapestry of life. It can even invoke an almost mystical sense of connectedness, particularly when one considers the very real changes that take place in that tapestry. (2009: 19)

Bokszański makes a similar comment. He regards continuity, as being the person who still identifies with "past values, thoughts and acts" 'przeszłymi wartościami, myślami i działaniami' (Bokszański 2007: 36), and, in a broader sense, salient for the analysis of Harrison's poetry, the concept of continuity assumes a link with the past, which is retained in individual, social and historical contexts. The abovementioned contexts remain in constant interplay in Harrison's verse and all pertain to the idea that the past takes an active role in the creation of individual and communal identities. This book discusses the (im)possibility of maintaining continuity with the past and analyses the ambivalent attitude of the poet towards his family history, visible in the autobiographical themes, for example, in the relation with his parents representing the class and culture to which Harrison cannot unambiguously

35 Emphasis added by the author of this book.
36 Emphasis added by the author of this book.
37 Emphasis added by the author of this book.
38 Emphasis added by the author of this book.

belong. The gulf between himself and his family reflects the otherness and alienation experienced by acquiring access to the world of eloquence, and it indicates the class chasm so characteristic for British society as a whole, becoming a metaphor of the South-North divide "instituted into media and public consciousness in the 1980s as a result of heavy job losses in the North" (Wales 2008: 210). The idea of a South-North divide is an important point of reference for understanding Harrison's poetry. As Katie Wales writes, despite all the social and political changes which took place in Britain since the 80s, this divide remains an important aspect of British identity. It is not exactly a geographical term, since "there is no 'North' on a map (or 'South of England')" (Wales 2008: 9) but an "idea … deeply embedded in the nation's cultural history in a variety of manifestations, including the linguistic; and the opposition itself [i.e. North/South] helps to determine the 'meaning' of the North and being Northern" (Wales 2008: 210).

The book shows how Harrison's autobiographical themes correlate with social and historical ones, which in itself can be interpreted as another type of continuity, namely, that between personal and general experience. As Annette Kuhn writes, "personal and collective remembering emerge again and again as continuous with one another … [a]ll memory text[s] … constantly call to mind the collective nature of the activity of remembering," (Kuhn 1995: 5) and so the private and the public must inevitably influence each other, their interdependence being almost a fact of life, like birth and death. This issue and its consequences are the subject of numerous poems by Harrison, vividly present in his war poems and in the poetry referring to the atrocities of the Holocaust[39], but also in the family elegies of the *The School of Eloquence*, in the politically engaged *v.* and in the colonial themes developed in *The Loiners*. The theme of (dis)continuity in its numerous versions and renditions[40] is given a prominent place in the thesis due to its importance in relation to the subject of constructing identity.

In Harrison's poetry, the concept of (dis)continuity is closely linked with the concepts of alienation, rejection and otherness, which are vividly reflected in a language that is for the poet not only a tool, but also a subject of discourse.[41] First of all, it represents the alienation of the poet from the community of the working

39 For a detailed discussion of Holocaust themes in Harrison's verse see *Tony Harrison and the Holocaust* a book by Anthony Rowland published in 2001 by Liverpool University Press.

40 One of the most important dimensions of continuity in Harrison's poetry is constituted by its dense net of inter-textual references. The book analyses the discourse of the poet within the literary tradition and attempts to define his place in the literary context.

41 See for example "Them and [uz]."

class he abandoned due to his education as mentioned above. But it is a simultaneous alienation from the middle-class community, caused by the fact that his roots lie in the North of England and that his working-class background remains an important element of his identity. Consequently, the sense of otherness of the poetic "I" is most vivid when Harrison makes an effort to come back to his roots, conducting a literary and metaphorical quest for the place of his birth, as exemplified by the multidimensional theme of Leeds in his work. The book focuses on the portrayal of Leeds as a real place reflecting the cultural and existential experiences of its citizens, and as a metaphorical city, a construct of poetic imagination. The main point of the discussion is not to create a full and comprehensive picture of the city seen through the eyes of the poet, but to address the degree of connectedness between the issue of "differential identity" tackled in Harrison's verse and Leeds. Leeds, which is for the poet, both a geographical place and a concept standing for that which is familiar as opposed to alien, familial as opposed to public, local as opposed to global, peripheral as opposed to central. But it must be kept in mind that the Leeds on Harrison's "memory map" is never an easily accessible place, as it can be reached only through the maze of meanings given to it by history. Recognizing the net of opposites into which Leeds is inscribed by Harrison, the book simultaneously interprets metaphorical images of Leeds in the context of his poetry as a whole and discusses the way in which the city of Harrison's birth epitomizes a source of identity which cannot be unambiguously identified with. Otherness on the one hand and continuity on the other are, for Harrison, closely connected with the issue of class differences and understood to a large extent as a source of conflicting forces, "the versuses of life," (v. 65) as Harrison would call them, which shape reality. At the same time, a continuity vs. otherness dichotomy is discussed in the book in relation to the question about the existence of factors that can unify rather than divide, factors which allow the reconciliation of contradictions and the synthesis of contrasts in the process of identity construction.

3. Identity—A Consequence of Conformism or Revolt

The third dimension, in reference to which the theme of constructing identity is examined here, focuses on "a working strategy of a subject" (Bokszański 2007: 37), which, in the context of Harrison's verse, is connected with the question of the role of a poet and poetry in the world. For Harrison, revolt and the issue of political protest are, first of all, forms of expression which characterize British class relations and form collective identities of different social groups operating within a system that destroyed the culture of the English working class (Bokszański 2007: 23). Being slowly deprived of an opportunity to fully participate in social, cultural and political life, the working-class community, or perhaps rather what is left of it, strengthens its survival instinct, assuming a position of aggressive resistance. At this point, we have to return once again to the issue of language, since revolt is reflected in Harrison's work most prominently in the theme of struggle for the recognition of the working class vernacular. Convinced about the role of eloquence in building social hierarchy, which is emphasised, among others, by the choice of Arthur Scargill's words for the motto of the (in)famous *v.*, Harrison gives the Yorkshire dialect prime place in his verse, and this in itself constitutes a revolutionary act. Equalizing the working class language with Standard English is described by the poet as a battle for poetic space occupied by the privileged middle class, the users of RP who want to secure their position of political and cultural dominance. Jonathan Barker believes that Harrison restores a public role to poetry (1991: 52) and obliges poetry to rage against injustice, and this book attempts to analyse the role revolt plays in the creation of individual and collective identities, including the identity of a poet. This problem seems to be especially pertinent if we consider the amount of critical texts devoted to the revolutionary character of Harrison's work. He has been called a poet of revolt; from the very beginning of his career, and throughout works that straddle completely altered political and social realities, he remains focused and vigilant, always ready to take a stand, even if it means offending the public or incurring the anger of both fellow writers and the politicians in power. Acknowledging an opinion often repeated by the critics,[42] that Harrison is, first of all, a political poet of the English working classes, this book proposes that he is perhaps primarily an engaged poet, or, to quote Jon Silkin, a "committed individual"[43] who inscribes the condition of the English working class into the larger context of turbulent and oppressive social relations where cultures, communities and identities cease to exist and are replaced by distorted versions of themselves. The question of whether they can undergo a process of reconstruction and restoration, whether they can be shored up against their own ruins, to use Eliot's expression, has obsessed Harrison from the seventies onwards.

42 See for example Douglas Dunn and Blake Morrison.

43 In 1973 Harrison's poems appeared in the *Poetry of the Committed Individual*, an anthology of poetry published originally in the *Stand* magazine and edited by Jon Silkin.

Chapter One
"Correct your maps: Newcastle is Peru!"

Continuity of Exploration and Exploitation in *The Loiners*[44]

The following chapter focuses on the theme of "constructing identity" in Tony Harrison's poetry while also commenting on themes developed in his subsequent collections: the theme of revolt, which originates in *The Loiners*, reappears in *The School of Eloquence* and acquires its most acclaimed shape in *v.*, and the theme of continuity, with its variations: continuity between public and private experience, between past histories and a present moment, between the author and the poetic persona Tony Harrison, between male and female as opposite but potentially complementary energies, but above all, the continuity of imperial structures of power which permeate the history of individuals, communities and nations. In Harrison's poetry, the theme of continuity is closely related to the problem of "difference," which often takes the form of estrangement from the speaker's home, family and class he grew out of.[45] The state of alienation of the poetic "I" is most acutely palpable in those moments when the poet returns to his roots, to a place literally and metaphorically understood as a source of poetic inclinations, of one's own voice and crude but continually renewable inspiration. Consequently, the city of the poet's birth and childhood years, Leeds—as a real place and a poetic metaphor—reoccurs in his poetry, its enduring presence already stressed in the title of Harrison's first book-form collection, *The Loiners*.

The following chapter begins with a discussion of a poem from Part IV of *The Loiners* titled *Newcastle is Peru*, which juxtaposes familiarity and otherness, setting commonplace Leeds and distant colonies side by side—both being peripheral in relation to the privileged centre of imperial power. As the analysis of selected poems will reveal, although a contained whole, *Newcastle is Peru* should not

44 Some of the ideas developed in this chapter constitute a part of a different publication: "A Contemporary Poet and his Identity: The Landscape of Leeds in Tony Harrison's Poetry." Maribor International Review. Vol. 1, no. 1 (2008).

45 Detailed analysis of the issue is undertaken in the second chapter of the book which focuses on *The School of Eloquence*—a sequence that foregrounds the theme of alienation from the poet's working-class background.

be read in isolation if it is to be understood in its whole complexity. The poem's implicit meanings are often born out of the dialogue the poem engages in with other texts of the sequence, creating a dense net of possible interpretations and reinterpretations of the themes of continuity, revolt and change; all of them rendered by the author as a possibility, never certainty. By extensive use of imagery reflecting the topography of Leeds, *Newcastle is Peru*[46] collects the autobiographical stories of first explorations, which are later inscribed into the problem of perpetual return to the place of origin characteristic of Harrison`s subsequent poetry (*v.*, *The School of Eloquence*), in which images of Leeds, imprinted or embossed in the poet's eye, undergo constant development into larger, multi-layered themes. The poem under discussion tells the story of the poet's return to England after living in Nigeria and Prague and, as N.S. Thompson suggests, his disorientation at the event (1997: 123), the poetic "I" taking the reader for a dizzying ride through memorable episodes from the past, exotic and local spots and scattered images remote in time and place. An attempt to light the fire with a Sunday newspaper "begins the process of regrouping impetus, memory, persona … from out of delirium into deliberate poetry" (Kelleher 1996: 14).

As "the fire sucks in the first cold air" (Newcastle is Peru 1987: 25), the reader manages to catch a glimpse of war and death, when the burning newspaper showing "lobbed mortar bombs" smashing the houses of Ontisha. In *Newcastle is Peru*, the social and the historical pervade the intimate experience as in many other poems of the sequence, for example in "Allotments," where the image of Auschwitz cuts into the scene of secretive love making. But the picture in the newspaper is consumed by the flame and swiftly replaced by other images which float and disappear, as if life is speeded up before the poet's eyes:

I lay down dizzy, drunk, alone,
life circling life like Eddystone
dark sea, but lighting nothing; sense
nor centre, nor circumference. (Newcastle is Peru 29–32)

In the process of moving through the subsequent images, the "remote and the intimate are brought together" (Spencer 1994: 35), with Leeds entering the context of other places like Newcastle and Prague, creating a sense of continuity between the familiar and the unfamiliar:

46 The poem published first as a pamphlet in 1969 (Byrne 1997: 101) was included in *The Loiners* (1970 edition) where it constitutes part IV of the collection.

the Blackpool Pleasure Beach Big Wheel
...
Leeds purposeful in its affairs.
Mercator; *miles*, school chapel glass
Transparencies to blood and brass.
....
The dizziness! That spiral stair
up St Vitus Cathedral; there
golden cockerel and great Prague
before us like a catalogue; (Newcastle is Peru 38, 54–56, 67–70)

Leeds ceases to be a fixed mark in Harrison's experience and becomes a shifting point whose boundaries cannot be easily outlined as "all the known Leeds landmarks blur / to something dark and circular" (Newcastle is Peru 47–48).

Introducing the poem in 1968, Harrison explained that the circles in the poet's mind seem to be concentric, a figure he relates to the figure of confusion, the labyrinth (Thompson 1997: 124). Images of concentric circles and spirals come back at different stages of the poem: in the staircase in St Vitus' Cathedral in Prague, in the whorls of a finger and its print, in the circular movement of a lover's hand over another's body. It seems that the movement of the poetic "I" is not a simple narrative but has a form of a spin, an up and down spiral. And the poet comes again and again to the same point but at a different level of his journey. Circular movement here is simultaneously a principle of the entire sequence's construction: As Romana Huk notices:

> The five sections of the book, set variously in the Leeds of Harrison's young adulthood, Africa, South America, Eastern Europe and Newcastle (where he now lives), *do move in a great circle out from the North of England into the world and back again*,[47] carrying what at first seem to be motifs of visionary discovery and globalized unity—as illustrated in the quotation from Thomas Browne's *Religio Medici* ... that heads part 2, 'There is all Africa and her prodigies in us; we are that bold and adventurous piece of Nature.' (1996: 200)

The idea of "globalized unity" (1996: 200) mentioned by Huk is present already in the title of *Newcastle is Peru*, which suggests that a commonplace English landscape can easily fall under the definition of the newly discovered land.

Although the poem, like *v.* written more than a decade later in 1984, is one of Harrison's works about the return to the North, the place inhabited in his youth, it is also a poem about the impossibility of the region's recognition. Perhaps it is not the topography of the northern landscape that changes but the speaker's perception, altered in an ironic mode by nine or ten pints of "Newcastle Brown," which

47 Emphasis added by the author of this book.

de-familiarizes the scenery and, as the poem develops, darkens and obliterates the previously familiar sites of Leeds. The method echoes the concept of de-familiarization developed by Victor Shklovski, who believed that as Habib explains that "the technique of art is to make an object unfamiliar and … to recover the sensation of life" (2008: 604). In the light of Shklovski's theory, it seems that the estrangement the poet experiences on his return to England is not entirely pessimistic since it offers the possibility of new discovery. The poem alludes to the metaphysical conceit ascribed to John Cleveland:[48] "Correct your maps: Newcastle is Peru" and suggests that a familiar place can be rediscovered as foreign and unknown (Barker 1991: 72). Harrison widens the field of exploration and brings together Newcastle, Peru, Prague and Leeds. Anywhere becomes anywhere else, and one place bears the features of another, or maybe the poet looks at Newcastle and Leeds through the prism of his experience in Nigeria and Prague and does not recognize the scenery he has carried under his eyelids through the whole journey. Whatever the reason, the imprint in the mind's eye does not match the reality and has to alter when the poet "reaches out to map" (Kelleher 1996: 15) the topography of the revisited landscape. N. S. Thompson suggests that Harrison records his own move to Newcastle as discovering a new world and setting a new empire (Thompson 1997: 127). That idea is reinforced by the breaking of the octosyllabic course in the word "New – / castle" (Newcastle is Peru 79–80) which becomes a stronghold, a landmark on the poet's route, and in its new form can be also read as an allusion to the "embattled fortress" (Newcastle is Peru 123) which appears later in the poem, built "against the world's bold cannonade / of loveless warfare and cold trade" (Newcastle is Peru 125–126).

Domestic images are followed by another depiction of an unknown landscape, the landscape of the body that offers itself to discovery. The exploration brings back the idea of circular motion. It is suggested by the movements of the lover's hands and the image of a woman's body compared to an endless maze that can be travelled through and through with undiminished fascination. The union achieved through love and sexual exploration is presented in *Newcastle is Peru* as an attempt to find a sense of completeness in the world of disruption and

48 As Byrne writes: "At the times of Newcastle's composition, the source of the poem's epigraph 'News from Newcastle' was thought to be by John Cleveland but the poem was later attributed to Thomas Winnard" (1998: 101). The same information is given in an explanatory note in Samuel Johnson's *The Lives of the Poets*, a selection printed in 2009 by Oxford University Press.: "'News from Newcastle: Upon Coal-Pits about Newcastle—upon—Tyne' … though printed in the early editions of Cleveland's works is now attributed to Thomas Winnard" (468).

opposites,[49] an issue characteristic of Harrison's poetry which, as Byrne writes, while "dramatizing the divisions ... seems to portray a displaced psyche in search for completion" (1998: 173). This is clearly visible in his later works, especially so in *v.* and in *The School of Eloquence* cycle, where "dramatizations of the tensions within the poetic persona 'Tony Harrison'" (Byrne 1998: 171) are balanced by the perpetual attempts at maintaining a continuity of working-class experience and a human bond that would make "his circle just" (Byrne 1998: 171), give it a "centre" and "circumference" (Newcastle is Peru 32). Nevertheless, the moment "when a man like Donne can brood over his woman and say, 'O my America! My new-found-land ... is a brief time"[50] (Huk 1996: 201) and the idea of male/female continuity giving a sense of completion, which appears among others in "Lords of Life"[51] and in *v.*[52], is usually questioned by Harrison as soon as it appears.[53] If it assumes a more definite, fuller character, it is in the poet's later works (Byrne 1998, 174) like "Cypress and Cedar," conveying the idea of unity in death

---

49 "we brave/harsh oppositions when we love" (Newcastle is Peru 119–120).

50 Huk's comment refers to the words of Tony Harrison, which can be found in *The Dictionary of Literary Biography*, where Catherine Lamb quotes the poet while writing about an event that triggered him to write *Newcastle is Peru*. Her words constitute an interesting backdrop for looking at the complex treatment of the issue of unity in Harrison's poetry.

> [Harrison] saw ... in a shop called Geographia hundreds of soiled, reduced price maps in dirty cardboard boxes. He discovered, with sinking heart, that every-one of them, without exception, was of Newcastle. He carried this depressing fact along with him to the British Museum, where leafing through the Metaphysical poets, he found in John Cleveland a line: "Correct your Maps: Newcastle is Peru!" This 'clue to my existence', as Harrison puts it summed up for him something he had been trying to do in his poetry: "Something which I desperately try to cling to in life, that although we are working with reach-me-down maps and second-hand charts, it is suddenly possible to cry out "Newcastle is Peru" .... I am interested in the point where one can say "Newcastle is Peru" ... and the point when a man like Donne can suddenly brood over his woman and say "O my America! My newfound-land." It is a very brief time. (158–159)

51 "curled in a circle, sucking its own tail, / the formed continuum of female/male" (Lords of Life 161–620).

52 "working marriage ... a blend of masculine and feminine" (v. 144–45).

53 It is related to the method of building poems out of opposite images which constantly clash and contradict each other. It seems that the poet searches for unity but continually finds disruption and consciously creates poetry out of it, and so, as Byrne writes, this is the poetry that "comes not from peaceful union but from embattled division" (Byrne 1998: 175) deeply engraved in the character of the abovementioned poetic personae

captured by an image of crematory smoke in which the two scents of wood representing the two sexes blend:[54]

> My love, as prone as I am to despair,
> I think the world of night's best born in pairs,
> one half we'll call the female, one the male,
> though neither essence need, in love, prevail.
> We sit here in distinctly scented chairs
> you, love, in the cedar, me the cypress chair.
>
> Though tomorrow night I might well sit in yours
> and you in mine, the blended scent's the same
> ....
> I'll have my coffin made of cedar wood
> to balance the smell like cypress from inside
> and hope smoke of both blends in the sky,
>
> as both scents from our porch do tonight. (Cypress and Cedar 127–134, 148–151)

Unlike in "Cypress and Cedar," in *Newcastle is Peru* the reconciliation of opposites, a unification of male/female elements occurs only as a tempting notion, sought but never achieved.[55] The "strong – / hold of love" (123–124) cannot hold and although "the lover offers the poet respite from the polyvalency and tension ... their unity ... is

---

"Tony Harrison (Byrne 1998: 175)" which is being created on the basis of internal tensions and versuses. Richard Eyre comments upon the topic as follows:

> The man is his work. It is not so much that it is autobiographical (though much of it of course is) but that the content invariably dramatizes the ambivalences at the heart of his character and attempts to reconcile them. Tony does not deal in the familiar English modes of ellipses and reticence, but in an unremittingly direct address that is at times almost unnerving. Those opposing valencies that he invokes in *v.* are not a poet's conceits but are the syntax of his daily life. Heart/brain, soul/body, male/female, family, freedom, class, culture, this is the divided territory in which he searches for harmony and despairs at its elusiveness. (Eyre 1991: 363)

54 Mureen Duffy observes that" the subtext of the poem seems ... to be from Donne, in particular 'The Ecstasy' and 'The Relic'. Harrison rejects, as Donne does, the traditional separation into male and female" (1991: 340).

55 Byrne states that although "the figure of lover and/or wife appears in many poems, often in contexts that gloss her as Eve to the poet's Adam (*Kumquat*, 'Following Pine'); sweetness and light to his bile and darkness ('Cypress and Cedar')" her presence cannot fill the void or assure "peaceful continuum" in the face of "social upheaval." (Byrne 1998: 175) The abovementioned characteristics, Byrne continues, "do not ... seem ... to be representations of Platonic *anima*, and they do not complement or complete the poet any more than any other poetic personae" (Byrne 1998: 175).

temporary and conditional and no permanent solution to or consolation for the things the poet encounters outside" (Byrne 1998: 175). If there is continuity it takes the form of perpetual return, of an ongoing exploration of the "maze" achieved through the projection of the images Harrison carries in his mind onto the place he discovers: in this case a geographical image of a new "landscape"[56] and a poetic image developed centuries earlier by Winnard. As a result of this projection, the body of a lover becomes another land the poet travels through, like Prague and Africa, which return at different points of the poem in their numerous incarnations, in a slide show manner. It is interesting that the body's labyrinthine character reflects the quality of the poet's whirling mind and the shape of his black fingerprints—marks of working-class identity. It gives an impression that the subject of his exploration seems to posses no integrity of her own—she assumes the character given to her by the explorer. "[W]art, mole, spot" (Newcastle is Peru 129) make up a harmonious, self-contained whole only when labelled Peru, only in correspondence to the metaphysical conceit, and consequently may be seen as becoming inscribed into the British literary canons as another appropriated literary landscape. It seems the body is being "read" by the lover's touch. According to Luke Spencer:

> [Following] … the geographical/topographical trope by which the wife's body becomes Peru, one can now identify the same masculine perspective that enabled John Donne to call his mistress 'my America! My new-found-land' without of course, questioning his right to exploit either the woman or the continent. For Harrison the woman's body functions as an object of his gaze.[57] (1994: 37)

Neil Hairsine assumes a different perspective, criticizing Spencer for not taking into account "the ironic detachment and self-criticism" and a "negative appraisal of … [his] own selfhood including an implicit critique of his masculinity" which Harrison "exhibit[s] in … verse" (1997: 151). Indeed, it is difficult not to take into consideration the way the speaker of the poem describes himself as being inherently dirty and his poetic visions and the perspective of his "gaze" as potentially unreliable; after all, they are a product of the excessive consumption of alcohol. Similarly, upon realizing the fact that the wood representing the male, poetic "I" of "Cypress and Cedar" actually "'stinks o' shite'" (Cypress and Cedar 25), it

56 "wart, mole, spot / like outcrops on a snowfield, dot/ these slopes of flesh" (Newcastle is Peru 29–31).

57 Spencer's usage of the term can be seen as related to the notion of "male gaze" developed by Laura Mulvey ("Visual Pleasure and Narrative Cinema" 1975) in relation to film studies, as it entails erotic treatment of the subject of observation which in turn remains passive. For analysis of the issue of gaze see: Marita Sturken and Lisa Cartwright. *Practices of Looking: An Introduction to Visual Culture*. Oxford: Oxford University Press, 2001.

is difficult not to see the speaker's words as endowed with a fair dose of irony. Hairsine underlines the importance of the metaphor of "négritude,"[58] ignored by Spencer (1997: 54),[59] which foreshadows Harrison's intertextual references to Aimé Césaire's[60] *Notebooks of a Return to the Native Land* in one of his most acclaimed poems "On Not Being Milton" and introduces an immediate association with a postcolonial tradition of text-reading:

> The designation in the poem of the female lover as part of generic Otherness ("you also are Peru")—linked, and in some way an equivalent, to the cultural and colonial Other—is reinforced by … reference to négritude. Throughout the volume the sexual and the colonial Other are implicitly aligned, both being defined by the binary oppositions of authoritarian culture as submissive or 'lower'. Here, however, the parallel between the two contains further significance. Not only is the repression of the Other invoked, but also the rebellion of the Other. The négritude movement promoted positive black identity and opposed colonialism. (1997: 154)

---

58 "The fire I laid and lit / … / flickers and struts upon the bed. / And I'm left gazing at full-page spread / of aggressively fine bosoms, nude/ and tanned almost to négritude,/ in the Colour Supplement's *Test / Yourself for Cancer of the Breast*." (Newcastle is Peru 161–168)

59 To be exact, Spencer does not ignore the négritude metaphor (see: Spencer 1994: 36) but rather dismisses it as not worth thorough analysis, seeing in the passage nothing more than a statement of Harrison's gender position:

> Harrison is looking at colour supplement photograph of 'aggressively fine bosoms' which mimic 'négritude' with their expensively acquired suntan, and are displaced not for sexual arousal but as an aid to self-examination for breast cancer. In other words, what might have been a celebratory image of female eroticism turns out to be a sobering reminder of malignant growths and possible mastectomies … And whose disappointment but a man's could possibly represent such a photograph as an unwelcome instance of how the world violates our privacy? (1994: 37).

It should be noted that the image suggesting "malignant growths" (Spencer 1994: 37) cannot be discussed in isolation, simply as a symbol of the intrusion of harsh reality into the intimate space the speaker inhabits, as it constitutes a part of a larger metaphor of illness developed in the collection which represents among others the condition of western culture and imperial consciousness of the colonizers, unable to function in the foreign land they invaded. The image under discussion has its numerous counterparts in the poem ("The White Queen") analyzed later in this chapter.

60 Aimé Césaire, in full Aimé-Fernand-David Césaire (1913–2008) was a "Martinican poet, playwright, and politician, who was co-founder with Léopold Sédar Senghor of Négritude, an influential movement to restore the cultural identity of black Africans." (http://www.britannica.com/EBchecked/topic/103729/Aime-Cesaire)

The reading suggested by Hairsine is especially pertinent if seen in the context of négritude understood as an attitude towards an oppressive culture,[61] a "posture of revolt" described by Aimé Césaire's in his address[62] given in Geneva on June 2nd 1978 on the occasion of the creation by Robert Cornman of a cantata entitled *Retour* which is said to have been inspired by the *Notebooks of a Return to the Native Land*[63]

> ...when it appeared the literature of Négritude created a revolution: in the *darkness of the great silence,*[64] a voice was rising up, with no interpreter, no alteration, and no complacency, a violent and staccato voice, and it said for the first time: "I, Nègre."
>
> A voice of revolt
> A voice of resentment
> No doubt
> But also of fidelity, a voice of freedom, and first and foremost, a voice for the retrieved identity. (Thébia-Melsan 2000: 28)

The words of Césaire can be applied to the attitude expressed by Harrison in many of his poems[65], in which he openly declares a need to give voice back to those deprived of it by the dominant culture of the privileged, and acknowledges the political role of poetry. In order to assume this role, poetry should be "public," which in turn means that it must be engaged in (re)constructing identity through maintaining continuity of experience, bringing back history to those who lost their right to it through different forms of imperial subjugation, among them the British working classes,[66] and elevating their language to a higher rank.

---

61 For a discussion on other dimensions of négritude (as ontology, as aesthetics, as epistemology) see online Stanford Encyclopaedia of Philosophy http://plato.stanford.edu/entries/negritude/

62 Reprinted in *Aimé Césaire, pour regarder le siècle en face*, edited by A. Thébia-Melsan, bublished by Maisonneuve & Larose in Paris in 2000.

63 For more information see: http://plato.stanford.edu/entries/negritude/

64 Emphasis added by the author of this book.

65 See for example "Heredity".

66 As Albert Memmi writes in his book *The Colonizer and the Colonized* (first time printed in 1957): "the most acute blow that the colonized received was to be removed from history" 'Najpoważniejszy cios, jaki otrzymał kolonizowany, polegał na usunięciu go z historii.' (Memmi quoted in Burzyńska 2006: 557) Harrison's poetry shows that a similar process took place in the case of the working class community in Great Britain whose history, language and culture undergo extinction as a result of marginalisation of the entire class and consequently of the North as a working-class region of the country.

The idea that blackness, associated in colonial discourse with backwardness and lack of eloquence, that which is lower and animalistic, and indirectly with silence[67], can be seen as a source of power is inscribed in the name of the movement itself, derived from the Latin "niger," meaning "black"—a word which functioned before the Négritude Movement was founded and which its creators appropriated to serve their own agenda. The word was used for the first time in a journal *L'Étudiant noir*, launched in years 1934–1935 by Aimé Césaire:

> It was meant to be (and, above all, to *sound* like) a provocation. *Nègre*, derived from the Latin "niger," meaning "black," is used in French only in relation to black people as in "art nègre." Applied to a black person it had come to be charged with all the weight of racism to the point that the insult "*sale* nègre" (*dirty* nègre) would be almost redundant, "sale" being somehow usually understood in "nègre". So to coin and claim the word "Négritude" (*Négrité*, using the French suffix *–ité* instead of *–itude* was considered and dropped) as the expression of the value of "blackness" was a way for Césaire, Senghor and Damas of defiantly turning "nègre" against the white supremacists who used it as a slur.[68]

In Harrison's poems, darkness and dirt are associated with the mining culture and coal, both a main asset and curse of the northern towns—which were built around collieries and whose plight came as a result of the collapse of the mining industry. The coal/mining metaphor developed in some of *The School of Eloquence* poems and in *v.* is foreshadowed in the penultimate stanza of *Newcastle is Peru*:

> My fingerprints still lined with coal
> send cold shudders through my soul.
> Each whorl, my love-, my long life-line,
> mine, inalienably mine,
> lead off my body as they press
> onwards into nothingness.
> I see my grimy fingers smudge
> everything they feel or touch. (Newcastle is Peru 153–160)

The idea that mining is quite literally a dirty job but also that being a miner, being working class, is "dirty and fallen" (Hairsine 1997: 152) is expressed in the metaphor of fingerprints, which uses the association between blackness and dirt. The speaker of the poem is a man identifying himself with the British working-class culture, he is not a colonial subject[69] but the notion that "sale" is

---

67 Both Césaire (see: the fragment of his address quoted above) and Harrison associate darkness with silence. See for example Harrison's poem entitled "Working": "the silence of the worked-out-gob" (16).

68 http://plato.stanford.edu/entries/negritude/

69 http://plato.stanford.edu/entries/negritude/

somehow understood *in* "nègre" constitutes a bottom line of the metaphor, developing an image in which dirt and blackness quite literally pervade his body, flowing like blood through his system. As Hairsine writes, "the image of 'grimy fingers' is the culmination of the conceit of personal identity. The author's 'fingerprints' are signs of his inheritance, they are 'still lined with coal'" (Hairsine 1997: 152) but also a personal badge of individuality, "they are uniquely his" (Hairsine 1997: 153). Hairsine writes that the stanza constitutes "a profoundly negative appraisal of the poet's own selfhood;" after all, he sees his fingers "contaminate 'everything' he comes into contact with" (1997: 153). However, through the association with Négritude, blackness (in the consciousness of the dominant culture tantamount to dirt) is being appropriated and used in a different context: taken from the discourse of the oppressors and endowed with a positive, revolutionary meaning.

So, it is risky to see "the image of fingers begriming everything" (Spencer 1994: 37) only as an unambiguous symbol of self-critique, as Spencer seems to suggest, as they are rather a subversive symbol of poetic identity of the speaker who allies himself with the rebellious movement of colonial subjects seeking their own, inalienable voice. The problem with defining interrelated images of coal, mining, darkness and dirt and their meaning within the larger issue of identity stems from the multiplicity of the sometimes contradictory meanings they acquire in Harrison's poetry. For example, the image of coal in *Newcastle is Peru* can be associated on one level quite "innocently," as Huk suggests (1996: 203), with fire and a home-like feeling of safety. It may be also understood as a sign of a revolutionary attitude mentioned above, but, read in the larger context of other poems from the collection, the image under discussion becomes much more complicated:

> The coal image ... doubles back ... to accumulate associations with this Loiner's [i.e. the poetic persona Tony Harrison] mining hometown as well as with the staithes and shipyards of Peru making him both a victim as a native of the industrial North of England, and a victimizer, as an indoctrinated, travelling representative of the same rapacious western culture that exploits his region and haunts him. (Huk 1996: 203)

Going back to Hairsine's commentary on Spencer's analysis of *Newcastle is Peru*, it should be noted that Hairsine agrees with Spencer that the male gaze prevailing in the poem as well as the "representation of women in the volume as a 'series of breasts, bellies and buttocks'" (1997: 155) might be "potentially reductive" (1997: 155). However, he sees the description of photographs (they are said to be "aggressively fine") as a suggestion of affirmation. Disturbing as they may be (from a male perspective as the poem implies) they are also potentially revolutionary (Hairsine 1997: 155) if seen in the context of the négritude metaphor.

It may be useful for the sake of our further discussion to focus for a moment on Harrison's tendency to portray women in terms of fragments, selected images of body-parts or different attributes ascribed to female characters in particular poems. In general terms, this method can be read as a visual representation of the human condition characterized by "fragmentation (or dislocation perhaps) of the self" (Van Wolputte 2004: 262). An image of a fragmented body or body represented by certain parts reflects the heterogeneous, differential identity of the subject, identity which is always in the process of construction. The idea of being in-between (unable to unambiguously identify with one point of reference, such as place, culture or language) which pervades Harrison's verse, in itself excludes the possibility of completeness, which can be achieved only as a transitory feeling, a fleeting moment. Van Wolputte describes this condition as characteristic for a contemporary self and metaphorically renders it as tantamount to being a Creole:

> We all are Creoles of sorts: hybryd, divided, polyphonic … This contemporary body-self is fragmentary, often incoherent and inconsistent, precisely because it arises from contradictory and paradoxical experiences, social tensions, and conflicts that have one thing in common: they are real, that is, experienced.… body and bodiliness … are questioned and lose their self-evidence and on the experience or threat of finiteness, limitation, transience and vulnerability. These embodied uncertainties do indeed challenge the autonomy of the in/dividual insofar as they no longer appear as a lack or deficinecy, but instead as as an existential characteristic of the human condition. (Van Wolputte 2004: 263)

A question then arises as to what sort of meaning can be attributed to the fact that in many cases, it is a woman, not a man, who is portrayed in terms of fragments? One way to look at this fact is to diminish its importance, following the line of thought suggested by Byrne:

> We should perhaps be wary of making too much of Harrison's habit of portraying women by piecemeal images of anatomical parts. The "I" of "Allotments" is not sketched in any more detail than the partners he takes to the cemetery and the abattoir. If the girls were represented by rumpled jumper, nylons, a bum embossed with an epitaph, the young "I" is also clammy mackintosh and winner vest, and usually, no more solid or complete an image. (1998: 175–176)

The difference is that "we are given an insight into the narrator's thoughts and feelings," (Byrne 1998: 76) which puts him in the spotlight, in the centre of the poem[70], thus becoming the poem's most important subject. The woman is created/constructed by the narrator, as the dedication to *Selected Poems* (Published by Penguin

70 It is the case of the majority of poems in the sequence with the powerful exception of "The Nuptial Torches" whose speaker and central character is female.

Books in 1987) suggests: "… son io poeta, / essa la poesia." From the perspective of feminist theory, the process of reification would be a product of what Laura Mulvey calls a male gaze "objectifying, fragmenting and fetishizing parts of the woman for its own pleasure, both implying and denying autonomous 'wholeness' to the woman and to the female body" (Ross 2010: 4). Undeniably, there is an element of voyeurism in Harrison's observations but as it is often in the case of his verse, it is not only pleasure, but also politics which come into play. Rick Rylance stresses the pertinence of Harrison's method of description. He comments on its political dimension in "Doomsongs: Tony Harrison and War," analysing "The Curtain Catullus" and "The Chopin Express" which "express yearning for sex to overcome political division" (1997: 159). In the former, whose title refers to the Iron Curtain, a woman is reduced to her calves followed by a voyeuristic eye of the observer, in the latter the body of a woman is compared to a foreign land undergoing a form of partition:

Your … calves
Bulge left, right, left. I'm out of breath and stop
To get a peep in at the skirted halves,
Those pale four inches past the stocking top. (The Curtain Catullus 1–4)

The bottom bunk. The blue nightlight
daubs Heaven over the white
uncovered parts. Breasts and thighs
the colour of clear, neutral skies
like Africa's. The fast express
makes our rhythms effortless.
Neutrality! Brave cocks and cunts
belong to no barbed continents. (The Chopin Express 17–24)

According to Rylance in "The Curtain Catullus" "voyeurism plays with and against Cold War context" (1997: 159). The speaker declares "I'm tired of stone bodies I want yours" (The Curtain Catullus 30) in an act of subversion against political divisions. Woman's calves resemble marching soldiers (Rylance 1997: 159), flesh bulging "left, right, left" (The Curtain Catullus 2) in an absurd, parodic way, but are in the same time symbols of desire, a source of pleasure and life-giving energy. "The Chopin Express" constructs images of bodily parts to suggest something more disturbing. "It is clear" Rylance writes "that Africa's imperialist condition is not one of 'Neutrality'. This speaker understands geopolitics in the same way he understands bodies, as an assembly of parts, some of them fantastically desirable" (1997: 159). Here, like in *Newcastle is Peru*, a fragmented female body is compared to the land seen as an object of possible appropriation.

Fragmentation of the body can be also discussed in reference to the theme of memory in Harrison's writing. Craig Raine claims that the difference between the "original experience and that experience when it is hallowed by remembrance" is that things which are "looked back on.… exist cropped out of context, shorn of explanation" (Raine 2009: 30). We remember an "anthology of snapshots" like those at the beginning of Joyce's *A Portrait of an Artist as a Young Man* "a snatch of baby talk, the sensation of wetting the bed; covering and uncovering your ears at refectory" (Raine 2009: 30). To reconstruct the whole picture means to fill in the gaps between the fragments using the power of imagination at the cost of losing the authenticity of experience. Being aware of this fact will not stop us from striving for completeness as if continual attempts to give a full story of the past could give it justice. "Anything fragmented" Raine continues "is given a penumbra of suggestion that we mistake and read as vividness of outline" (2009: 30–31). The one trying to remember is always tempted to fill in the gaps between Wordsworthian "spots of time" (*The Prelude* 257) like the viewer of René Magritte's "L'Evidence eternelle" 'The Eternally Obvious' is tempted to fill in the gaps between the fragments of the female body. In this case, wholeness is in the eye of the observer, not in the thing observed, it is being born on the verge of what one sees and what one imagines. Raine quotes Kundera's *Ignorance*, suggesting that one reason for the need to obtain a continuity of remembrance is nostalgia, "the suffering caused by an unappeased yearning to return" (Kundera 2002: 5) which forces people to retell their histories other and other again.

Raine recalls the way Proust describes instances of memory as extremely pleasurable (Raine 2009: 33) and develops the topic further:

> I suggest that the pleasure, the joy really experienced by Marcel, and the rest of us, is bound up with sensation of immanence, suspense an arrival—common to sex and simile. Memory is metaphorical in its operations …. The pleasure of memory is the pleasure we experience when we read a good simile—the pleasure of difference between the two things being compared, the pleasure we take in the justice of the comparison and the sensation of comprehension. (Raine 2009: 35)

Perhaps this is why girls in "Allotments" and the lover in *Newcastle is Peru* are described in fragments. Their images, retrieved shreds and snatches of the past, constitute a part of a larger story, continuously (re)constructed, in which even the most intimate experience is always underpinned by historical and political context. Memories of a bum embossed with an epitaph, nylons, jumper or naked calves are "sexual" but also "metaphorical" in their "operations" (Raine 2009: 35) as they always stand for something else than what they literally are: parts of female bodies or the garments they wear. Fragmentation represents vulnerability of life. In a sense our memories represent the ruins of the past, removed further and further from what is now, always endangered by being forgotten. They fade unless they are not recalled, unless they have an important place in the present. Retelling old stories, reviving experiences, mourning the dead, archiving events, repeating rituals, taking photographs and many other human activities which are to keep the past alive can be seen as acts of defiance against oblivion. Memory is revolutionary is its operations. As Raine notices, the "word 'remember' is in itself an implicit rejoinder to death. Its etymology counters dismemberment" (2009: 35–36).

What is characteristic of the way Harrison uses memories in the constructions of his characters (including the poetic persona Tony Harrison) is that "memories are" for him "themselves interpretations" (Lawler 2010: 17) and not only in the sense, although as Lawler says it is a fact, that they are not reliable (Lawler 2010: 17) but in a sense that they are "social products" since "what we remember depends on the social context" (Lawler 2010: 17). Lawler suggests that all men are engaged in *memoro-politics*—a process described by Ian Hacking (1994, 1995) "by which the past is interpreted in the light of the knowledge and understanding of the subjects' present" (Lawler 2010: 18), which means that personal memories become reconstructed within the frame of the public context. Steedman explains it as follows:

> We all return to memories and dreams … again and again;[71] the story we tell of our life is reshaped around them. But the point doesn't lie there, back in the past, back in the lost time at which they happened; the only point lies in interpretation. The past re-used through the agency of social information … interpretation of it can only be made with what the people know of a social world and their place within it. (1986: 5)

Lawler comments upon Steedman's thought, concluding that there can be no "unmediated access to … experience … as the past is remembered it is interpreted and reinterpreted …. what we know of 'experience' depends of what we know about the ways in which those experiences relate to the wider social circumstances" (2010: 18). What matters to Harrison is precisely that link between the experience of the individual, which becomes a part of his personal history, and the social, communal experience. The interplay between the two is the subject of

---

71 It is characteristic for Harrison to go back to the same "places" from the past, events from his life's narrative which resemble one another and parallel images belonging to the autobiographical landscape of his working-class childhood and youth. The imagery of concentric circles Harrison often employs in his poems can be interpreted in reference to the issue of continuities between past and present and the problem of memory, especially if seen in the light of Ricœur's opinion that "Memory … is itself the spiral movement that, through anecdotes and episodes, brings us back to the almost motionless constellations of potentialities that the narrative retrieves." (Ricœur, 1980: 186)

many of his poems. It is visible, for example, in the abovementioned image from *Newcastle is Peru*, where an attempt to light the fire with a Sunday newspaper, a vignette of personal memory, is inscribed into the context of war or in the scene from "Allotments,[72]" where an intimate moment of love-making is suddenly set beside an image of a Nazi concentration camp. In the latter, the "past," which is brought back by the old citizen of Leeds and catches the kids "at it," is "*interpreted*[73] through the present"[74] (Lawler 2010: 19), translated into the language of urban imagery, seen "through the lens" (Lawler 2010: 19) of industrial landscape[75] but it also "*informs*[76] the present" (Lawler 2010: 19). The process in which the past exercises its influence upon the present is vividly exemplified by the way

---

72 "Allotments" belongs to the group of so called "Childhood Poems" (Hairsine 1997: 9) which together with "Thomas Campey and the Copernican System" form Part I of the sequence. "Ginger's Friday," "The Pocket Wars of Peanuts Joe" and "Allotments" move "from a depiction of sexuality as innocent and life-affirming to an account of 'fallen sex' which is permeated by guilt and death" (Hairsine 1997: 9) portraying the way in which authority suppresses the power of (Spencer 1994: 21) "emergent sexuality" (Hairsine 1997: 9). It cannot escape unnoticed that the whole sequence is pervaded by sexual imagery and, as Spencer bluntly puts it simply is "centrally concerned with sex" (1994: 22) not only in its life-creating aspect connected closely to issues of inheritance and generation continuity but also with sex in its political aspect as a potentially revolutionary activity. In *The Poetry of Tony Harrison* Spencer opens his chapter on *The Loiners* with an epigraph taken from Herbert Marcuse's *Eros and Civilisation*: "… human freedom is not only a private affair—but it is nothing at all unless it is also a private affair." and adds that in the sequence under discussion, the private affair is defined in terms of sexuality endowed with "subversive potential" but limited by "authoritarianism and violence" (Spencer 1994: 22). For further discussion see pages 21–43 in Luke Spencer's *The Poetry of Tony Harrison*, London: Harvester Wheatsheaf, 1994.

73 Emphasis added by the author of this book.

74 "present moment" understood here as the moment in personal history of the speaker positioned in relation to the past histories of the Holocaust, a moment in which the action of the poem takes place, contemporary to the young boy. It should be stated that the poem offers three time-planes: distant past (Holocaust) the past (the speaker's youth described in the past tense) and the point in time in which the poem is being written (which is not acknowledged in any straightforward way).

75 The image of concentration camps and its crematoria is superimposed on to the image of chimneys belonging to Leeds abattoirs, memories of the Holocaust "materialize" in the industrial urban landscape: The Pole who caught us at it once had smelt / Far worse at Auschwitz and at Buchenwald / he said, and pointing to the chimneys, *Meat*! / *Zat is vere zey murder vat you eat.* / And jogging beside us, *As a man devours* / *Ze flesh of animals, so vorms devour ours* (Allotments 27–29).

76 Emphasis added by the author of this book.

the intrusive interference of the death image prevents the moment of pleasure, quenches lust, which becomes entangled in the net of horrific associations with death and remains in the mind's eye to haunt the dreams of the speaker:

> Nearly midnight and that gabbling, foreign nut
> Had stalled my coming, spoilt my appetite
> For supper, and gave me a sleepless night
> In which I rolled frustrated and I smelt
> Lust on myself, then smoke, and I felt
> Street bonfires blazing for the end of war
> .... and I cried
> For the family still pent up in my balls,
> For my corned-beef sandwich, and for genocide. (Allotments 34–39, 42–44)

Harisine points out to the role which the past, invading the present in the form of war-time memories, plays in the movement from innocence to experience, to use Blake's antithesis:

> Primarily, the passage [lines 34–44] dramatizes the youth's assumption of new kind of personal identity. The secure but illusory shell of privacy, described in the first section, is broken. It is replaced with an anguished awareness of his own involvement in the continuities of history (and of the human condition: these are the existential "allotments" of the punning title). Significantly, the smell of smoke is located on his own person. The blending of smells of lust and smoke suggests the way in which sexual appetite is adulterated by the appalling connotations of the abattoir smoke. (1997: 11)

As the example of "Allotments" shows, the social context used in Harrison's poems is not always the immediate one; sometimes the scene which cuts into the private experience comes from a distant time and place, but the private experience is almost always reinterpreted and reshaped by the social, political, communal one. If memory is reconstructive (Misztal 2003: 82) and if tales of the past "mash with the rest of the world and with other people's stories," (Hacking 1995: 250–251) then "public voice for poetry" can be obtained only through exercising private memories or, to put it differently, through the negotiation of the autobiographical experience which, in turn, will be always influenced by the social context.[77] The public, politically-involved voice in *The Loiners* touches upon several subjects, one

77 Liz Stanley discusses the difficulties with interpreting the autobiographical material in her book *The Auto/biographical*, developing an issue which proves important for reading of Harrison's poems and understanding the construction of the Tony Harrison persona: "The self who writes has no more direct and unproblematic access to the 'self who was' than does the reader; and anyway 'the autobiographical past' is actually peopled by a succession of selves as the writer grows, develops and changes" (Stanley, 1992: 61).

of them being an issue relevant for many of Harrison's later poems,[78] namely the issue of the dominance of authoritarian culture over the culture of the suppressed. The poem that develops this theme extensively is "The White Queen[79]," in which the backdrop for the interplay of private and public affairs, the intimate and the political, is Colonialism and consequently Imperialism, presented as powerful forces that shape the western consciousness and British identity. The continuity of the colonial experience, which manifests itself in "authoritarian concern with power" (Hairsine 1997: 56), is transferred in Harrison's later work into the national context. The relations between the privileged culture of the higher classes and the working-class culture of the English North in Commonwealth Britain are based on the dichotomy between the "dominant" and "subject," similarly to the relations between the colonizers and the colonized[80] (Hairsine 1997: 56) in the times of the British Empire. "The White Queen" creates the basis for this analogy, delving into the concept of "oppressive hierarchies which structure personal and political relationships" (Hairsine 1997: 53) but also comments upon the problem of identity of the suppressors and the suppressed, revealing different continuities between private and public experience, which in the colonial context assume the form of "the continuity between the interior, psychological repression and the exterior, political violence" (Hairsine 1997: 54).

According to Spencer, Harrison introduces in "The White Queen" "a deviant but defiant character, whose very marginality is a source of insight" and who remains strongly inscribed within the social context of Britain, especially the 1960s, when "whole categories of the despised and rejected began to gain some sympathetic recognition" (Spencer 1994: 27). He is a homosexual man who enjoys the company of African boys and so shows, according to Spencer, paedophile inclinations, which consequently means he is "undeniably beyond the pale of English … respectability" (Spencer 1994: 27). However, his occupation (he is a professor of English) and the fact that he is a white man imply that "his nickname itself can be seen as … setting his sexual deviancy alongside the skin colour, education and income by which he is socially empowered in a black African country" (Spencer 1994: 27). The perspective from which he describes his own actions shows awareness of his

78 See *The School of Eloquence* and *v.*

79 "White Queen" is composed of five parts: Satyrae, The Raiload Heroides, Travesties, Manica, *from* The Zeg-Zeg Postcards.

80 In "The White Queen" it is the Loiner who is the colonist, a representative of the dominant culture. In the subsequent poems from *The School of Eloquence* the Loiner is given a different position—he becomes the member of the suppressed, marginalized strata of the society.

moral condition and the position he holds, awareness of "racism and sexism which infect his own 'liberated' conduct" (Spencer 1994: 27):

> Black, black. What's the use? I can't escape
> our foul conditioning that makes a rape
> seem natural, if wrong, and love unclean
> between some ill-fed blackboy and fat queen. (Satyrae I, 37–40)

This blunt identification with the unnamed group ("our conditioning") which shapes his identity and gives him the right to exploit seems to come solely from his belonging to the dominant, authoritarian culture and makes him a representative of the colonial consciousness but also alienates him in the foreign African context. He is an example of an ambivalent hero whose identity cannot be easily defined, who excludes and abjects but at the same time, undergoes exclusion and abjection himself, empowered by the same social background which rejects him and censors his sexual preferences.

As Hairsine writes, Harrison endows the main character of the poem with the world-view characteristic of the authoritarian, western consciousness saturated with the idea of "hierarchical divisions generat[ing] the forms and categories in which the world is defined," (1997: 53) but at the same time offers the readers a different perspective, "dismantle[ing]," if only for a brief moment, "the dichotomies which sustain authoritarian culture" (1997: 53). A pertinent example of this method, a poem that echoes the image of the lover's body as a foreign land in *Newcastle is Peru*, comes from the "Travesties." It is titled "The Ancestor" and alludes to the lines by the Cuban poet, Nicolás Guillén:

> Lover, under your bleak landscape are
> rivers of strange blood, where you may see
> lily and lotus, rose and nenuphar;
> and there you'll see a restless spirit stare
> and turn, your ancestor's dark shadow flee,
> who gave the frizzle to your golden hair. (9–14)

It is a close-up of an intimate encounter and a social comment. The white body seen in *Newcastle is Peru* as a "snowfield" and "slopes of flash" (130–131) in "The Ancestor," functions even more powerfully as at the same time an object of personal desire and a political entity, with its latter role brought to the foreground. Showing a white man through the eyes of his African lover, the poem, which tackles the question of inheritance, central to understanding of the later *The School of Eloquence* sequence, exposes the way "Europeans disclaim any evolutionary or cultural kinship with blacks" (Spencer 1994: 31) but, simultaneously, points to the ancestral continuity between the two. This is perhaps the most significant difference between the image of "body as landscape" in "The Ancestor" and the parallel one constructed in *Newcastle is Peru*, which seems to postulate the possibility of "overcoming cultural and habitual myopia," to use Huk's words, by "rediscovering the world in the familiar" (Huk 1996: 201): the former poem stresses the inherent connection between the speaker and the object of his desire whereas the latter does not. The speaker of *Newcastle is Peru* moves across the surface of the discovered land, which metaphorically represents the superficiality of his perspective[81], astonished by the infinitely new landscape, at risk of getting lost[82] as he possesses no knowledge either of its history or topography, whereas the speaker of "The Ancestor" describes the world "under" as if he sees that which is not immediately noticeable, that which escapes the eye of the ordinary or reckless onlooker. In Harrison's poetry, the movement "under" is often tantamount to movement into the past, as in "Travesties," where the idea of ancestral lines running back in time indicates the possible existence of an anthropological bond between the colonizer and the colonized.

As Lawler claims, "in European and North American culture inheritance is held to lead to identity," (2010: 31) and so the issue of looking back in search for one's roots inscribes itself into a larger task of constructing "identities within the context of a kin structure" (2010: 31). The problem of "kinship," mentioned pertinently by Spencer, is introduced in the poem most powerfully by the metaphor of "rivers of strange blood," suggestive of the side of human experience which is biologically determined or inborn, which in turn corresponds to the following perspective assumed by David Schneider. Schneider suggests that considering kinship involves the conceptualization of two basic orders: "the order of blood and the order of law" (1968: 24), which means that people can be "related through blood (children and parents, siblings, cousins, etc) or through law (spouses, in-laws). The author of *American Kinship* notes that "unlike legal ties … [blood ties] cannot ordinarily be dissolved," a fact contributing to the emergence of "a cultural belief that the blood relationship is 'an objective fact of nature" (Schneider 1968: 24) and encourages people to see "'blood' links" as crucial in the creation of identity (Lawler 2010: 38). As Schneider claims:

> A blood relationship is a relationship of identity. People who are blood relatives share a common identity, they believe. This is expressed as 'being of the same flesh and blood'. It is a belief in common biological constitution, and aspects like temperament, build,

---

81 "Discovery! Wart, mole, spot / like outcrops on a snowfield, dot" (Newcastle is Peru 129–30).

82 "your body like an endless maze" (Newcastle is Peru 134).

physiognomy and habits are noted as signs of this shared biological makeup, this special identity of relatives with each other. Children are said to look like their parents, or take after one or another parent or grandparent; these are confirming signs of the common biological identity. A parent ... may speak of a child as 'a part of me'. (Schneider 1968: 25)

Nevertheless, according to Lawler, the "blood/law distinction" should not be understood as a simple reflection of "nature/culture divide" (2010: 37) and Schneider does not suggest it (Lawler 2010: 37). Lawler understands blood as symbolizing connection, not a connection in itself (Lawler 2010: 37), which as a consequence, makes it possible for Americans (and Europeans) to "build cultural relations of kin" (Lawler 2010: 37). "Kin relations are" Lawler continues "by definition cultural. Kin are ... those we *recognize* as kin ... according to the two orders of blood and law" (Lawler 2010: 37).

What the poem presents, and what makes it an instance of "dismantle[ing]" the above-mentioned "dichotomies which sustain authoritarian culture," (Hairsine 1997: 53) is a moment of establishing continuity. The perspective assumed by the African lover who, despite the surface "biological constitution" (Schneider 1968: 25) different than his own, claims common ancestry with the white man, is essentially an act of *recognition*. If "kinship" is "a way of constituting relationships that include and exclude others" then the European "disclaim" Spencer writes about (1994: 31), in combination with the politics of supremacy, must result in denying African people any type of identity apart from the one imposed upon them by the colonizing culture. The "European perception of African realities," (Nicholson 2010: 73) entailing superior position and a harassing gaze which appropriates and subdues, is one of the main topics of "*from* The Zeg–Zeg Postcards" the fifth movement of "The White Queen":

I watch you pour the pure
well water, balanced up the mountain,
in blinding kerosene cans,
each lovely morning, convict,
your release date, nineteen years from now,
daubed in brown ink on your rotten shirt. (Zeg–Zeg Postcards V 2–7)

The image unfolds from a description of a body in motion, enchanting in its simplicity, into a sinister comment upon the enslavement of the colonized in Africa, illustrated most disturbingly by the "(mis)placing of 'lovely' [which] speaks subliminal appropriation of a figure of desire destined to rot" (Nicholson 2010: 73). As Nicholson suggests, the speaker's sense of sensual pleasure is derived from the fact that the object of desire he repeatedly observes is subjugated (Nicholson 2010: 73) and powerless, his position inferior and confined. The continuity of the appropriating gaze[83] runs in the fragment parallel to the continuity of the colonial "structures of power" (Nicholson 2010: 62), which are not only reflected in the act of watching but also reinforced by it, since the voyeuristic activity of the speaker seems to be unhindered and self-indulging. A similar effect is achieved in the sixteenth Postcard of the sequence, in which the body of the Other is looked at through the prism of western civilization, here represented by an iconic drink. The Colonizer's gaze turns the colonized into an erotic object who passively, maybe even unconsciously, assumes the role superimposed on to him by the observer:

> The shower streams over him
> and the water turns instantly
> to cool Coca-Cola. (Zeg–Zeg Postcards XVI 1–3)

The poet adds a fictional context to this part of the poem under discussion (i.e. *from* The Zeg–Zeg Postcards) in a short note which explains the origin of the series of short, haiku-like impressions:

> These short poems are from a collection written on the backs of postcards and gradually accumulated over the years in a card-index cabinet. The postcards are all from, or of, places in Europe visited by the 'White Queen' on leaves from Africa, and the poems on them are, almost without exception, about Africa ... It is curious that those that were actually posted are addressed to a completely *illiterate*[84] lover. (The Loiners 46)

The addressee of the postcards, uneducated, according to a western understanding of what education is, embodies Africa, inscribed into the colonial discourse as its subject with no possibility of becoming an interlocutor. Desire mixed with awe lies close to violence, and the White Queen knows it. As Spencer suggests one of the most straightforward "stab[s] of self- and social awareness" (Spencer 1994: 28) of the sequence comes with the "*from* The Zeg–Zeg Postcards IX" (not reprinted in *Selected Poems*) when the speaker notices that "What begins in honest lust can end/with innocent blood on its hands," (Zeg–Zeg Postcards IX 1–2) revealing his awareness of colonial reality. Subordination of the colonized is symbolized in the poem by the silence of illiteracy; and consequently, the image of the African lover denied a voice, absurd as the addressee of the White Queen's postcards, illustrates "distances separating construer from construed" (Nicholson 2010: 73). Seen from the perspective of western cultures, the African lover possesses no proper language skills. Deprived of his own voice, he is denied "the

83 "I watch you ... each lovely morning" (Zeg–Zeg Postcards 2–5).
84 Emphasis added by the author of this book.

right to claim an identity as distinct from an ascribed and enforced classification" (Bauman 2004:39). Commenting on Bauman, Lawler suggests:

> An identity is imposed and there is no official space allowed where this may be contested or different identity affirmed ... Those with a power to name[85] can identify both themselves and those without such power. Further, those who are denied any chance to name and define themselves tend to be defined in terms of 'mass' or a 'mob' and to be contrasted with an 'us' who are individuals. (Lawler 2010: 146)

It seems that the postcards address a concrete individual. He is referred to in the poem most frequently in terms of sensual qualities, which can satisfy the lust of his white lover, a man in "pursuit of variation" and "maximisation of sexual opportunity" (Nicholson 2010: 74) and so exhibits the characteristic behavior, as Ronald Hyam explains in *Empire and Sexuality,* of a representative of colonial Britain (Hyam 1991: 3). The African lover seems to exist only as a projection of the white man's desire, a member of an underclass whose existence is subordinated to the power of the socially and morally superior. Bauman explains:

> The meaning of 'underclass identity' is an absence of identity; the affacement or denial of individuality, of 'face'—that object of ethical duty and moral care. You are cast outside the social space in which identities are sought, chosen, constructed, evaluated, confirmed and refuted. (2004: 39)

The issue of silence or lack of voice returns, although from a different perspective in part three of the poem under discussion titled "Travesties," which is based on the section of the poetic work *Syphilis sive Morbus Gallicus (Syphilis or the French Disease)* by Hieronymus Fracastorius (1483–1553). In "Distant Ophir"[86] opening "Travesties," the lack of a speech organ is, in a paradoxical way, presented as an inherent feature of the one whose job is to deal with words and produce utterances. Harrison informs the reader in a note following the poem that "Hieronymus Fracastorius (1483–1553) was born as perhaps befits a true poet,[87] without a mouth. The fact is celebrated in the well-known epigram of Julius Caesar Scaliger

---

85 The issue, frequently appearing in Harrison's poetry returns among others in the *School of Eloquence* sonnet titled "Fire-Eater" where the speaker, equipped with and empowered by the "tongues of fire," (Fire-Eater 11) a bitter-sweet inheritance he obtained from his ancestors, names the world like biblical Adam.

86 As Nicholson writes: "Book III of Syphilis combines Columbus's numerous landings into one event and relates how he and his crew set down on Haiti (Ophyre)" (2010: 70). Ophir is also a place mentioned in the poem by John Masefield entitled "Cargoes".

87 A parallel image namely of an orator with a speech impediment returns in "Them and [uz]" a poem from *The School of Eloquence* sequence.

(1484–1558), Fracastorius died, after apoplexy, speechless." Acknowledged by name as the author of the original version of the travesty, Fracastorius becomes, in Harrison's poem, a Tiresias-like character: he can deliver a poetic prophecy despite being speechless, just as the mythological prophet of Thebes could foresee the future despite being blind. In Harrison's poem, the prophecy concerns the bearers of the colonial legacy, referred to as "Westerners," (Distant Ophir 1) the name used by Fracastorius in a narrower sense, to denote the French, the invaders of Italy who crossed its borders between the years 1494–1528, in the author's lifetime (Hairsine 1997: 86). Harrison's "Westerners," or, as Hairsine calls them, "hubristic transgressors," have their "western history reduced" in the poem "to the dual themes of continuous political violence and existential degeneration" which correspond to "the cataclysms of the twentieth century ... both located and circumscribed within this continuity" (Hairsine 1997: 88). The speaker of the poem, "the dark bird"[88] (Distant Ophir 31), enumerates both the dreadful deeds of the colonizers and the plagues which will descend as their result:

> 'Westerners, who laid their Sun's fowl low,
> The flocks of Apollo now stand and hear
> The dreadful sufferings you must undergo.
> ...
> Self-lumbered pilgrims of San Lazaro's
> brothels and gold bars bring you no joy,
> porphyry and rape bring you no repose!
> ...
> *worse wanderings after*[89] with more thousands lost,
> comrades you fitted out search parties for
> hutches of bleached ribs on our bare coast. (Distant Ophir 1–3, 10–12, 16–18)

The continuity of colonial experience and colonial hubris stretch forward on to the post-colonial era, where the overseas voyages and bold explorations which "cost destruction greater than the siege of Troy" turn into "wanderings" (Distant Ophir 15–16) deprived of destination and hope, tantamount to the fall of western

---

88 Nicholson explains Harrison's reference to "the dark bird" as follows:

> Importing European power into Haiti Spaniards using the new weapons of gunpowder shot 'ornate birds [with] blue flashing wings contrasting with their red beaks, who [until then] passed untroubled through their native grove's wilderness'. Inserting European valences, Fracastorius invokes these Caribbean birds as sacred to Apollo, Mediterranean god of poetry but also of constitutions and codes of law, and describes how they retreated 'flocking together in terror' to the high rocks. (Nicholson 2010: 70)

89 Emphasis added by the author of this book.

civilization. The protagonists of Harrison's poem, the Westerners, roam the land as a result of their invasions and destruction of native cultures but also the inability to acknowledge their "universal affiliation" with the Other (Hairsine 1997: 89) or, to use Lawler's terminology, an inability to recognize the principle of "common humanity" (2010: 3) which makes all people kin. Colonialism, Harrison seems to be saying, does not vanish with the dismantling of the Empires but takes its toll and influences those who come next and have to endure the "wanderings after," described as "worse" (Distant Ophir 16) than all previous sufferings. The perpetual loss that accompanies them is metaphorically represented in "Distant Ophir" by "hutches of bleached ribs on our bare coast" (18) an image strangely reminiscent of Eliot's "rats' alley/ Where the dead men lost their bones" (The Waste Land 115–16) in which the protagonists of "The Waste Land," devoid of strength and spirit, find themselves. According to Hairsine "symptomatic aimlessness, restlessness and essential incoherence connoted by wandering" constitutes "an existential inheritance of the (contemporary) Westerner … deprived of physical and metaphysical home" and signifies "a disintegration of social identity" (Hairsine 1997: 90).

Analysing the poem from the perspective of Bauman's sociological thought, one notices that the condition of the constant wanderer corresponds in some of its aspects to Bauman's description of a vagabond—a metaphorical representation of a post—modern identity type: a man who travels constantly, not by choice (Bauman 1996: 14), but because he is uprooted, displaced and/or rejected by the given community he temporarily became a member of (Bokszański 2007: 256–257). The similarity of the condition of Harrison's Westerner, who stands for both the colonizer and his inheritor, to the condition of Bauman's vagrant becomes apparent if one takes into account the Homeric references developed in "Distant Ophir" and aptly commented upon by Hairsine:

> The Homeric allusion extends into stanza six of the poem [quoted above] … On one hand such "wanderings" are suggestive of the flight of Aeneas and other Trojan survivors of the war; and so of the future sufferings of the displaced peoples and refugees. More central to the themes of 'Distant Ophir' … is the reference to the fate of the victors of the war, to 'the wanderings of Odysseus' in particular … The poem implies a mythic structure underlying the Homeric epics which is comparable to the Christian story of The Fall. In the aftermath of 'the fall' of Troy the victors (and also the vanquished) *are forced to wander*[90] because they are excluded from, or denied a return to, their homes. (Hairsine 1997: 89)

90 Emphasis added by the author of this book.

The way a free-moving tourist, the post-modern consumer, can turn into his underprivileged alter-ego, the vagabond (Bauman 1996: 14) bears resemblance to the way the colonizer, travelling in the name of new discoveries, turns, in Harrison's poem, into a wanderer. What connects these two transformations (tourist to vagabond, colonizer to wanderer) is the fact that they both entail the abovementioned loss of freedom to choose one's fate. As a result of the transformation, Harrison's traveller, a man of power, a domineering conquistador who draws his own maps of the lands he crosses,[91] designating the boundaries of the world, changes into an exile who finds his surroundings "unbearably inhospitable" (Bauman 1996: 14). His new identity is depicted as an ongoing curse as he is "losing more and more/to the sea, the climate" (Distant Ophir 19–20), and perhaps, Harrison seems to be suggesting, it is a perpetual condition of the westerner which will be passed on to the next generations like a disease, like syphilis described in the sixteenth century by Fracastorius. A fatal "*discubrimiento*" (Distant Ophir 29) which makes the travellers curse the hour they decided to conquer and appropriate the foreign land casts a shadow on the joyful image depicted in *Newcastle is Peru*. A metaphorical new-found-land acquires a much more disturbing undertone, or, as Huk puts it, "darkens into analogue for its domination … translated into sexual terms," (Huk 1996: 203) turning the delighted explorer of the "slopes of flesh" (Newcastle is Peru 131) into a ruthless exploiter for whom his lover is not only as unknown as Peru but also "as distant" (Newcastle is Peru 137).

The idea, hinted at in *Newcastle is Peru*, that colonized land is at the same time under control and out of reach, conquered but unintelligible, is translated in "The White Queen" into an imagery of nothingness which like an "endless maze," (Newcastle is Peru 134) becomes a figure of confusion and alienation. The unavoidable feeling of emptiness the westerners experience in Africa, proves that "[t]he nightmare of history is not only outside but inside" (Huk 1996: 202), that is within the geographical borders of England but also deeper, in the souls or perhaps, to read Harrison's metaphors closely, in the guts of the colonizers and their envoys, who are more or less devoted to the imperial cause. One of the characters of the "Satyrae," a Russian medical officer named Boris, one of those, "unwitting representatives" (Huk 1996: 202) of the colonizing system, sees the abyss as an integral part of the human constitution, an intrinsic feature of life (Hairsine 1997: 80). He can detect it listening to the pulse, to the rumbling rhythms of the

91 This land, where you are now, is that Ophir/your flashy maps show off like a jewellery (Distant Ophir 4–5).

body, its rooms being empty holes which echo sounds without meaning.[92] Emptiness brings despair, boredom, hopelessness; all ascribed in the poem to western thought. They constitute a part of its heritage which in "Satyrae" is essentially devoid of everything alive, passionate or regenerative. The escape from nothingness attempted by one of the characters, Lisa, brings only short-term relief. The change of one empty landscape (sand) to another (snow), both equally cold and uninviting, disillusions the escapee. In her disillusionment, she is no different from other western characters of the "White Queen" who, according to Huk, often "try to break out of one stereotype only to fall into another" (1996: 202) and eventually find themselves caught in the labyrinthine sequence of false moves and misguided ventures.

> The Nothingness! Lisa—she couldn't stand
> the boredom and packed off to Switzerland.
> She sends him a postcard of a snowblown slope:
> *Boris, ich bin frei ... und friere.* He can't cope
> Here alone. (Satyrae V 27–31)

This failed attempt at closeness between an estranged couple (Hairsine 1997: 83) is described in terms of a black/white antithesis, often used by Harrison: after a moment of shared life the woman escapes boredom to inhabit a seemingly better place and leaves the man on the opposite pole, in black Africa, which he is sick of and despises, yearning for a white promised land. Boris becomes a fallen man "eternally exiled from the mythically pure St Petersburg," (Hairsine 1997: 83) where he will never be able to return. The state of frigidity and lifelessness in which the protagonists find themselves is stressed by the words of Lisa who writes on the postcard that she is "free and ... freezing" 'frei und ... friere' (Satyrae V 30). "Nothingness," (Satyrae V 27) which in the poem constitutes a separate entity, a state of things, a condition of the contemporary European, refers in the passage, first of all, to the lack of human bond. This idea is strengthened by the formal arrangement of the lines where "Nothingness" is inserted between the image of the "double bed" where Boris sleeps alone and the image "Lisa"[93] who chooses Switzerland over Africa. Harrison's "Nothingness" (Satyrae V 27) is a reference

92 "The space, the gaps, the darkness, that same void / He hears vibrating in clogged adenoid / And vocal chords. Through his cool stethoscope / He hears despair pulsate and withered hope / Flutter the failing heart a little, death/ Of real feeling in a laboured breath. / He knows with his firm finger on a pulse / It is Nothingness and nothing else / Throbs in the blood." (Satyrae V 9–17)

93 "... their double bed. / The Nothingness! Lisa—" (Satyrae V 26–27).

to Pascal, mentioned three times in the "Satyrae," and to Pascal's discussion of the human condition, which is in essence "inconstancy, boredom [and] anxiety," a man is "equally incapable of seeing the nothingness from which he emerges and the infinity in which he is engulfed" (1962: 95). It seems to be a condition of perpetual torment:

> Nothing is more intolerable to a man than a state of complete repose, without desires, without work, without amusements, without occupation. In such a state he becomes aware of his nothingness, his abandonment, his inadequacy, his dependence, his emptiness, his futility. There at once wells up from the depths of his soul weariness, gloom, misery, exasperation, frustration, despair. (1962: 90)

The state of futility in which Boris finds himself is a condition of a man deprived of the superficial badges of belonging to European culture. Those cultural signs of identification, a certain style of living appropriate for an affluent European and represented in the poem by Swiss winter resorts, dining out, gardens and Scotch whisky,[94] lose their meaning in the foreign context of Africa, which strips the newcomers of the layers of cultural context. Africa reveals the void—the core of western existence. Europe is presented in the poem in terms of absence, in terms of non-being rather than being.

> Northwards two hundred miles, emptiness
> As big as Europe; *Sah'ra*; Nothingness.
> South six hundred, miles of churning sea
> Make of the strongest swimmer a nonentity. (Satyrae V 1–4)

The comparison of the size of the Sahara to the size of Europe also serves to compare Europe itself to the Sahara, which from a European perspective stands for "Nothingness" (Satyrae V 2) In the foreign environment a European feels lost; Africa, perceived as the Other, cannot be understood since any possible attempt of identification with the otherness is rejected at the very beginning of the encounter. The word *Sah'ra* is written in italics like the voices of dialect speakers in *The School of Eloquence* (Harrison 1991: 229) it represents the cultural Other. The image of the Sahara stands in opposition to the image of a garden, a form of artificially created environment, tamed nature which seems frail and perishable in comparison to the destructive and omnipotent force of the Sahara, a desert depicting the emptiness of the European soul, desolate and barren. As Hairsine writes:

---

94 They belong to the same category of tools of colonial subordination as "'phlegm, firepowder, cerebral caution, exercise' … mental attitudes and physical equipment" (Nicholson 2010: 74) enumerated by Harrison in "Black and White and red all over: the fiction of Empire," an article published in *London Magazine* in 1972.

> The obsessive designation of Africa as Other has led to a profound alienation from the African environment and inability to discover or assign comprehensible meaning to it … The limits of Eurocentric values and systems of thought are exposed by the failure or refusal to find a foothold of recognition … or any sense of belonging, within this environment. The European consciousness instead transfers its own fears and anxieties onto the Otherness." (1997: 81)

Consequently, in the European consciousness, "Emptiness" becomes synonymous with the Sahara since it is an ultimate representation of cultural Other—"nothing" seen as an opposition to "something". The poem plays with the idea of a desert seen as nothingness and offers a different perspective. Paradoxically, Harrison says, it is the western culture, which offers nothing but despair, as it is built of gaps and darkness.

The European man who asks for sleeping pills to kill the void gaping inside him projects his fear onto the Sahara like the man from Pascal's writings projects his "inner desolation … onto a universe" (Pascal 1962: 105):

> I see the terrifying spaces of the universe which imprison me, and I find myself planted in a tiny corner of this vast space without my knowing why I happen to be here rather than in some other place, or why the brief space of life that is mine has been allocated to me at this point rather than another in all the eternity of time which preceded me and all the eternity of time that will come after me. I see only infinites on all sides which enclose me like an atom and like a shadow which only lasts for a second and which will not return. (Pascal 1962: 105)

By alienating the Other, Europeans project their own perception of the human condition onto that which they don't know and don't comprehend, and so onto that which they perceive as inferior and potentially threatening to their value system. Western hierarchical order, symbolized in the poem by the structure of the garden, yields to the force of "churning sea" (Satyrae V 3) of the desert—to the chaos of the Other. By colonizing Africa, imposing their own world view, enforcing their rules, westerners only deepen the feeling of despair they carry within. Colonizers neither identify nor sympathize with the Other, and so Africa is inaccessible and illegible for them, closed like a rock, impenetrable like a mirror surface that reflects their soul as they approach it but does not open itself. It may be broken but it gives nothing and remains, from a western point of view, "an accursed heritage" (Burzyńska 2006: 556) as one of Joseph Conrad's characters puts it, which has no culture, no history and consequently no identity of its own.

Harrison quotes his famous predecessor in the title of the poem immediately following "The White Queen," namely, "The Heart of Darkness," which perpetuates "pervasive imagery of circularity," (Huk 1996: 201) representing, according to Huk "the progress of history" where "constructions of … power root themselves in historical/discursive precedents and thus perpetuate their cyclic, eternal return" (1996: 201–202). This is the idea underlying the opening poem of the third part of the book, titled "The Nuptial Torches," which takes readers back in time and removes them from a British context.[95] The main character of the poem is Isabella of Spain, speaking as she observes the mass burnings of heretics, among them Carlos de Sessa and Ponce de la Fuente, executions ordered by her newlywed husband Philip II, who "exemplifies" in the poem "the death instinct as both a sexual perversion and a principle of political action" (Spencer 1994: 26). Spencer finds this poem the most original one in *The Loiners*, among other things, due to its seeming incongruity:

> It is the only poem that deals with people and events unconnected with … England … [and] the twentieth century … a poem that gains in stature and significance the more it is compared with other poems of the collection. Its inclusion can be justified, on structural grounds only by its overwhelming relevance to the central themes which Harrison is examining.… Only here is a woman treated as a moral subject whose feelings form the bedrock of compassion on which the text's meaning is centred. Isabella's is the authentic voice of … [the] exploited … [and] has the authority to speak for the other victims in the poem. (1994: 25–26, 40)

Isabella's narration sets the private starkly against the public, for Harrison inseparably combined in a shocking, conceit-like metaphor of burning stakes. The stakes are horrific symbols of "organised barbarism" (Spencer 1994: 26) but also symbols of wedding torches lighting the way to the couples' marriage bed, in whose smoke "pitch-stained children" go "to the upper air" (The Nuptial Torches 44) and which evoke an oblique association with the atrocities of Auschwitz and Buchenwald present in "Allotments." In "The Nuptial Torches," Harrison creates, once again, the image of the body in close-up:

> Young Carlos de Sessa stripped was good
> For a girl to look at and he spat like wood

95 Apart from "circular progress of history" described by Huk, due to which the same barbaric laws of oppression subsequently return in new historical eras, another type of continuity the poem evokes is commented upon by Harrison in the interview with Haffenden: "When I give readings I often begin with 'Nuptial Torches': a woman who stands for life and continuity is married on the day when she sits next to her husband watching people burning at the stake, and there is a struggle between what she sees and her instinct for continuity" (Harrison 1991: 227). Harrison mentions also other poems which tackle a similar problem: "A 'Kumquat for John Keats' is also about the same subject but from a different end: how does joy exist in a world which the intellect tells you is full of pain? 'Cypress & Cedar' is also about the same duality in one" (Haffenden 1991: 227).

Green from the orchards for the cooking pots.
Flames travelled up his flesh into dry knots.
....
O yellow piddle in fresh fallen snow—
Dogs on the Guadarramas ... dogs. Their souls
Splut through their pores like porridge holes.
They wear their skins like cast-offs. Their skin grows
Puckered round their knees like rumpled hose. (The Nuptial Torches 11–14, 24–28)

This time, the human body is not explored as it was in *Newcastle is Peru* but destroyed (heretics) and sexually abused (Isabella) by "repressive civilization," which in the case of Isabella's fate takes the form of "patriarchal power in marriage" (Spencer 1994: 27). In the context of the colonial theme of *The Loiners*, upon which the central part of the book is based, exploration and exploitation, embodied in the character of the great conquistador Philip II, constitute one act that can be interpreted differently depending which point of view is assumed: the one of the transgressor or the one of the invaded subject.

Considering the construction principle of *The Loiners*, which moves, as noted, "in a great circle," (Huk 1996: 200) it seems justified at the end of the chapter to go back for a brief moment to the first part of the sequence and examine the continuity of colonial structures of power (Nicholson 2010: 62) that permeate domestic affairs and determine the fate of a northern periphery subordinate to the culturally and politically privileged centre. The opening poem of the sequence titled "Thomas Campey and the Copernican System," centres around the character of the street-card trader and junk-dealer who comes from the records of Harrison's childhood memories (Nicholson 2010: 61) and who, according to Spencer, takes after Dickens's "gnarled and knotted Krook," a protagonist of *Bleak House* (Spencer 1994: 23). Nicholson sees in his "wretched and lingering condition ... a 'third world' portrait of life in the 'first world' urban economy" (Nicholson 2010: 61) an epitome of exclusion, and traces in this image of Campey references to Frantz Fanon's *Black Skin, White Masks*:

> Harrison has unsettling things to say about these [i.e. colonial] habits of mind and their associated will to power, and beguiling ways of saying them: taken together they position *The Loiners* as a volatile but radically sympathetic response to Frantz Fanon's revolutionary call ... Fanon traced social coordinates for the psychic structure of the colonial relation in the colonial city's racially divided native and settlers zones: the first *Loiner* Poem focuses on segregation in an English city. (Nicholson 2010: 61)

Campey's *tabes dorsalis*, which in *The Loiners* functions as "metonymy for all the cross-infections caused by territorial greed," (Spencer 1994: 30) shadows Fracastorius' *Syphilis* from "Distant Ophir" and stands for the "diseased" state (Hairsine

1997: 5) of the authoritarian culture of the West.[96] Within the frame of this culture, Newcastle is indeed Peru and Leeds can be compared to Haiti[97] since the same laws segregate the cities in distant colonies and in the North of England. This oblique connection that can be drawn between Leeds and Ophir, a mythical land of gold, as presented in John Masefield's "Cargoes,"[98] has its deeply ironic undertones. Both poems construct an image of cargoes, a list of objects which represent the land of their origin and constitute a commodity meant for sale. In the case of Masefield's celebratory poem, these are the goods of imperial trade hauled by Quinquireme and Spanish galleon.[99] In Harrison's text, Campey's back is "bowed by the weight of old, crack-spined volumes" (Byrne 1997: 5) and Victoriana, coming from the waste land of a post-industrial town.[100] The first stanza, which is the first movement of the entire collection, is as Hairsine affirms, "an image of the shadow of the past hanging over, and then descending upon, the present ... influence of the colonial ... inheritance upon Leeds" (1997: 4–5, 7).

> The other day all thirty shillings' worth
> Of painfully collected waste was blown

---

96 This reading is reinforced by an allusion to the fall of the Roman Empire established in the text by references to Spengler, Mommsen and Gibbon who wrote, respectively, *Decline of the West*, *History of Rome* and *The History of the Decline of the Roman Empire*.

97 As was stated above "Ophir" in Fracastrorius' work denoted Haiti.

98 Harrison was definitely aware of Masefield's poem while writing "Distant Ophir" since "Cargoes," which romanticizes the age of discoveries, was a school anthology poem at the time. Spencer claims that it was the main source of Harrison's poem's title.

99 Quinquireme of Nineveh from distant Ophir,
Rowing home to haven in sunny Palestine,
With a cargo of ivory,
And apes and peacocks,
Sandalwood, cedarwood, and sweet white wine

Stately Spanish galleon coming from the Isthmus,
Dipping through the Tropics by the palm-green shores,
With a cargo of diamonds, Quinquireme
Emeralds, amethysts,
Topazes, and cinnamon, and gold moidores. (Cargoes 1–10)

100 Northern, early nineteenth century industry is represented in Masefield's poem by the image of British coaster hauling a cargo of "Tyne coal, / Road-rails, pig-lead, / Firewood, iron-ware, and cheap tin trays." (Cargoes 13–15) This is perhaps a cargo significantly less magnificent than colonial spoils but representing technological progress and industrial development. Coal and firewood constitute definitely a more prominent array of goods than the stuff Campey is "hauling" in his handcart.

> Off the heavy handcart high above the earth
> And scattered paper whirled around the town. (Thomas Campey 1–4)

Other dwellers of Leeds described in Part I are presented similarly to Thomas Campey, disturbingly haunted by Queen Victoria (Huk 1991: 83), as social victims (Spencer 1994: 22) repressed by the authoritarian system represented by such institutions as school and church ("Ginger's Friday") or by patriarchal culture ("The Pocket Wars of Peanut Joe"), which leaves them "cornered and alone" within their "sexual identity" (Spencer 1994: 22). It is the system that harnesses Loiners' sexuality, this "dynamic force … leading human beings into relationship" (Barker 1991: 48) and makes them "loners … who bear their loins through the terrors of life" (Harrison, The Inkwell of Dr Agrippa, 1991: 35). Even if their actions, like for example Ginger's "disobedient sexual behaviour" stand as a "symbolic threat to authority" (Hairsine 1997: 13) and are potentially revolutionary in nature, the characters that undertake them are unaware of this potential, oblivious to issues of "collective resistance to … repression" (Spencer 1994: 22), just as the possibly illiterate Campey, who "hoards words with a greedy, superstitious appetite for their cumulative physical weight and appearance," (Spencer 1994: 23) is indifferent to the meaning those words carry. What the "*Loiner* poems" (Nicholson 2010: 61) of the sequence clearly show is that "constructions of … power," with their "attitudes, hierarchies and pedagogies … exported and practised wherever Britain planted its flag" (Nicholson 2010: 61) did not perish with the dismantling of the British Empire but continued to operate in the working-class Britain of the '70s. *The Loiners* revolves around continuities of subjection and revolutionary resistance (Nicholson 2010: 61), which will find their further development in *v.* and *The School of Eloquence,* and whose main focus is on the idea, pervading Harrison's work from the '70s onwards, that "colonialism in the English example … was no marginal activity on the edges of British civilization" (Nicholson 2010: 61). Quite the contrary, operating both home and abroad reveals itself as a fundamental force for the self-representation (Nicholson 2010: 61) and ongoing construction of British identity, influenced by the phenomenon that Harrison calls "British imagination in its imperial phase, when the gaps had all been filled and the maps coloured cochineal [that] projected its fear of itself onto the dark peoples it 'pacified,' and the shadowy creatures of its own Id onto the vastness of the Dark Continent" (1972: 91).

Chapter Two
"Wherever did you get your talent from?"

Continuity of Poetic Heritage in *The School of Eloquence*[101]

> Poetry is all I write, whether for books, or readings or for the National Theatre .... All these activities are part of the same quest for a public poetry, though in the word public I would never want to exclude inwardness. I think how Milton's sonnets range from the directly outward to the tenderly inward, and how the public address of the one makes the clearing for the shared privacy of the other. (Harrison quoted in Astley, 1991: 9)

In the abovementioned quote Harrison sets out a clear poetic task for himself, most boldly fulfilled in his acclaimed verse *The School of Eloquence.*[102] The poet must be able to express both the inner world of the individual and the outer world of historical and social turbulence: in other words, the public and the private. In his book entitled *Identity: Conversations with Benedetto Vecchi* Bauman quotes the Spanish-language writer Juan Goytisolo who observes, "intimacy and distance create a privileged situation. Both are necessary" (2007: 14). Intimacy and distance are the most important features of Harrison's poetic perspective. Inextricably linked, these two attitudes stem from the experience of his working-class boyhood, his entrance into the school of eloquence and how he became a poet and stranger within his own community. As Harrison duly noted in one interview, from the moment he began his formal education at Leeds Grammar School, he never felt fully "at home" in either "the world of literature with [his] education and identity of the poet" or "in [his] working-class background" (Haffenden 1991: 234). Alienated from both, he never sought "redemption or ... respite in a dream of belonging" (Bauman 2007: 14). This kind of attitude, succinctly described by Zygmunt Bauman in *Identity: Conversations with Benedetto Vecchi*, allows Harrison to navigate with ease in "several different linguistic universes" (Bauman 2007: 14) and continually transgress the boundaries of these two conflicting worlds. In

---

101 Some of the ideas developed in this chapter constitute a part of a different publication: "On (Not) Being Milton: Tony Harrison's Liminal Voice." in *Text Matters: A Journal of Literature, Theory and Culture*. Vol. 6, no. 1 (2016).

102 *The School of Eloquence* was a name for the "London Corresponding Society," a radical organization of the 1970s. For the history of the organization see E. P. Thompson *The Making of the English Working Class*. London: Victor Gollancz, 1963.

consequence, Harrison's poetry occupies a place in a broader literary tradition produced by such widely differing authors as Samuel Beckett, Vladimir Nabokov, Jorge Luis Borges[103] and others whose work benefits from an intercultural and interlinguistic identity. According to Bauman, the question of identity can only occur in a situation where a man is pulled out of "wherever could pass for his natural habitat" (2007: 12), which is as much to say that it is always "born out of the crisis of belonging" to a given community (Bauman 2007: 20). Contemporary sociology defines two basic types of community: *communities of life and fate* whose members (according to Siegfried Kracauer's formula) "live … in an indissoluble attachment" (Bauman 2007: 11) and communities which are "welded together solely by ideas and various principles".[104] The first type of community has been denied to Harrison as a result of his education and profession.[105]

The process by which eloquence is attained and thereby creates a simultaneous feeling of loss of belonging is one of the sequence's most essential themes. Exclusion from the working-class *community of life and fate* made Harrison question his own feelings and attitudes towards his background. His new identity was to hoist those "social anchors which made it look … predetermined and non-negotiable" (Bauman 2007: 24) and became a target of an effort, "an objective," something which he would need to "build from scratch" (Bauman 2007: 16). The following analysis attests to a prerequisite for understanding the theme of continuity and otherness in *The School of Eloquence* and rests squarely on the assumption that:

> 'Belonging and 'identity' are not cut in rock … they are not secured by a life long guarantee, they are eminently negotiable and revocable; and that one's own decisions, the steps one takes, the way one acts—and the determination to stick by all that—are crucial

---

103 Although the abovementioned writers, their names quoted after George Steiner in Bauman's *Identity* (2007:14), belong to the group of authors whose identities transgress the boundaries of different nationalities whereas Harrison's self-definition transgresses the boundary between two different classes, the mechanism is parallel.

104 See Siegfried Kracauer. *Ornament der Masse*. Frankfurt am Main: Suhrkamp. 1963.

105 Harrison always saw poetry as his trade. As Astley writes:

> He is one of the few poets who make a living entirely from poetry, something he always wanted to achieve in order to prove to himself and to his working-class parents that writing poetry was as much a proper job as being a baker (like his father) or a teacher (what his mother wanted him to become, to make use of his education) [.]" (1991: 10).

In the interview with John Haffenden Harrison asserts that he wanted "to make poetry a *real job*, and that's a question of hazarding the whole of your life on what you do; for … years I've done nothing but write verse for a living. I wanted *my job* to be the whole enterprise [.]" (1991: 246).

factors of both. In other words, the thought of 'having an identity' will not occur to people as long as 'belonging' remains their fate, a condition with no alternative. They will begin to entertain such a thought only in the form of a task to be performed, and to be performed over and over again rather than in one-off fashion. (Bauman 2007: 12)

The loss of belonging to a particular community in Harrison's poetry results in the problem of resolving the issues of la-memete (the continuity of our identity over time[106]) and l'ipseite (the coherence of whatever distinguishes us as a person) (Bauman 2007: 13). *The School of Eloquence* addresses both these issues, as the poem's speaker principally assumes the perspective of a man who cannot unambiguously identify himself with the class of his origin, and who sees his identity as a poet and his identity as a working-class man as conflictual, if not mutually exclusive. The struggle he undertakes is the struggle to "work up a relationship between the two selves" (Garofalakis 1991: 205), to provide connecting lines "between two societies, two classes, two languages that were always in versus relationship" (Garofalakis 1991: 205).

One of the problems closely related to the construction of identity (Hall 2008: 2) in modern man facing the crisis of belonging (Bauman 2007: 24) is the issue of *identification*. The following chapter discusses the way in which the problem of *identification* is tackled in *The School of Eloquence* and its subsequent role in the development of themes of continuity and change. According to Stuart Hall:

In common sense language, identification is constructed on the back of a recognition of some common origin or shared characteristics with another person or group, or with an idea, and with the natural closure of solidarity and allegiance established on this foundation. In contrast with the "naturalism" of this definition, the discursive approach sees identification as a … process never completed—always 'in process'. It is not determined in the sense it can always be 'won' or 'lost', sustained or abandoned. (Hall 2008: 2)

If we are to understand the issue of identification in Harrison's *The School of Eloquence* from the perspective of the abovementioned discursive approach, then it is only to view Harrison's identity as an ongoing construction. The speaker of Harrison's poems is unable to identify himself within society and is bound therefore to constantly question and re-establish his feelings of belonging and rejection. Within the social context described by Harrison in *The School of Eloquence*, the speaker is beset by difficulties of self-definition emerging from, among other

106 It is connected, according to Bauman, with the fact that people in the contemporary world who do not belong to the *community of life and fate* cannot avoid "the passage through more than one *community of ideas and principles*" (2007: 13).

things, the "politics of exclusion" (Hall 2008: 4–5) to which the speaker finds himself constantly subjected. The sequence observes the development of a character who recognizes his working-class origins but who at the same time feels estranged from his own family and class. While he affiliates himself with the world of newly acquired eloquence, he does not accept its elite set of values. Accordingly, the position of the speaker—the knowing subject—in Hall's terms, is always "displaced" and "decentred" in relation to the surrounding context (2008: 2). In order to follow the process of *identification* described in the sequence, the reader is obliged to concentrate on the relation between the displaced "knowing subject and the discursive practices" (Hall 2008: 2) which the subject undertakes in a given context.

This aforesaid character of *identification* is one of the reasons why a feeling of political solidarity with the working class in the sequence often appears problematic. The speaker, who at the same time approves and criticizes the class of his origin, belongs simultaneously to two different "cultural ideals" (Hall 2008: 2) characterized by values which exist frequently in very real conflict. As a result, the "ego" of the speaker is composed of "identifications which are not necessarily harmonious" (Hall 2008: 3). The speaker of such poems as "Them and [uz]" or "Book Ends" explores the boundary between the two worlds to which he belongs and from which he feels alienated. His *identification* obeys the "logic of more-than-one" (Hall 2008: 2) and can never amount to a totality as it "operates across difference" (Hall 2008: 2) and always "requires what is left outside, its constitutive outside, to consolidate the process (Hall 2008: 2).

The following chapter discusses the process of *identification* and the issues of belonging in relation to the themes of continuity and otherness in *The School of Eloquence*. It focusses on the role of this newly acquired eloquence and the role of the working-class legacy in the construction of the speaker's poetic identity. The issues thus far mentioned are further broken down into the following problems: cultural transition from a working-class background to a middle-class community, the struggle to maintain connections with one's roots, the continuity of experience of the working classes and the search for connections between the individual and social, personal and general aspects of human existence. Firstly, the chapter discusses the structure and form of the sequence in relation to the themes of continuity and change. Following this, the chapter analyses two poems from the original group of sonnets of *The School of Eloquence*, "On Not Being Milton" and "Them and [uz]," which contain germs of ideas unfolding in the subsequent poems of Harrison's sequence. The two poems establish a powerful relationship between the issues of the individual identity of the poetic "I" and the identity of the English working-class[107] as a stratum of society. The two poems are the core of an extended theme of the sequence concerned with the changing dynamics between the heterogeneous poetic "I" and working-class "us" (or rather [uz] to use Harrison's deliberate phonetic rendering of the pronoun). The complexity of the sequence's development, its changing dynamics and main turning points, require a separate discussion in the following chapter, which is chiefly concerned with a group of selected elegies from *The School of Eloquence.* The starting point for the discussion undertaken in the two chapters concerned with *The School of Eloquence* is an observation by Luke Spencer, namely, that the eighteen poems comprising "the first public airing" (Spencer 1994: 89) of the sequence[108] were primarily about "language as an instrument of power and therefore inescapably, of political struggle" (Spencer 1994: 89). According to Spencer, the development process of the sequence is characterized by a shift of focus from a social identity to an individual identity, which results in the absence in the later poems of "the idea of language … as the means of emancipation for the inarticulate masses" (Spencer 1994: 90). The extension of the sequence:

> Left the overtly political poems outnumbered by poems which are instead absorbed with the details of family and neighbourhood life … the general direction of development of the 'School' has been away from committed … view of the class, in all its historical, cultural and personal dimensions, and towards a characteristically liberal concern with individual experience … This change of perspective … has been achieved at some cost. (Spencer 1994: 90)

The following analysis challenges the abovementioned opinion and demonstrates how the issue of linguistic, political and social hegemony remains, in Harrison's poetry, inextricably linked with the problem of identity and, more specifically, with the themes of continuity and change and their various manifestations.

The structure of *The School of Eloquence* reflects a centrality of the themes of continuity and change for the entire sequence. The sequence grew from ten

107 As with other works in *The School of Eloquence*, Harrison presents the reader with individual working-class characters but also, on a different level, with a working-class community which can be called a collective character of the sequence.

108 Spencer refers here to the Rex Collings Edition of *The School of Eloquence* titled *From The School of Eloquence and Other Poems* (1978), which is often mentioned by the critics as the first publication of the sequence and treated as the foundation of *Continuous*: 50 *Sonnets from The School of Eloquence* However, an earlier publication of the sequence, mentioned in the subsequent part of the chapter, does exist.

poems published in a private edition (Rex Collings 1979[109]), to eighteen in *From The School of Eloquence and Other Poems* (Rex Collings 1978) and later to fifty in *Continuous: 50 Sonnets from The School of Eloquence* (Rex Collings, 1981). In 1984, Harrison added another 17[110] poems to the sequence (*Selected Poems*, Penguin, 1984) and then expanded it further in 1987 to seventy-eight in the second edition of the *Selected Poems* (Penguin, 1987[111]). Even if, by 1981, the sequence had a "clear thematic, tripartite frame"[112] (Morrison 1991: 56) which was retained in the latest publication of *Collected Poems* (2007), Harrison has never proclaimed the sequence complete. Its open-ended structure, as further analysis of the individual poems will confirm, grows out of their subject matter and reflects the search for continuity and the inevitability of change—two major themes exploring the issue of identity central for Harrison's discussion. Jem Poster claims that Harrison's "resistance to conclusion, or at least, to any simple forms of foreclosure" (1997: 84) of the sequence should be seen as a poetic statement on the affirmative quality of the act of writing.[113] The "continual enterprise" (Haffenden 1991: 228) of the sequence

---

109 It should be stated, however, that individual poems of the sequence appeared in periodicals and anthologies before the release of this publication, for example, in *South Bank Poetry and Music* (London 1971), in *Planet* 24/5 (Aug. 1974) and in *A Decade and Then Some* (London 1976) edited by Allen de Laoch. The first publication included "On Not Being Milton." The second a group of three sonnets titled "The School of Eloquence." The third the poems later re-titled as "Rhubarbarians."

110 The number of poems given here, correct according to my estimation, in its accordance with the count made by Luke Spencer (1994: 78). Blake Morrison (1991: 56) counts only 64.

111 1987 was also the year of publication of a selection from the sequence titled *Ten Poems from 'The School of Eloquence'* (London Penguin Books).

112 Blake Morrison and Rick Rylance describe it as follows:

> The intimate commemorative family poems of Part 2 are preceded by the densely wrought political poems of Part 1 and followed by a looser set of poems (about politics, history, art and morality) of Part 3: the Elegies at the centre acquire their meaning from the context in which they are set. (Morrison 1991: 56)
>
> The second [part] is a sequence of elegies for [Harrison's] parents ... The first [part] deals mainly with communally-based issues, such as those focused on language or nineteenth century subjects ... The third ... deals with the relationship of art to socio-political events. The meditation on dislocation, on family and class history, and the place of art, remains, but to these are added meditations on ecological catastrophe ... and ... resuming the issue raised in section one, imperial history. (Rylance 1991: 120)

113 For Harrison's comment upon the "celebratory impulse" (Poster 1997: 84) of writing see an interview conducted by John Haffenden, a reader in English Literature at the University of Sheffield. Haffenden's books include *The Life of John Berryman* (Faber,

challenges the same historical pessimism and feelings of despair that characterize so many of the poems.

Both Blake Morrison (1991: 56–58) and Luke Spencer agree that the familial elegies in Part 2 of the sequence are "supported and enhanced by their placing within a contextualizing historical perspective" of Part 1 and 3 (Spencer 1994: 79). The political and social overtone of the familial poems of Part 2 are strengthened by the particular structure of the sequence, where two parts function as an "intellectual support" (Morrison 1991: 56) for the central section and hold its powerful content together gives shape to the book as a whole. Being clear and concrete, the structure of the sequence is, at the same time, "capable of infinite extension" (Morrison 1991: 56) and it extends through the years within its tripartite frame. In 1983, Harrison commented in an interview on the way the sequence is changing.

> The bones of *Continuous* are already sketched out. The area where I've had difficulty is in the central section, where a number of things seem to be happening. One is what I designate by the italic[114] … It seemed as if the italic could somehow take over from the roman … so that in the end I could become a mouthpiece. The other direction is suggested by the line "My mind moves upon silence and Aeneid IV" as if there could be some sort of meeting in the afterworld, both with my father and everything implied by his class and forebears … Another section … goes into so-called uneducated poets[115] in the North in the nineteenth century. (Haffenden 1991: 229)

Since 1983, even if the number of the poems has grown, it should also be noted that, as the author stated, the development of the sequence is not strictly linear, since each of the three major parts develops at a different pace. As a result, the interplay between parts and individual poems has a fluctuating character, since each addition slightly alters an existing order to introduce new types of links and new continuities within the larger structure of the sequence.

1982), two collections of interviews, *Viewpoints: Poets in Conversation* (Faber 1981) and *Novelists in Interview* (Methuen 1985). The interview with Harrison took place in Newcastle in 1983 and appeared for the first time in *Poetry Review*, 73 no. 4 (January 1984). Since then, it has been widely quoted by Harrison's poetry critics.

114 "The form of type which represents, at times, the voice of 'the other' in Harrison's poetry" (Garofalakis 1991: 207) whereas a roman type represents his voice, the voice of the poet.

115 Harrison poetry refers to a group of working-class poets writing in England in the eighteenth and early nineteenth century (the Thames waterman John Taylor, shoemaker James Woodhouse, pipe-maker and trumpeter John Frederick Bryan, the "Bristol milkmaid" Ann Yearsley, the "thresher-poet" Stephen Duck and others), so-called pitman poets from the North of England writing in the nineteenth and early twentieth century.

Spencer and Morrison assert that the "balance between the politico-historical and familial has shifted significantly since the first collection and that the shift is later consolidated in *Selected Poems* (1984)" (Spencer 1994: 57–58). Out of eighteen poems published in *From The School of Eloquence and Other Poems*, thirteen belong to what later became Part 1, three to Part 3 and only two to Part 2 of *Selected Poems* (1984), which means that the poems that form the basis of the sequence are the politico-historical poems of social class inequality and "linguistic oppression"[116] (Morrison 1991: 56). In *Selected Poems* (1984), Part 1 is further extended to 14 poems, Part 3 to 18 poems and Part 2 becomes the longest part of the sequence, now extended to include 35 poems. The next publication brings another extension of Part 2, to which another 11 poems are added with no increase of other parts. The expansion of the part dealing with familial issues reflects their significance (Morrison 1991: 59); most importantly, it strengthens the close coexistence between public and private themes in Harrison's poetry which concurs with the wider task involved in the poet's undertaking. For Harrison, the politico-historical, from which stems the sequence proper, and the familial, are two sides of the same coin. Consequently, the task of the poet is to search for 'connections' between the individual and the social, for the shared experience of people living in different times and places, and for continuity between personal and general experience.

The fact, as Morrison suggests, that "at the early stage the sequence was more bluntly and single-mindedly a thesis about political and linguistic oppression" (1991: 56) to be later enriched by the familial themes, leads us to the conclusion that the individual experience from the outset is, for the author, tainted by the politico-historical context in which it occurs. In an interview conducted in 1983, John Haffenden (1991: 230) asked Harrison, rather provocatively, to what extent it would be true to say that in *Continuous*, he addresses personal and psychological issues whilst adding the historical and social context in order to give his poems a larger authority (1991: 231). Harrison replied:

> I see them all as intimately related: the historical, the autobiographical and the metaphysical if you like … I always remember the way kids at school used to write out their addresses in full, starting their name and school and going on with 'Beeston, Leeds, West Riding, Yorkshire, England, Great Britain, Europe, The World, The Universe': I think I have a mind and sensibility which keeps running up and down that kind of ladder, that scale or spectrum, and it seems to me that what you call psychological issues

116 As Morrison and other critics assert, Harrison makes allusions to his family in Part 1 of the sequence but the familial theme does not develop fully until the beginning of Part 2.

are as historical as the historical issues are psychological. I see them as a part of the same scale, the same historical spectrum. (1991: 230)

If the personal and the individual stems from historical and social aspects, as the construction of the sequence appears to suggest, the historical and social can be perceived and understood only from the perspective of the intimate and the private, which is "an earthing area for the lightning of … political struggle" (Haffenden 1991: 231). In *Continuous*, then, the impossibility of separating those issues, their constant, stormy and turbulent co-existence, is a separate theme in itself and an important factor in shaping the identity of the speaker.

The coexistence of political and familial issues is further reinforced by the three epigraphs to the sequence[117], which foreshadow, among other things, the themes of continuity and otherness. The first epigraph, taken from E. P. Thompson's *The Making of the English Working Class* (1963), explains the title of the sequence by providing the context in which the phrase originally appeared and "identifies the learning of eloquence as a vital element in the education of radical artisans" (Spencer 1994: 67).

In 1799 special legislation was introduced utterly suppressing and prohibiting by name the London Corresponding Society and the United Englishmen. Even the indefatigable conspirator, John Binns, felt that further national organization was hopeless … when arrested he was found in possession of a ticket which was perhaps one of the last "covers" for the old LCS: *Admit for the Season to the School of Eloquence.*
(E. P. Thompson, *The Making of the English Working Class*).

The character of John Binns,[118] an "indefatigable conspirator," as Thompson would have him (Thompson 1963: 174), exemplifies a man for whom social change must start with the individual's education. According to Spencer, it is a language or rather linguistic ability which mobilizes working-class "people *en masse*" (1994: 68) and gives them their own communal voice, a chance to be heard or seen by the rest of society. However, eloquence means nothing, if it is not accompanied by deed, "as power lays with those who have wealth, status and a developed class identity" (Spencer 1994: 68), for example those who "could (and did) pass legislation 'utterly

117 *Continuous* is additionally dedicated to the memory of the author's mother (who died in 1976) and father (who died in 1980).

118 "John Binns, a young man from … Dublin, who was working as a Plumber in London. He … joined the L.C.S. in 1794, rose rapidly to the Chairmanship of committees …He belonged to the majority of members who argued that … the society should propagate its message more widely, and should organize large public demonstrations so that the Government might be 'compelled to grant a reform'. And the reform for which he was working was, in effect, reform by revolution" (Thompson 1963: 139–40).

suppressing and prohibiting' the London Corresponding Society," of which Binns was a prominent member" (Spencer 1994: 68). By introducing the political and historical context, the epigraph positions eloquence alongside the realities of class hegemony[119] and political power and heralds one of the main themes of the sequence: "the suppression of working-class speech" (Morrison 1991: 56).

The politico-historical and familial themes do not develop along the same lines. Rather than moving "up and down the ladder" (Haffenden 1991: 230) the author sensibly seems to be moving up and down the spiral,[120] as it continually comes back to the same point but at a different level, and explores layers of connections and interrelationships between the "historical, autobiographical and metaphysical" (Morrison 1991: 56) elements of human experience. The highly intertextual organization of the entire sequence described above is first introduced by the structure of the first epigraph. That the fragment of Thompson's *The Making of the English Working Class*, a quotation itself, contains two other quotations, hints at the polyphonic and heteroglossic (in Bakhtinian terms)[121] character of *The School of Eloquence* in which Harrison, with a greater force than ever before, introduces a powerful interplay of different discourses.

The second epigraph comes from Milton's "Ad Patrem" 'To My Father,' a poem in which the author pays tribute to his father and justifies his intention to become a poet (Morrison 1991: 56). The epigraph foreshadows the autobiographical theme of *The School of Eloquence* while at the same time introducing the problem of resolving the issue of l'ipseite as a result of a conflict between being a poet and the son of a working-class father. Harrison chose only the opening and concluding pages of the poem for the epigraph, but Morrison (1991: 57)

119 The term "hegemony" is used here and in the subsequent parts of the book in accordance with its definition by Antonio Gramsci (1891–1937), to denote relations between the ruling class and the rest of society, which are established and sustained by means of public (legal, political, military, educational) institutions (Burzyńska 2007: 529). The problem of cultural hegemony and its various manifestations (for example in the sphere of language), is one of the central issues in Harrison's literary work.

120 Images of spirals, circles and circular movement are characteristic for the sequence as a whole. See, for example, "Illuminations," "Timer." Hereafter, that which is described as Harrison's "Cycloidal Imagery" in this book will be discussed in the following chapters.

121 For a discussion on heteroglossia see: M. M. Bakhtin, *The Dialogic Imagination*. Ed. Michael Holquist, trans. Caryl Emerson and Michael Holquist, University of Texas Press, 1981. Garofalakis states that "although according to Bakhtin 'only under the conditions present in the genre of the novel can dialogic heteroglossia be achieved'" Harrison, a poet, achieves it when "various voices in history intersect in his lines" (1991: 202). A similar point is argued by other critics (for example by Helga Geyer-Ryan).

draws the reader's attention to the line of the omitted part of "Ad Patrem" 'To my Father:' "Do not dismiss the sacred Muses' efforts" (To my Father 67). The line heralds those poems of the sequence which discuss the role of newly acquired eloquence in the construction of poetic identity and in the destruction of family ties. In many of the poems from *The School of Eloquence*, the speaker is faced with the irreversible disintegration of the family circle and, in consequence, with the disruption of la-memete, the continuity of identity over time. The attempt to "create new wholes out of the disruption" (Haffenden 1991: 249) is one of the themes of the sequence but also an ongoing task undertaken by Harrison the poet as he tries reconcile in the sequence his newly acquired eloquence with his working-class legacy—the two elements of his identity which remain inseparably and explosively combined. The figure of the father, an important persona of the *The School of Eloquence* who symbolically represents the characteristics of the disappearing working-class culture, is illuminated by another line from the missing part of the quotation from Milton's poem: "Apollo, wishing that he could divide himself in twain, / gave some of his gifts to me and others to you, / so that we, father and son, comprise the divided god" (To my Father 66–68).

The ironic overtone of the line is telling, since Harrison provided the autobiographical context of his father who was a baker, not a man skilled in music and composition like Milton's father and so had neither time nor desire for poetry. However, Harrison's father's influence and the influence of the father's craft-in-trade upon Harrison's work remained strong regardless of the fact that he persisted "in contempt for the sacred Muses" (To my Father 57) and never read his son's verse.[122]

In his book, *W brzuchu wieloryba: Szkice o dwudziestowiecznej poezji brytyjskiej i irlandzkiej* Jerzy Jarniewicz states that Harrison explicitly identifies with his northern legacy and wants to be perceived as a poet of everyday speech, the speech of his father and the working class of Leeds. The third epigraph, a short poem entitled "Heredity," comments on the nature of Harrison's ties with his working-class background:

How you became a poet is a mystery!
Wherever did you get your talent from?
I say: I had to uncles, Joe and Harry
one was a stammerer, the other dumb.

All those incipient trains of thought present in the two earlier epigraphs combine in this quatrain to bring together the political and the familial, and open

122 See: Interview with John Haffenden (1991: 246).

up discussion of the nature of both individual talent and social stigmatization. Though they may not necessarily agree on the inspiration, many critics have commented upon this particular short poem. According to Morrison, the epigraph implies that the poet's legacy is a linguistic struggle, (1991: 57) and that the following poems, with their "strained syntax" and their "awkward articulacy" (1991: 57) are born out of the experience of the laboring classes. Spencer argues that although "mute ingloriousness" is "unquestionably part of Harrison's inheritance," (1994: 80) it is not enough to explain his talent and prefers to see the epigraph as a "confession of bafflement at the sheer arbitrariness of it all-dumbness to Harry; poetic talent to Tony" (1994: 80). Since the development of the identity of the poetic "I" is one of the most complicated and multi-layered themes of the sequence, reading the sequence's subsequent poems turns both those statements into glaring oversimplifications. It is hard not to agree with the opinion of Marylin Hacker (1991: 249), who considers the development of self-consciousness to be the major defining feature of *The School of Eloquence*. Hacker claims that the sequence has features of Bildungsroman[123] and more precisely Erziehungsroman, which is a variation of the former and focuses on formal education and its impact on the growth of the individual:

> *The School of Eloquence* is something between a Bildungsroman and a novel of retrospection … A bright, working class boy … is educated to "rise beyond his class." His parents encourage him, even as his education, particularly the different spoken language it requires, separates him from them. As a young man he becomes a writer; as a grown man he realizes that the matter and substance of his art must be the very language above which he "rose," and its incorporation into literature: the occupation of literature by those it had excluded, silenced. (1991: 248)

The silenced and the excluded are represented in the epigraph by the two uncles, who reappear later in the sequence "Harry in Part I, a deaf-mute who had 'eloquent' recourse to a dictionary when refuting 'Tory errors'; Joe in Part III, a printer who could 'handset type much faster than he spoke'" (Morrison 1991: 57). Jarniewicz suggests that Harrison's declaration of kinship with the voiceless comprised in "Heredity" makes the quatrain his "ars poetica" (Jarniewicz 2001: 88). As

123 According to Hirsch:

> A Bildungsroman is, most generally, the story of a single individual's growth and development within the context of a defined social order … The growth process, at its roots a quest story, has been described as both 'an apprenticeship to life and a search for meaningful existence within society.' …. To spur the Hero or heroine on to their journey, some form of loss or discontent must jar them at an early stage away from the home or family setting (293–312).

the poet wants to speak in the name of Harry, Joe and others "whom the feeling of inadequacy drives towards silence" (Worpole 1991: 68), who have no "privilege of literacy" (Haffenden 1991: 231) and in that language, which, according to many, has no literary potential, the speaker's answer to the question of an interlocutor whose surprised tone expresses an assumption that two such concepts as "working-class" and "poet" contradict each other, is highly subversive. He "slyly endorses" (Spencer 1994: 80) the questioner's prejudice lingering behind the praise, and at the same time proves the assumption false. In subsequent poems, the Northern dialect, the "awkward articulacy" of the working classes and silence of those deprived of language, become the foundation for poetry.

The first line of the quatrain is not so much concerned with poetic identity itself but with the mystery of its origin, and correlates with the perspective adopted by Bauman, Bokszański, Skarga, Hall and other scholars who see identity as a process. As noted in the introduction, the consequence of adopting such a viewpoint is that the most important questions one may ask in relation to identity "are about the way in which it is being created and the way it changes not about what it is" (Bokszański 2007: 34). According to Bokszański, this attitude to the problem of identity involves an assumption that the effort of self-definition will never be rewarded with the ultimate adjustment of the individual to a given cultural order (2007: 37). The question asked by Harrison's quatrain initiates the theme by dealing with the way in which the poetic identity of the speaker is born and how it constantly evolves, and so the most important problems encompassed by the theme concern the engagement in the historical and social turmoil of the modern world, Harrison has an acute awareness that there is no hiding place from the social and the political, that the private and the public are permanently combined. The task of the poet is not only to acknowledge that fact but also to continue examining it on different levels of human experience, in the changing context of history, even if the conclusions remain pessimistic and the fate of the individual seems predetermined. Only a defined and concrete form can contain the horrors of reality, can enable the poet to look into darkness with his eyes wide open and prolong that gaze making the "continuity of poetic enterprise" (Haffenden 1991: 234) possible.

According to Burton, the use of formal restrictions in Harrison's poetry can be compared to the use of masks in Greek tragedy which separated the naked human face from the terrors they had to confront.[124] "His verse can be seen as a mask through which he faces up to the world" (1991: 26) Burton concludes. Following this same line of thought, Spencer suggests that in the "metrical underpinning" of

124 The issue of the mask is further discussed in the final chapter.

Harrison's poetry "there is a strong suggestion of sanity saving craft" (1994: 16). Such craft prevents the one who gazes into darkness from succumbing to it in the manner of Conrad's Kurtz, "defeated by the lack of restraint" (Spencer 1994: 16). The restraint of the sonnet forces Harrison to be brief,[125] so to filter his thoughts through the structure of sixteen lines and to contain in a short poem the essence of an overwhelming abundance of voices and images characteristic of his work. As the author explained in an interview with Richard Hoggart, the rhythm carries his emotions and prevents them from bursting out, channels anger, distress and grief, like a medical instrument, makes the transfer of essential substance possible:

> That rhythmical thing is like a life-support system. The meter … is like a pulse…. I feel I need a way I can control what I say. It's not restrained, isn't the word itself, it's like giving blood. If you are dying I can't give you blood by slashing my wrists; it has to go through a sterile jar. (1991: 43)

In the fragment quoted above, poetic content is metaphorically represented by blood, needed for the human organism to survive. The image of poetry as an inherent attribute of life, basic and intimate, remains in agreement with Harrison's belief that writing is a celebratory enterprise. However, the difficulty with sustaining that enterprise lies in the fact that each act of writing, a "momentary defeat of pessimism" (Haffenden 1991: 227) as Harrison calls it, is an act of subversion that takes place in the context of history. The organic and technical metaphors of the life-support system, of the heartbeat and pulse, which Harrison uses to describe the importance of rhythmic patterns, are usually read by the critics (maybe because of the explicitly autobiographical character of Harrison's work) as referring directly to the uncertain situation of the author who faces the threat of being carried away by emotions or stands on the edge of the abyss. However, the meter in Harrison's poetry is primarily the life-support system of the poem, sustained by the frame of the formal structure.

In the case of *The School of Eloquence* this pattern is predetermined by the choice of the Meredithian sonnet as a leading form of the sequence. The iambic pentameter in which the sonnets are written is not an obvious pattern to measure the rhythm of the subject matter stemming from political dominance, social exclusion or the terror of history. The degree to which the iambic pentameter

125 In the interview with Haffenden, Harrison explains that the brevity of the sonnet allowed him to tackle autobiographical themes, especially those touching upon the death of his parents: "[T]he sixteen-line sonnet … leads itself to a kind of broken narrative, since—at the time I wrote them—many of the sonnets in the sequence were so painful that the attention I could bring to bear on them had to be brief" (1991: 228).

endorses elite forms of writing and pronunciation, has been noted by Anthony Easthope in *Poetry as Discourse:*

> Unruffled smoothness, flowing elegance, poise: these are qualities that counterpoint of pentameter facilitates in two respects. Through counterpoint the abstract pattern of the metre is relatively backgrounded. Recognition of the work of metric production—and so of the poem as constructed artifice—suppressed in favor of a notion of the poem as a spontaneously generated product … Pentameter makes verse especially compatible with the received Pronunciation of Standard English … It does so because it legislates for the number of syllables in the line and therefore cancels elision, making transitions at word junctures difficult …. Such pronunciation … signals 'proper' speech; that is a class dialect. (1983: 67–69)

However, Harrison's choice is not accidental but subversive. Instead of rejecting the forms associated in the public consciousness with the "bourgeois establishment" (Spencer 1994: 17) he decides to "occupy"[126] them and yield their regularity to the "unmannerly interruption of subaltern voice" (Spencer 1994: 17). The surprised reader often discovers therefore that Harrison introduces formal constraints only to break them. The hesitancy and vulnerability of formal structure are what interests him. His poetry "counterbalances the claims of poise and order" (Spencer 1994: 17) to become a poetry which yields ostensibly to an order of acceptable decorum in versification while his locution remains at odds with what those same claims and orders have historically prescribed. For Harrison, this comes as an inevitable consequence of speaking the language of working-class people, his poetry wrought from speech not fully expressed, perhaps even denied, down the centuries. The words come awkwardly, all effort spent with the utterance, the labour of phrase-making expended in deference to the same manual labour once expected from his working-class antecedents. According to Ken Worpole, the tension resulting from bringing together the "classical form … and the colloquial nature of the subject matter," (1991: 68) is one of the greatest strengths of Harrison's poetry.[127] The "sharp sense of irony and self dignity" (1991: 68) which Worpole describes, comes additionally from the fact that Harrison is

126 The term used by Harrison in relation to writing poetry in a regional dialect in one of his most widely recognized poems of the sequence "Them and [uz]" later analyzed in detail.

127 A similar comment is made by Sandie Byrne, who suggests that Harrison's method of incorporating material traditionally excluded from canonical forms "enables [him] to have it both ways: to use the rhetorical possibilities of the sixteen-line sonnet while implicitly attacking it…. Harrison both exploits and resists a fruitful poetic convention" (1997: 59).

not afraid to move a step further, "closer to the fire" (1991: 68), and makes the dialect of the north the living tissue of his poems (Jarniewicz 2001: 92).

The introduction of the dialectal voices marginalized in the literary discourse (Rowland 2001: 269), into the old and well-established tradition of the sonnet, the mainstream of the poetic canon, may put the reader's expectations to the test but not necessarily go against the grain of the sonnet's original tradition. Indeed, it is worth remembering "that the word sonnet derives from Italiano sonneto, diminutive of suono, meaning 'a little sound' or 'a little song'" (Hirsch 2008: 39). Harrison restores the forgotten function of this poetic form, which was originally associated with the regional language of Italy as opposed to the more sophisticated Latin and was meant for reading aloud. As Worpole acknowledges, the sonnet "is a highly appropriate form in which to write about language or speech" (1991: 68) and it can be no accident on Harrison's part that he makes it one of the predominant topics of *The School of Eloquence*. For Harrison, writing sonnets in his working-class dialect, the origin of the form serves as an intercultural reference to the oral literary tradition of the British working classes[128], whose strength lay "in the strong identification of the authors, with the place and the language of the English North" (Parkinson, 1972: 108). Songs of "impressive technical skill" (Parkinson 1972: 108) reflected the realities of the working-class experience and sustained working-class traditions, as they were created continually, in response to the political and social events of the community's life. The abovementioned "continuity of poetic enterprise," (Haffenden 1991: 228) in the face of such moments of crisis as the 1831 and 1841 Durham Strikes or the 1872 Durham Lock-out, is what Tommy Armstrong, one of the pitman poets, describes as the most important responsibility of the poet towards his audience:

> When you're a pitman's poet and looked up to for it, wey, is a disaster or a strike gans wi'oot a song from you, they say, what's wrong wi'Tommy Armstrong? Has someone druv a spigot into him an let oot the inspiration! (Armstrong qtd in Parkinson 1972: 109)

The voices of pitman poets, whose work created the foundation of the written tradition of the North, serve as an inspiration for several poems in the "familial" part of *Continuous*. Harrison's affiliation with their work is based on a belief in the necessity of a strong "creative relationship between the individual and the community" (Parkinson 1972: 108) that he himself grew out of. The "hard circumstances of working-class life, crushing industrial conditions" (Parkinson 1972: 108) and

128 According to W. E. Parkinson, the author of "Poetry in the North East" oral working class tradition existed in the North-East of England from the early Industrial Revolution and died out in the early part of the twentieth century (1972: 108–109).

social and political turbulence fed the poetic imaginations of Tommy Armstrong, Thomas Wilson and and Joseph Skipsey, and continue to inspire Tony Harrison equally with the works of Milton and the Classics. The continuity of inspiration, or "holy daftness" as Armstrong called it (qtd in Parkinson 1972: 108), is what allows Harrison to revive the old traditions of working-class poetry and open it up to different, intertextual and cross-cultural influences. In *The School of Eloquence*, regional literature[129] runs up against the canon. The sonnet is written in the language of a pitman in order to reveal the poetic potential of a vernacular, which as David Craig puts it:

> Comes from a society with its own strong character which lives to a great degree in its language—the spoken—and the tongue which is close to the movement of an alert feeling for life. Speech has its being in the mass of individuals who use it, with the run and stress, the direction and depth and the force of feeling at work as they live out their kind of life. It is a force of life in action, alternately affecting and itself being played upon by particular phases of experience. (1961: 55)

Harrison's public readings of the sequence (Worpole 1991: 68), accompanied by his explanatory remarks, constitute a further attempt to continue the lost tradition of the sonnet as a form "derived from the importance of the human voice" (Worpole 1991: 68) and refer to a working-class tradition of "literature as a shared experience" (Worpole 1991: 68). Reading aloud, institutionalized in the late nineteenth century in the form of "penny readings,"[130] was part of a wider social phenomenon, called "Mutual Improvement." This so-called "self-help" among working-class members, extensively described in *Intellectual Life of the British Working Classes* by Jonathan

---

129 A definition of regional literature adopted for the purpose of this book comes from W. E. Parkinson's "Poetry in the North East." According to Parkinson, regional literature is something more than the writer's reflection upon his or her environment, "[it] should include a regional awareness, a response to those features that make a region distinctive … its history, political struggles, economic adversities, traditions, folklore, myth, people, humour and language" (1972: 108).

130 Invented by Samuel Taylor, penny readings began in 1854, when Russell's Crimean War dispatches for the *Times* were read "from a terrace in Hanley's market square" as Rose notices.

> The first 'war readings' attracted 8,000 to 10,000 people. The authorities welcomed them as a means of keeping the lower orders out of pubs and music halls, so they offered Taylor the free use of the Town Hall for other readings.… At first the events were free but soon the attendance was so great that 1d. admission had to be charged.… Between October 1857 and April 1858 Staffordshire towns were staging penny readings for overflow crowds, with total admission of 60,000 to 70,000—this in district of population of 100,000. (Rose 2002: 84)

Rose, was forged primarily by the numerous Mutual Improvement Societies,[131] which organized discussions, lessons and lectures to encourage literacy, and in consequence, induce working-class people to read. Though these same societies very often took on more advanced forms of reading rooms and Sunday schools where predominantly working-class teachers gave classes in English, drawing and arithmetic (Rose 2002: 62), the fact that they relied on the support of working men meant they were liable to be short lived, "vulnerable to economic downturns and internal squabbles" (2002: 65). Nevertheless, their role in the rise of self-awareness and independent thinking among working-class members was undeniable as they "reinforced the importance of … education" (Rose 2002: 87) and hastened the development of readership. Reading aloud was one of the most widely practised forms of education, both at home and during communal readings,[132] contributing to the creation of shared literacy culture within which books were treated "practically like public property" (Rose 2002: 84) as they circulated among readers. There is truth to be had, albeit faintly ironic truth, in the fact that Harrison's audiences did not comprise working-class men, but his public readings place *The School of Eloquence* within the frame of that working-class experience of communal book culture. The sonnet, a seemingly bourgeois literary form, served him as a tool to maintain the continuity of this experience and to revitalize the old forms of literary expression, which would be inclusive in its nature. This is clearly visible in "On Not Being Milton" and "Them and [uz]," two sonnets from the sequence examined in detail in the following part as central texts from the point of view of the problem of identity construction.

Bauman claims that identity in the contemporary world has to be understood as the goal of an effort and as an ongoing task. In the opening sonnet of the

131 Such as the Institute in Hebden Bridge, Culloden Collage or more permanent organizations: The Huddersfield Mechanics' Institute and The Mechanics' Institute in Bradford. They were not necessarily political organizations but as Rose notes, "discussions during the meetings were politically oriented. The association of mutual improvement with political radicalism, made by nineteenth century middle-classes was not completely unfounded" (2002: 63). After all, The London Corresponding Society, "the first laboring class political organization, was organized on the mutual improvement model" (Rose 2002: 62).

132 Rose states that in an "oral history investigation of social life between 1870 and 1918, half working-class interviewers indicated that reading aloud (including Bible reading and parents reading to children) was practised at homes were they were raised" (Rose 2002: 84).

sequence, "On Not Being Milton," Harrison identifies this task as writing. His chosen method of constructing the poet's identity:

Read and committed to the flames, I call
These sixteen lines that go back to my roots
My *Cahier d'un retour au pays natal*[133]
My growing black enough to fit my boots. (1–4)

Lines of verse which "go back to … [his] roots" (On Not Being Milton 2) become lines which restore continuity with the past and have the power to sustain the connection. The first stanza of the poem uses "elemental" imagery of fire and earth[134] which, together with the verbs denoting movement, gives the act of writing the character of physical transformation. The destructive force of the flames, the processes of growing black and returning to one's roots suggest the transformational power of a language, which penetrates the layers of personal and public histories described in the poem. Writing acquires a concrete direction in time and space: the movement in the poem is the movement into the past and back to the native land, the place of origin. Additionally, the usage of a set metaphor "to go back to one's roots" suggests that the return may be read as a vertical journey, into and underneath: in other words, an inverted growth whose image is strengthened by referencing the blackness of coal as the main natural resource of the English North East. This movement *under* metaphorically establishes the intention of the poet who wants to re-establish the position of language spoken as "from below," a language which constitutes the periphery of literary experience but whose roots lie deep in the history and culture of the native land Harrison left in order to read books and gain the privilege of literacy.

The title of the poem, "On Not Being Milton," a negative definition of the speaker's self, immediately places the issue of identity in the framework of literature. The reference to Milton, primarily the quotation from Gray's elegy,[135] sets the poem, according to Rick Rylance, "in the persistent tradition of the mournful alienation in English writing about the dispossessed" (1991: 118). In his elegy,

133 The quotation from Aimé Césaire's poem "Cahier d'un retour au pays natal" meaning "Notebook of return to a native land."

134 Imagery characteristic of Harrison's poetry. The image of earth (with related images of growth and decay) is an organizing image of Harrison's first collection of poems *Earthworks*. The image of fire reappears in many of the poems of *The School of Eloquence*, for example: "Fire-Eater," "Cremation," or "*Dichtung and Wahrheit.*"

135 "Three cheers for mute ingloriousness" (On Not Being Milton 12) is an allusion to the line from "Elegy Written in a Country Churchyard" by Thomas Gray: "Some mute inglorious Milton here may rest" (1993: 59).

Gray sympathizes with the inglorious Milton from a distance and in a highly literary voice befitting the distinguished elegiac form. Harrison recognizes his affiliation with the tradition of Milton and Gray but does not grant it the privilege of superiority, setting Gray's lines alongside those written by shoemaker Richard Tidd.[136] His spelling mistake, which produces a pun and makes "writing" tantamount to "setting to rights," proves in Harrison's rendering to be no less poetic than Gray's sophisticated metaphors. The merging of these two ideas in one word "clinches the connection between articulacy and political activism" (Rylance 1991: 116) and signals the analogy between the lack of linguistic eloquence and social marginalization reappearing frequently throughout the sequence. The concluding line, "*Sir, I ham a very bad hand at righting*" (On Not Being Milton 16), italicized within the print of Harrison's poem suggests a quotation and also locates the perspective from which the problem of identity is to be viewed in the subsequent part of *The School of Eloquence*. The speaker of the line does not describe his problem with literacy in terms of aptitude: He does so in terms of identity and as lacking a command of language that might determine who he is. The line develops the meditation on the issue of identity initiated in the title of the poem and may be read as a provocative starting point for a discussion on the nature of social and cultural exclusion. The poem describes the scale according to which the value of language, and thus the position of the individual in the society, is summarily estimated. At the top of the scale reside Milton and Gray, and the elite tradition of art they represent; at the bottom, the regional voice, barbarian diction unfit for poetry. The poem establishes the position of the speaker assumed in the majority of subsequent poems. He is a man occupied with the language of Milton and Gray but a man who consciously chooses to speak with the voice of Richard Tidd and thereafter makes feasible the coexistence of the two languages.

The referencing to Richard Tidd is characteristic of Harrison, who dramatizes "personal crisis as representative of larger problems," (Rylance 1991: 115) while associating lack of literacy with social degradation. This citation strengthens the analogy "between political and linguistic violence" (Rylance 1991: 118) developed in the second stanza of the poem:

---

136 Charged with high treason and executed with other co-conspirators in 1820 for an attempt to assassinate the British Cabinet. For more information see: *The Lives of Thistlewood, Davidson, Brunt, Tidd and Ings: The Leaders of the Cato Street Conspiracy who were lately executed at the Old Bailey*. London: Printed by C.A. Madden for Kelleher, Guardian Office Strand, 1820, 31–35.

The stutter of the scold out of the branks
of condescension, class and counter-class
thickens with glottal to a lumpen mass
of Ludding morphemes closing up their ranks.
Each swung cast-iron Enoch of Leeds stress
Clangs a forged music on the frames of Art,
The looms of owned language smashed apart! (On Not Being Milton 5–11)

The voice of the scold, the troublemaker identified in the poem with nineteenth-century Ludditism[137] interferes in the matters of "Art" (On Not Being Milton 10) while disturbing the rules of mainstream culture. The clash between the standardized version of language, represented by the capitalized "Art," (On Not Being Milton 10) and Harrison's native variation, the voice of a rebel and a poet,[138] is rendered in terms of armed conflict. The Leeds accent destroys the "frames of Art" (On Not Being Milton 10) just like Luddites destroyed "the knitting-fremes that were depriving them of livelihoods" (Rylance 1991: 117). Art, and consequently, dominant language variation, is framed, constructed, exclusive, and, like the knitting-frames, owned, by representatives of a dominant social class. If language is owned, Rylance suggests, "expression is a cultural as well as political activity" (1991: 117) and a privilege the working class has rarely been granted.

Harrison's return to the eighteenth and the nineteenth century gains an additional dimension in the light of Tony Crowley's analyses[139] of the history of standardization of English in Great Britain. Crowley argues that the emergence of the "standard language" was spurred by the social and economic development of the South-East[140] rather than by any linguistic factors (1989: 198–200). Standardization was followed by codification, which led to the "suppression of optional variability" (Milroy and Milroy 2005: 178) and stigmatization of non-standard

137 A member of the band of English workers who destroyed machinery, especially in cotton and woolen mills, which they believed was threatening their jobs. (Oxford Dictionary of English).
138 "scold" (or "skald")—and Old Norse poet.
139 Namely: *The Politics of Discourse: The Standard Language Question in British Cultural Debates*. London: Macmillan, 1989.
140 The South-East is understood here in accordance with Linda Thomas's definition as "the area in central to south-east England which includes capital, London, and the cities of Oxford and Cambridge, the homes of England's two oldest and most prestigious universities" (1996: 189). According to Thomas "if the political, social and commercial heart of England had been elsewhere, the current standard form of language would look different, since it would have been based on a different English variety" (1996: 177).

forms. The fact that a large part of British society continued to speak one of the non-standard varieties, which were and still are perceived as culturally inferior, shows, as Milroy and Milroy argue, that "the universal adoption of the standard has failed" but "promotion of an ideology of a standard has been very successful" (2005: 179). According to Crowley, since the beginning of the nineteenth century, "whenever political or cultural crisis threatened, the English language was offered as evidence of underlying or unconscious unity that held together despite all superficial differences" (1991: 70). The creation of "social-bonding" (Rylance 1991: 119) on the basis of the standardized version excluded those who had no command of the prestigious dialect—that is, among others, members of the British working-class—from the circle of the "shared cultural heritage" (Rylance 1991: 119). In the poem Harrison creates a set of analogies: between linguistic and social suppression, between the linguistic and physical attack and between the "frames of Art" (On Not Being Milton 10) and the knitting-frames, symbols of the establishment. They shed new light on the seemingly benign "ideology of the standard" (Watts 2002: 189) which associates standardized English with "'positive' social behaviour" (Watts 2002: 189) and aesthetic superiority (Crowley 1989: 198–200) and by analogy / in consequence, non-standard English with their opposites. The nature of language standardization provides strong historical ground for Harrison's extended metaphor of linguistic expression as rebellion. Harrison looks back to the eighteenth and nineteenth century for historical facts which can give credibility to his metaphors, but, first and foremost, as Rylance suggests, such facts maintain the continuities of linguistic and political working-class experience (1991: 119). The metaphors created in the poem such as: "the looms of … language" and "Enoch of Leeds stress" (On Not Being Milton 9, 11) reveal these two lines of experience (the linguistic and political) as inextricably bound. In the poem, "lines" go back to the "roots," (On Not Being Milton 2) to the native land of the speaker, but also encompass larger social, cultural and political debate; the "historicity of [Harrison's] poems extends far beyond Beeston"[141] (Rowland 3: 2001) towards global issues.

The poem is a revolt against the marginalization of the non-standard forms wrongly labelled as intellectually, morally and aesthetically disadvantageous, but this revolt does not imply unambiguous identification or, as Rylance calls it, "naive solidarity with the non-literary 'other'" (1991: 118). Harrison knows that literature is produced primarily outside the working-classes, and that makes incorporation

141 The south Leeds district where the poet was born.

of a working class voice into literature a difficult task. The pun on "forged"[142] (On Not Being Milton 10) introduces the idea that the music of working-class expression runs the risk of being a mere imitation of the mainstream art, of the language owned by a privileged minority. An example of such "forged" literature according to W. E. Parkinson, are the poems of the pitman Joseph Skipsey (1832–1903), who, like Harrison, climbed the social ladder to leave his place of origin. After moving to London to become a curator of Shakespeare's house, Skipsey re-wrote his early work in "acceptable literary language" (Parkinson 1972: 110), modelling his diction on the works of Dante Gabriel Rossetti (Parkinson 1972: 110). This act of domesticating translation from the source language of the working classes into the target language of a middle-class audience resulted in poems that were culturally sterile. The new versions could no longer express the complexity of working-class experience; they have lost touch with the reality from which they originally stemmed. Parkinson sees the main threat to regional and class poetry as the "conscious literariness" (1972: 110) of the poets, who chose to write in "a mainstream literary language and expect a middle-class literary audience", but the poetry of Harrison, not so much a "cultural bastard" but an "immigrant" (1972: 107–122) to use Parkinson's label, proves that eloquence is not tantamount to the abandonment of regional voice.

The opening poem of *The School of Eloquence* renders rejection of the poetic achievements of Milton and Gray purely on the basis of political argument[143] as dubious and unsettling. Smashing the "frames of Art" (On Not Being Milton 10) may lead to the victory of "mute ingloriousness," implied in the poem by an ironic "three cheers," (On Not Being Milton 12) but will not necessarily result in the creation of an original voice of the working classes. Moreover, the victory itself will be unsatisfactory and short-lived, such as that of the nineteenth century Luddites, who were unable to stop the progress of mechanization. In "On Not Being Milton," the scold/skald character, the outsider and the rebel, is a type of ambivalent hero described by William Empson as a man outside society because he is "too poor for its benefits" and so "independent, as the artist claims to be" (1995: 20–21). He is allowed by the author to become:

> [A] judge of the society that judges him. This is a source of irony both against him and against the society, and if he is a sympathetic criminal he can be made to suggest both

142 To forge: 1. Create a shape (a metal object) by heating it in a fire or furnace and hammering it. 2. Create something strong, enduring and successful. 3. Produce a fraudulent copy or imitation of something (Oxford Dictionary of English).

143 Namely, that they represent the value system of the ruling class.

> Christ as the scapegoat ... and the ... tragic hero, who was normally above society rather than below it, which is a further source of irony. (Empson 1995: 20–21)

In "On Not Being Milton," the hero has multiple incarnations, with a greater number of "shadowy identities" (Byrne 1997: 22) whose nature is always oppositional and indeterminate. The rebellious scold associated with the Luddites and thus representing a collective rather than individual identity of the underprivileged and the dispossessed, is given a specific face in the character of the scapegoat[144] and/or usurper Richard Tidd. Other historically documented heroes of the poem are Sergio Vieira and Armando Guebuza, from the Frelimo movement[145] who articulated their grievance and judgment through political action but also through poetry. Seemingly less ambivalent[146] than the scold, Tidd and the Luddites, they belong in the same category because they are outcasts, both dispossessed and rebellious. Incorporation of their histories into the poem emphasizes the "relationship between poetry, education and politics" (Rylance 1991: 121) and invites an analogy between the history of the English working class and the history of the colonial and post-colonial independence movements (Rylance 1991: 121). The most important element of this analogy is "the experience of a condition of cultural exile," (Rylance 1991: 120) a point of contact between the story of Harrison and the story of Mozambican poets engaged in armed conflict and political discussion.

Another persona in the poem, one whose identity remains oppositional and deeply ambiguous, is that of Milton. A fuller discussion of Milton's persona necessitates an examination of two key issues: the issue of the ambiguity of the poem's attitude towards Milton, as analyzed by Rick Rylance and Sandie Byrne, and the ambiguity of the poem's attitude towards Milton, created through

---

144 The important feature of the figure of a scapegoat is the fact that it is "someone blamed for the wrongdoings of others, especially for reasons of expediency" and is "traditionally associated with the idea of being an outcast. In the Bible, a scapegoat is a goat sent into the wilderness after the Jewish priest had symbolically laid the sins of the people upon it." (Oxford Dictionary of English).

145 Frelimo is a name of "a political and military movement that initiated Mozambican independence from Portugal and then formed the governing party of newly independent Mozambique in 1975." (Encyclopedia Brytannica).

146 Although the moral ambivalence of the characters is not suggested directly in the poem, it can be claimed on the basis of historical context, and precisely on the disputable nature of Guebuza's political success and his party's electoral victory. For more information of Frelimo and Mozambican fight for independence see J. Cabrita, *Mozambique: The Tortuous Road to Democracy*, New York: Macmillan, 2001.

metaphor and literary allusion within the semantic and formal framework of the poem. The first issue presents itself in *From The School of Eloquence and Other Poems* and is further emphasised in *Continuous* by the addition of a sixteen-line epigraph culled from Milton's famous elegy "Ad Patrem." The Epigraph wrought to resemble one of Harrison's own sonnets (Rylance 1991: 118), suggests a "humble" (Rylance 1991: 118) reading of the title: I am not Milton, my poems are not as good as his. Conversely, the title, especially if read in the light of subsequent lines, opposes "Milton's Latinate language and his learned classicism" (Rylance, 1991: 118). The author identifies his own poetry in unison with the poetry of Milton and, revolting against its elite status, both "celebrates the literary and criticizes it" (Rylance, 1991: 118). This latter type of ambiguity, inherent to Milton's persona, is constructed on the basis of an intertextual reference to Gray's poem and the character of the "mute inglorious" (On Not Being Milton 59) namesake of the famous poet buried in the country churchyard. His understated presence might easily be overlooked by the reader, since this paraphrase is in no way signposted. Quite the opposite, "mute ingloriousness" (On Not Being Milton 12) is made to look as if it was Harrison's utterance: immediate, contemporary and general. The switching of the adjective (inglorious) for the noun (ingloriousness) changes the aspect of a person into a state characteristic of a whole stratum of society which remains, like Gray's Milton, buried and silent. Noteworthy too is that the adjective "inglorious" contains two meanings: "unknown,"[147] as in Gray's intentional meaning and pointedly relevant for Harrison, and "disgraceful,"[148] which achieves a specific overtone in the context of Harrison's social discussion. The lack of command of language or, as the following poems of the sequence bear out, a lack of command of the privileged dialect, is for a working-class speaker, a source of shame, designating his inevitable marginalization within society. Whereas "ingloriousness" refers to the condition of the working classes, the adjective "mute" binds this condition with the inability and/or impossibility to speak out and suggests the silence surrounding the issue of language hegemony, which had become an inherent element of an accepted social order.

---

147 "Not glorious; not bringing honour or glory; not accompanied with fame or celebrity; as in an 'inglorious life of ease.'" (Webster 1828 Dictionary) This meaning is also apparent in the etymology of the word: "Latin *inglorious*, from in - + *gloria* glory … not glorious; lacking fame or honour 'made an *inglorious* comeback.'" (Merriam—Wbester's Collegiate Dictionary. 11th Edition 2003).

148 "Shameful, disgraceful. He charged his troops with inglorious flight" (Websters 1828 Dictionary); "Shameful, ignominious 'an inglorious defeat'" (Merriam—Wbester's Collegiate Dictionary. 11th Edition 2003).

The understated presence of the inglorious Milton, suggested by the paraphrase, raises both the question of meaning in the poem's title and a corollary question about the identity of the speaker. Stuart Hall argues that identities:

> Emerge within play of specific modalities of power, and thus are more the product of the marketing of difference and exclusion, than they are the sign of identical, naturally—constituted unity—an identity in its traditional meaning (that is, an all—inclusive, seamless, without internal differentiation) … identities [are] constructed through, not outside, difference. (2008: 4)

Hence, identity can be constructed only through the relation to the Other, to "what it is not, what it lacks," to a so-called *constitutive outside* (Derrida 1981; Laclau 1990, Butler 1993). The point Harrison makes in his opening sonnet is that the identity of Milton the poet functions "because of [its] capacity to exclude, to leave out, to render outside" (Hall 2008: 5) the abject element, that mute ingloriousness embodied by Gray's Milton, his silent alter ego[149] absent from literary history and collective memory. Every identity, continues Hall, "has its margin, an excess, something more" (2008: 5) which, even if "silent and unspoken" (2008: 5) is necessary to achieve, even if only temporarily, a certain form of unity of the self (2008: 5). A constitution of the self as Laclau persuasively argues, "is an act of power" since:

> If … an objectivity manages to partially affirm itself it is only by repressing that which threatens it. Derrida has shown how an identity's constitution is always based on excluding something and establishing a violent hierarchy between the two resultant poles—white/black, man/woman, etc. What is peculiar to the second term is thus reduced to the function of an accident as opposed to the essentiality of the first. It is the same with the black-white relationship,[150] in which white, of course, is equivalent to 'human being.' 'Woman' and 'black' are thus marks (i.e. marked terms) in contrast to the unmarked terms of 'man' and 'white.' (Laclau 1990: 33)

In following Laclau's arguments, it is important to note the relation on the social level between two Miltons, represented by a violent hierarchy, the privileged and the dispossessed, the voice of "Art" (On Not Being Milton 10) and the awkward articulation, standard English and the non-standard dialect: fraught dichotomies

---

149 A parallel construction is created in Harrison's *v.* (discussed in detail in one of the following chapters of the book) where on return to his native Leeds, the poet meets the skin, his working-class Other.

150 The way in which this dichotomy functions in Harrison's verse is especially interesting in the case of the "colonial theme" of *The Loiners* discussed in the previous chapter of the book.

within which the identity of the ruling class is established through the abjection of working-class values. The established ruling-class identity must be then inevitably threatened (Hall 2008: 5) by the marginalized, who assume the position of outcasts and outlaws, as embodied in Harrison's poetry by ambivalent heroes. To emphasize the game of acceptance and exclusion in the abovementioned poem also means to confirm its presence on the level of an individual "self." The two Miltons comprise one contradictory internal identity,[151] one part of which is under constant destabilization by the Other, by "what it leaves out" (Hall 2008: 5) what it opposes, and what it argues against. On this level, where the glorious Milton stands for poetic eloquence and the inglorious Milton for working class origin, both terms (poet/working-class man) are marked as dependent upon that set of values the speaker acknowledges as his own in a given instance of discourse. This is as much to state why he cannot fully identify with either and remains in a state of continual transgression of boundaries, feeling "alienated from both" worlds and seeking to "give justice to this alienation" (Haffenden 1991: 234).

Any dichotomy between these two contrasting poles is used as a central device in a pair of sonnets titled "Them and [uz]," which represent a larger group of *The School of Eloquence* poems[152] analyzing the continuity of working-class experience and the class content of individual existence (Spencer 1991: 7). The title itself (i.e. "Them and [uz]"), so suggestive in its pledge of conflict, or "at best a dialogue" between "two different voices" (Crucefix 1997: 166) and consequently between two conflicting cultures and two sides of the speaker's identity, is personified in the opening poem by the two Miltons. The first line of "Them and [uz]" incorporates "aiai" of "the classical dramatic lament" (Crucefix 1997: 167) and the "ay ay!" "of the music hall comedian" (Crucefix 1997: 167), and can easily be taken by the reader for a "howl of inarticulacy." (Crucefix 1997: 166) This same line introduces the "unresolved drama" (Crucefix 1997: 166) of conflicting voices but also grafts the voice of a popular culture entertainer on to that of a Greek orator or, as Sandie Byrne puts it, it creates a "conjunction of music-hall stand-up comedian and Demosthenes" (1998: 104). The juxtaposition of the two phrases, and thus two images, introduced by the intertextual contexts of "ai ai" and "ay, ay!," affects a closeness to that offered by a particular metaphysical conceit, in which two contrasting ideas are traditionally brought together to reveal and elicit their striking correspondence. In this case, the correspondence is based on a homophony of

151 The dichotomy can be treated as a metaphorical rendering of speaker's "trouble with resolving the issue of l'ipseite (coherence of whatever distinguishes us as a person)" (Bauman 2007: 13) as discussed in the initial part of this chapter.

152 "Working," "National Trust," "Classic Society," "Study," "Me Tarzan" and other.

syllables sharing the same pronunciation but referring the reader to different cultural contexts. That this correspondence takes place on the level of pronunciation sharpens the contrast between (democratic) speech and (elite) writing (Jarniewicz 2001: 90) and constitutes an "ironic comment upon the subject of what really is in language … gibberish, and that which belongs to the sophisticated field of literary language"[153] (Jarniewicz 2001: 90). Harrison names the sound of the four syllables that will become in the poem the stutter of a future orator. The image of Demosthenes, fighting to improve his pronunciation by trying to achieve the impossible, shouting down the roar of the ocean, constitutes a metaphorical rendering of the speaker of the poem fighting to "occupy" the "speech of Kings" (Them and [uz] II 1, 7) in order to recover "his native voice suppressed by schooling in the tradition of 'dozing Daniel Jones'"[154] (Rylance 1991: 119) and others anointed by the system. Demosthenes then, in Harrison's poem, is an example of a "poet born without a mouth"[155] who has to struggle for his voice, and whose gob[156] full of pebbles, is made to resemble the worked-out seam of a mine[157] which is after all nothing more than a dark, useless hole. As a part of the human body and as a part of the northern landscape, the gob implies some form of deficiency, standing for a lack of voice and for a lack of coal, for both silence and darkness. It is not by chance that many poems of the sequence characterize the place from which Harrison's poetry stems and sufficiently describe those factors shaping his poetic identity. In

---

153 My translation of: "ironiczny komentarz na temat tego, co tak naprawdę jest w języku … bełkotem, a co należy do dziedziny wyrafinowanego języka literackiego" (Jarniewicz 2001: 90).

154 Author of *The English Pronunciation Dictionary* (1917) who "gave a further currency to the term 'RP' (Received Pronunciation), first used it in the late nineteenth century, and offered as a standard of correct speech, that of the public school-educated natives of the south of England. Jones also used the term Public School English, or PSE, to describe the form of English he presented" (Byrne 1998: 23).

155 As was discussed in the first chapter the description refers to Hieronymus Fracastorius (1483–1553), the author of *Syphilis*, referred to in a note to the "White Queen".

156 A recurring image in Harrison's poetry usually associated with working-class people speaking local dialects. Having a gob stands in *The School of Eloquence* in opposition to having a mouth, as it implies the inability to pronounce words in a socially accepted way.

157 A "gob" means a "mouth" but it is also as Harrison explains in the *Collected Poems* "an old Northern coal-mining word for the space left after the coal has been extracted" (2007: 135) and a British slang word meaning "to spit." (Andrew Tomlinson, Private Conversation, 28 March 2013, London)

"Heredity," "Dark Times," "Cremation," "Working" characterizing his poetic roots by negative properties denoting absence rather than presence (like lack of light and lack of sound) is a part of his larger strategy. He often speaks with silences (Byrne 1998: 167) and presents images of empty spaces created by the destructive power of inevitable change, extinction of cultures, places and languages (see for example: "Art and Extinction," "The Earthen Lot," "t'Ark"). Darkness and silence as two factors shaping the poetic identity of the speaker characterize the nature of the land of his roots (On Not Being Milton 2) which slides slowly into an abyss (a process illustrated in *v.* by the image of earth collapsing into the worked-out seam of the mine), but also imply multiple continuities, breaks and ruptures, which mark the experience of the poet.

Harrison uses "the phonetic alphabet to differentiate between the RP version of 'us'" and the regional "flattened vowel" of the northern [uz] (Spencer 1994: 72) and thereafter allies himself with the latter. His identification with the regional pronunciation of the pronoun implies a further identification with the working-class tradition whose voice intertwines in the poem with the voice of hegemonic culture, personified by a school master:

> 4 words only of mi' art aches and … 'Mine's broken,
> You barbarian, T. W.!' He was nicely spoken
> Can't have our glorious heritage done to death!'
>
> I played the Drunken Porter in Macbeth.
>
> 'Poetry is speech of kings. You're one of those
> Shakespeare gives the comic bits to: prose!
> (Them and [uz] I 3–8)

His "claim to possession [and] to authority in the matters of language" (Crucefix 1997: 167) based on the false assumption that Keats spoke RP, can be forcefully refuted by the speaker, the adult Harrison, who by now is a scholar himself and who realizes "the implications of Keats being Cockney" (Spencer 1994: 73). However, the young Harrison, whose voice is being silenced, endures an act of marginalization: his role in a larger society represented on a smaller scale by the role he is given in a school play of *Macbeth*. The school master's utterance of the phrase "you are one of those" (Them and [uz] I, 7) lays both a dividing and divisive line running between the cultured and the barbaric.[158] Further discussion of those ramifications entails an understanding of how the word "barbaric" is employed

158 For a detailed analysis of the coexistence of the two categories see Anthony Rowland *Tony Harrison and the Holocoust.* Liverpool University Press, 2001, 254–261.

to refer to a lack of culture.[159] An unfamiliar type of pronunciation or taking a different perspective, a lack of correct pronunciation is, according to the representatives of the hegemonic social group, a sign of barbarism. *The Oxford English Dictionary* defines barbaric as follows:

> The use of words or expressions not in accordance with the classical standard of a language, especially such as are of foreign origin ... The mixing of foreign words or phrases in Latin and Greek; hence, rudeness or unpolished condition of language ... absence of culture; uncivilized ignorance and rudeness ... cruelty.

Furthermore, an implicit understanding of the term is enhanced by its etymology: "Originating in the Greek world for a 'foreign mode of speech,' it indicated the creation of a specifically linguistic 'other'" (Rowland 2001: 257). According to Julia Kristeva, the onomatopoeic expression was created by the Greeks, who perceived a foreign language as meaningless "bla-bla, bara-bara," (1991: 51) as incomprehensible gibberish. Interestingly, the term "barbarians" was applied not only to foreigners but also to Greeks who used a non-standard version of their native language[160] (Kristeva 1991: 51). As Jarniewicz points out, Harrison is akin here to fellow poet Douglas Dunn:

> It is interesting that two contemporary British poets, Tony Harrison and Douglas Dunn, use the concept of 'barbarism' in their works dealing with the situation of the working-class in Britain. The word initially applied to alien tribes is used here to refer to a social class within one nation to the effect of evoking the idea of *foreignness* and *alienation*[161], a split that devides social classes and which makes communication between them difficult. (Jarniewicz 1994: 110)

The abjection of the linguistic Other, thereby labeling a working-class culture as foreign and alien, enables the school master to constitute his own identity as a non-barbaric member of society. In Harrison's poem the school-master, in order to exclude, establishes "a violent hierarchy" (Laclau 1990: 33) between standard and dialect pronunciations, the inferior, or to use Laclau's terminology "marked," (1990: 33) version of his own native language. He is a representative of a whole section of British society whose group identity is to a large extent created on the basis of rendering outside the barbaric element. His attitude echoes the opinion

---

159 See definition given in *The Concise Oxford Dictionary*. Oxford, 1982.

160 Harrison is aware of the diversity of Greek and of the inferior status of some of its forms, for example Doric Greek (Byrne 1998: 26). See Preface to *Aikin Mata: The Lysistrata of Aristophanes*. Ibadan, Oxford University Press, 1966, 10.

161 Emphasis added by the author of this book.

on non-standard forms of speech expressed in *Newbolt Report*,[162] published in Great Britain in 1921, which among other things, sought to define the role of elementary school education:[163]

> It is emphatically the business of the elementary school to teach all pupils who either speak a definite dialect or whose speech is disfigured by vulgarisms, to speak standard English, and speak it clearly. The great difficulty of teachers in elementary schools in many districts is that they have to fight against the powerful influence of evil habits of speech contracted in home and street. The teacher's struggle is thus not with ignorance but with perverted power. (*Newbolt Raport* qtd in Worlpole 1991: 63)

The "perverted power" which, according to the authors, teachers have to face in approaching the speakers of non-standard versions of the language, suggests a link between the ability to speak Standard English and the "morality of a well ordered world" (Thomas 1996: 189). The barbarians, so easily distinguished from other members of the society by their lack of that ability, could potentially destabilize the social order (Watts 2002: 155–172). Their manner of speech is associated in a public debate with that which is evil and perverted[164], or even criminogenic and filthy, and by default, with that which should be eradicated in order to maintain status quo. As an MP, Norman Tebbit said in 1985:

> If you allow standards to slip to the stage where good English is no better than bad English, where people turn up *filthy*[165] at school ... all these things tend to cause people to have no standards at all, and once you lose standards than there's no imperative to stay out of *crime*[166]. (qtd in Cameron 1995: 94–96)

The above comment treats the lack of ability to speak a standard form of language as tantamount to being unclean, similarly to the *Newbolt Report*, which suggested that a dialect is comparable to using vulgarisms. In both cases, non-standard

---

162 It should be noted that *Newbolt Report* advocated changes in the literary canon taught at British schools and expressed a need for wider access to education which should stop it being a privilege attainable only for the rich. However, intellectual advancement of the lower classes could, according to the author, take place only if the students abandon their non-standard way of speaking. In *Newbolt Report*, the term English refers solely to Standard English. Its superiority lies in the fact it is tantamount to thinking, which makes dialects unfit for cultured discourse.

163 For additional comment on the subject see: Margaret Mathieson *The Preachers of Culture: a study of English and its teachers* London: Rowman & Littlefield Publishers 1975 (Chapter 6).

164 See the fragment of *Newbolt Report* qtd above.

165 Emphasis added by the author of this book.

166 Emphasis added by the author of this book.

speakers of English are marginalized as those who do not obey the social norms of the society they live in.

As stated in the poem the headmaster establishes his own identity in opposition to the speakers of non-standard versions of English. Just as with the identity of the poetic "I" of the poem, the identity of the headmaster can only be understood as a process. In terms of Hall's reasoning, his identity "can only be read against the grain—that is to say, specifically not as that which fixes the play of difference in a point of origin and stability but that … which is constantly destabilized by what it leaves out" (Hall 2008: 5). In this light, the beginning of the second "Them and [uz]" sonnet i.e. "So right, yer buggers, then! We'll occupy / your lousy leashold Poetry," (Them and [uz] II, 1–2) can be read as a promise of "destabilization" (Hall 2008: 5), a threat directed at "Them," and in consequence, a further claim of identification of the poetic persona with the "[uz]," with the barbarians, the speakers of a dialect. However, the identification can never be fully successful. According to Sandie Byrne, "although Harrison insists [uz] [uz] [uz] and expresses a longing to restore the continuous of … geographical and social group, it is 'my name' and '[my] own voice' which is the loudest, not 'we' but 'I'" (Byrne 1998: 168). In "Them and [uz]," as well as in other poems of the sequence (for example, "Me Tarzan"), the "loss of membership of a group" (Byrne 1998: 168) and the loss of a "sense of place" (Byrne 1998: 168) lead to an existential dislocation (Bokszański 2007: 21) of the poetic persona.[167] As Byrne points out: "Them and [uz]" may be "a defiant declaration of affiliation to the group whose standard is Leeds dialect," however, although the poetic "I" refuses to identify with [us], "dropping T.W." does not mean automatic "assimilation with [uz]" (Byrne 1993: 168). The impossibility of full identification is caused, among other things by the fact that the poetic "I" is forced to face what Jawłowska calls "the drama of recognition," 'dramat uznania' (2001: 51–52).

The choice by the adult Tony Harrison to identify with working-class culture is at odds with the will of a social group he enters, which does not want to grant him the freedom of that choice. Eloquence makes it possible for Harrison to occupy poetry but his act of defiance and his consequent decision to rename himself Tony is ignored: "My first mention in the *Times* / automatically made Tony Anthony!" (Them and [uz] II, 16). His attempt to establish his personal and social identity by maintaining continuity with his working-class origins (Tony

167 The problem of alienation from working-class culture and impossibility of communications with the working-class community is further developed in the familial elegiac poems of *The School Eloquence: Continuous* and will be analyzed in the next chapter of the book.

was a name he was called at home) proves difficult in a new social context. According to Joanna Thornborrow:

> Personal identities are socially constructed through the use of names ... The giving of a name can be a part of the acceptance of an individual into a particular culture or religion, establishing individual identity.... The attribution of names is only one part of the story, however. Once you have your name, how people use it becomes very important. The way names are used ... is central to the process of constructing individual identities within a group .... What you get called is not necessarily a matter of your personal choice though. Names can cause problems, particularly if they don't fit in with the conventions of a community. (2005: 160)

Harrison's chosen name, i.e. Tony, definitely does not fit with the conventions acceptable for the community of RP speakers referred to in the poem's title as "Them" and identified by Harrison with the written, "cold" (Jarniewicz 2001: 90) version of language, as opposed to the spoken one which is seen in the poem. Similarly, the diminutive version of his name is regarded as "warm" (Jarniewicz 2001: 90)[168] and familiar. It is not then accidental that the act of renaming "Tony" as "Anthony" takes place in the public domain of the printed word.

One pertinent adjective chosen by Jarniewicz (i.e. "warm") to describe the quality attributed to the spoken language in the poem, gains additional meaning in the literary context of Richard Hoggart's *Uses of Literacy: Aspects of Working-class Life with Special References to Publications and Entertainments.*[169] In the chapter entitled "'Them' and 'Us,'" Hoggart describes the working-class peoples' sense of being members of the group" (Hoggart 2005: 54) as a "sense of group warmth" (Hoggart 2005: 55) which "exercises a powerful hold, and continues to be missed when individuals have moved, financially and probably geographically, out of the working-classes" (Hoggart 2005: 55). The sense of working-class community Hoggart refers to is not particularly "self-conscious" (2005: 55), it is natural and inherent as opposed to taught and constructed. Herein, communality precedes

---

168 My translation of:

> W sonecie 'Them and [uz]' ... Harrison zaznacza kontrast między (chłodnym) językiem pisma a (ciepłym) językiem mowy. To zasadnicze dla wiersza słowo 'uz' czyli 'my', pojawia się tu w transkrypcji fonetycznej ... jakby w ten sposób Harrison chciał przypomnieć, że to, co 'nasze', a więc to, co autentyczne i wiarygodne, należy do dziedziny mowy, a nie pisma. (Jarniewicz, 2001: 90).

169 The poem is dedicated to two people: Leon Cortes, a stand up comedian, and Professor Richard Hoggart. The title of one of the chapters of his widely acclaimed but also heavily criticized *Uses of Literacy* became a basis for the title of Harrison's "Them and [uz]".

any organized political or social action just as spoken precedes written language, and just as a spoken literary tradition is primal to a written one:

> [the sense of community] does not draw its main strength from—indeed, it precedes, and is more elementary than—the belief in the need to improve each other's lot jointly which gave rise to such organizations as the Co-operative movement. It arises chiefly from the knowledge it can give. (Hoggart 2005: 56–57)

Harrison's choice to make his poems "essentially speech" (Barker 1991: 46) may be understood as an attempt at continuity of belonging to the working-class community—a task which can be seen in terms of possibility but not in sureness since the working-class community "works against the idea of change" and imposes on its members "an extensive … pressure to conform" (Hoggart 2005: 58). Those who do not, such as a scholarship boy from "Them and [uz]" and "Me Tarzan," "become different through education" (Hoggart 2005: 58) and are likely to find themselves in the position of outcast.[170] In Harrison's poetry the pursuance of continuity of belonging of the poetic "I," which cannot be definitely achieved and remains in process, is historicized and contextualized to represent a continuity of the experience of the working classes, the barbarians, the speakers of dialect. Some of them, such as Hoggart, and in the same way as Harrison, become writers occupying liminal spaces, some, like Harrison's father, die labeled linguistically inferior. All of them, though divided by issues of "gender, family, war, politics" (Astley 1991: 10) become in *The School of Eloquence*, the "agents of *agon*" (Byrne 1997: 23), ambiguous heroes, and oppositional characters participating in Harrison's struggle to maintain a continuity of culture endangered with extinction. This inclusiveness[171] (Astley 1991: 10) resulting in multiplicity and diversity of voices in Harrison's *The School of Eloquence*, is probably "the strongest legacy of [the poet's] … upbringing" (Astley 1991: 10).

---

170 Another reason is the extinction of the working-class community itself. This issue will be discussed in the subsequent parts of the book in connection with his elegiac family poems and *v.*

171 Astley uses the term in reference to Harrison's verse, drawing on the linguistic claim that "we punctuate our speech with 'sociocentric tags': Middle-class speakers tend to say *I think* (giving their opinion), an exclusive tag, where working-class speakers will say *you know* (drawing the listener into a shared conversation)" (Astley 1991: 13).

Chapter Three
"The still too living dead"

Continuity of Mourning in the Selected Elegies from *The School of Eloquence*

In his paper entitled "Mourning and Annihilation in Tony Harrison's *The School of Eloquence*," Anthony Rowland places Harrison's "family sonnets" within a larger context of "poetry of mourning," which is "conventionally explicated within the recognized … and transgressive structure of elegy" (Rowland 1998: 1). Rowland focuses on theoretical approaches to the issue[172] although he does not ignore the importance of literary models of elegy, applied to Harrison's work by Rebecca Smalley in her (unpublished) thesis *The Role of Memory in the Poetry of Douglas Dunn and Tony Harrison*. Undeniably, structures of elegy and theoretical models concerning mourning cannot be treated as "a rigid interpretative grid" (Rowland 1998: 1) while explaining Harrison's "complex and elusive" (Rowland 1998: 1) approach to the process of mourning. Nevertheless, they are useful in interpreting the theme of loss and, as the following analysis will prove, its relation to the issue of constructing identity in *The School of Eloquence*. The reason for this is that structures of elegy and theoretical models concerning mourning lay great stress on "identity's diachronic relation to its past," in other words, they focus less on the "contingent in-the-present character (i.e. the social construction of identity) and more … [on] the ways in which past experiences appear to 'hard-wire' or determine categories of identity" (Prager 2009: 142). That is not to say that the issue of social construction of identity ceases to be important in the case of "family poems," which contrary to the opinion of Luke Spencer, retain a strong social and political[173] tone and whose protagonists "orient their actions vis-à-vis other

---

172 Applying the theoretical framework of Sigmund Freud, Nicholas Abraham and Maria Torok.

173 In his critical study titled *The Poetry of Tony Harrison* Spencer suggests somewhat scornfully that the shift towards personal experience in the second part of the sequence resulted in nothing more than a production of "some moving observations on Harrison's family life" (1994: 89). Spencer states:

> The original group of sonnets that made up *From 'The School of Eloquence' and Other Poems* were primarily about language as an instrument of power and therefore, inescapably, of political struggle.… Subsequent extensions of the *'School'*

'identity' groups co-existing with one another, each defining social action with respect to a particular moral vision of a world-in-the-making" (Prager 2009: 142). However, due to the elegiac character of the poems which constitute the second part of the sequence, the influence of a traumatic past experience on the process of constructing identity becomes even more explicit than in the case of the poems of part I and part III, and as such requires close analysis.

The speaker of the "family poems," in which personal grief and the historical context become, as Rowland points out, strongly entangled (Rowland 1998: 1), can be seen as an agent of "the genealogy of identity … [a] process by which individuals vertically place or imagine themselves into ongoing social categories of experience and construct their own understanding of themselves in relation to those categories" (Prager 2009: 142). Influenced by his own past but also by numerous public and private histories which constantly intersect and overlap in *The School of Eloquence*, the speaker of "family poems" undertakes a task, pertinently described by Eric Stantner in *Stranded Objects*, as a process of "integrating damage, loss, disorientation, decentredness into a transformed structure of identity … of an individual, a culture, or an individual as a member of a cultural group[174]" (Stantner 1990: xii). Stantner continues his argument by claiming that this process can be discussed in relation to "what Freud called Trauerarbeit, or 'work of mourning'" (Stantner 1990: xii) and to Freud's categories of "mourning" and "melancholia" described in his famous essay, written in 1915 and published two years later. To follow the direction outlined by Rowland, who applies Stantner's "concept of mourning in a cultural context" (Rowland 1998: 1) to Harrison's "family sonnets," it is necessary to refer to the source of Stantner's model (Rowland

---

> sequence have left … political poems outnumbered by poems which are instead absorbed with the details of family … life…. the general direction of the development in the '*School*' sequence has been away from a committed … view of class, in all its historical, cultural and personal dimensions and towards a characteristically liberal concern with individual experience. (1994: 89)

However, it is difficult to disagree with an observation that the second part of the sequence revolves around personal experience, to be precise, the personal experience of loss, but as the close analysis of individual texts will prove, this fact does not weaken the social edge of Harrison's statement. The private and the public in the familial poems remain closely related.

174 The problem described by Stantner has its equivalent within the frame of elegiac tradition in the issue of narration of lack and imagery of absence characteristic for Harrison's verse.

1998: 1) i.e. Sigmund Freud's "Mourning and Melancholia" and to a related study by Nicholas Abraham and Maria Torok.[175]

In his essay Freud distinguishes two categories of mourning. There is true, healthy mourning, described as "a reaction to the loss of loved person, or the loss of some abstraction which has taken a place of one, such as fatherland, liberty, an ideal and so on" (Freud 1937: 144). Since the loved object is gone "the subject needs to detach his/her libido from it in order to redirect cathetic[176] energy onto a replacement" so that at the end of the mourning process, the ego "becomes free to attach itself to an alternative" (Freud 1937: 144). And there is the second category, i.e. melancholia, where the mourner "recognizes the loss of the loved object but not how it affects him/her" (Freud 1937: 145). What occurs here is an "indefinitely extended period of disreality" (Freud 1937: 146), in which the subject remains attached to the "ideal of the object" in a "hallucinatory wish-psychosis" (Freud 1937: 144). As a consequence "the ego remains cathected to the lost object and becomes poor and empty; this results in a pathological loss of self-esteem" (Freud 1937: 146). In other words, "in mourning it is the world that has become poor and empty; in melancholia it is the ego itself" (Freud 1937: 146). Of the many attempts at literature analysis based on Freudian theory, Kennedy's analysis of Wordsworth's *The Prelude* should be mentioned as especially relevant for discussion of Harrison's poetry.[177] Commenting on Book IV of the poem, which "reads like a scene of a canonical elegy" (Kennedy 2007: 37), Kennedy juxtaposes two contrary states: "self-possession" and "half-absence" (Kennedy 2007: 37) and compares them to the balanced state of mind one can regain as a result of Trauerarbeit and to melancholia. "Self-possession" obtained by Wordsworth during his solitary night excursion is contrasted in the poem with the mental state of a discharged soldier, whose "demeanour of nameless loss prefigures to some extent," (Kennedy 2007: 37) according to Kennedy, "Freud's account of the

175 i.e. "Interjection and Incorporation: Mourning or Melancholia," first published in 1872.

176 The word "derives from 'cathexis', a word coined by Freud's translators to translate the German *Besetzung* ('investment') which describes the amount of energy invested in any attachment, mental process or mental structure.… Mourning is work because the libido has to be detached from 'each single one of the memories and expectations' bound up with the lost object" (Kennedy 2007: 40–41).

177 Harrison states that *The School of Eloquence* is his own version of *The Prelude or Growth of a Poet's Mind.* (Jarniewicz 2001: 89), which is also an ongoing poetic task written by Wordsworth throughout his whole life.

melancholic" (Kennedy 2007: 37). He appears in front of Wordsworth's eyes as a "shape," a ghost-like figure unfit for the world of the living:

Was Never seen before by night or day.
Long were his arms, pallid his hands; his mouth
Looked ghastly in the moonlight: from behind,
A mile-stone propped him; I could also ken
That he was clothed in military garb,
Though faded yet entire. Companionless,
No dog attending, by no staff sustained,
He stood, and in his very dress appeared
A desolation, a simplicity,
To which the trappings of a gaudy world
Make a strange back-ground. From his lips, ere long,
Issued low muttered sounds, as if of pain
Or some uneasy thought; yet still his form
Kept the same awful steadiness—at his feet
His shadow lay, and moved not. From self-blame
Not wholly free, I watched him thus; at length. (The Prelude IV 394–409)

The most characteristic feature of his condition is painful in-betweenness, a state of limbo, in which he finds himself neither fully alive nor dead. He is half-sitting, and half-standing, murmuring "sounds, as if of pain / or some uneasy thought," (The Prelude 405–406) expressing himself in a voice which seems dead. His presence, disturbing but also fascinating, symbolises the allure of death, of withdrawal into the world of shadows, described by many authors throughout the ages, the state of not-being which attracted Eliotean protagonists and the speaker of "Stopping by the Woods in a Snowy Evening," a poem by Robert Frost. The fact that melancholy can metaphorically represent a death-like state is relevant for understanding Harrison's sequence, where the two reactions to loss i.e. mourning and melancholia, function on a metaphorical level as two options the speaker has in the face of grief: the former being tantamount to consciously facing the horrors of life and the latter to the reluctance to admit the truth about the human condition.

One of the most significant developments in psychoanalytic theories of mourning since Freud's essay is Nicholas Abraham and Maria Torok's article "Introjection—Incorporation: *Mourning* or *Melancholia*", first published in 1972. "Introjection" is described as a "real" process in which the subject recognizes the loss of the loved object and sublimates the pain into language (Abraham and Torok 1980: 6). This operation can be indicated figuratively through the sharing of food, an activity common in Western societies after the funeral service: "such communion can mean that, rather than the person of the deceased, it is our mutual presence that we are taking into our bodies in the form of assimilable food; as for the deceased, we shall deposit him in the earth and not in ourselves" (1980: 8). In contrast, during "incorporation", the subject refuses to admit the loss of the loved object and fantasises "swallowing" the latter to "avoid the need for hyper-cathection" (1980: 4–5). Abraham and Torok typify incorporation as a result of linguistic silence: "because the object is narcissistically indispensable, the subject cannot admit its loss" (1980: 6–7). Their theory differs from Freud's in that they realize that some subjects refuse to recognise loss in the first instance, whereas "Mourning and Melancholia" has absence as its premise. Both theories, according to Rowland, remain locked in their oppositional rationalization: at first glance, Freud's mourning and melancholia seem to remain in an oppositional either/or relationship similarly, there is no sense that a mourner could shift between Abraham and Torok's introjection and incorporation (1998: 4). In his study, Rowland states, and subsequently proves, that in Harrison's poetry, both this shift and a shift between true mourning and melancholia can be observed. The latter shift, or as Rowland calls it, a "vacillation between the two poles" (1998: 3), is in accordance with the opinion of Freud himself who, as his theory develops, acknowledges, according to Rowland, that the "opposition he makes between the two entities [i.e. mourning and melancholia] is not fixed and irrefutable" (1998: 3). Freud's new perspective on mourning and melancholia attained in his essay *The Ego and the Id*[178] proves especially interesting in the context of Harrison's family sonnets, as it opens up new interpretative possibilities and broadens possible understanding of Harrison's treatment of the issue of mourning.

In *Mourning and Melancholia*, Freud suggests that the passing of time "for the melancholic does not relieve the … suffering that comes from the trauma of a world disrupted" (Freud 1937: 146), one reason being that the melancholic has "very little capacity to have ambivalent feelings come into the open"[179] that

178 Prager asserts that:

> Loss, mourning and melancholia were problems that preoccupied Freud largely during the middle part of his career.… [he] significantly amends his theory between 1917, when *Mourning and Melancholia* was published, written prior to the onset of the wartime experiences of deep loss, and 1923 when *The Ego and the Id* was published, following the experiences of death and destruction of the First World War and subsequent to profound losses he personally suffered. (2009: 152)

179 The ambivalent feeling the melancholic might have towards the object "expresses itself as an agent of criticism and judgment (that Freud would later call super-ego) that mobilizes, in the name of an idealized object, a sustained internal attack against the self" (Prager 2009: 152) and consequently becomes a destructive force.

would help to forge "the detachment process" (Freud 1937: 146). Consequently, the detachment process is never initiated; the idealized object remains internalized, leaving the melancholic unable to complete mourning (Prager 2009: 152). In *Mourning and Melancholia,* the main fact distinguishing the mourner from the melancholic is that while the mourner does not internalize the lost object, the melancholic does. This point of view changes in *The Ego and the Id* where Freud:

> No longer asserts that normal mourners libidinally detach themselves fully from the lost object. He now proposes that common to all is an internalization through identification with those who were lost. *Mourning never truly ends.*[180] The [former] distinction collapses between mourner and melancholic. (Prager 2009: 153)

Melancholia remains in *The Ego and the Id* a pathological condition distinct from mourning. What changes is the perspective from which Freud observes the distinction. In the most general terms, the main difference between mourning and melancholic loss is attributed to ambivalence. According to Prager's interpretation of Freud's theoretical model, a healthy mourner:

> Has a capacity to mobilize ambivalent feelings toward the lost object … In contrast to a melancholic … the mourner learns to tolerate the ambiguity of his relation to the … object. Stated differently the ego possesses within it the ability … to hold conflicting stances toward the internalized object and the abandoned love-relation …. [the mourner has] a capacity to access hateful as well as loving feelings toward the same object (even as it remains as an … internal presence). (2009: 154)

In consequence, not only does mourning remain an ongoing process, as it does in *The School of Eloquence*, it also acknowledges and encompasses difficulties the mourning subject may have with relating to the past. In her reading of Freud's late theory, Tammy Clewell concludes that "the mourning subject may affirm endurance of ambivalent bonds to those loved and lost others as a condition of its own existence" (2004: 65). As a result "mourning, rather than diminishing or weakening the individual, enables self-strengthening" (Prager 2009: 154).

As the following analysis will show, an ambivalent attitude towards the lost object is one of the main characteristics of the speaker of Harrison's elegiac sonnets, who makes constant attempts at affirming the "endurance of ambivalent bonds" (Freud 1937: 154). The impossibility of unambiguous identification, described in the previous chapter, which occurs as a result of the ambivalent attitude, encourages the continuous development of the speaker's identity based on conflicting attitudes towards the past, a disappearing working-class culture and the dead parents who represent it. According to Ramazani, whose *Poetry of Mourning: The*

180 Emphasis added by the author of this book.

Modern Elegy from Hardy to Heaney tries to characterize the main features and themes of modern elegiac verse, the ambivalence is a typical characteristic of the contemporary elegy which engages with "unresolved [and] violent" mourning (1994: 4) and whose authors "attack the dead and themselves, their own work and tradition and they refuse such orthodox consolations as the rebirth of the dead in nature" (1994: 4). It is hard to disagree with those critics (W. David Shaw, Celeste M. Schenk, Abbie Findlay Potts) who see this attack as closely related to the negation of traditional elegiac conventions[181] (Ramazani 1994: 1–2) and ceremonial patterns (Schenck, When the Moderns Write Elegy, 1986: 108) and observe that as a result, modern elegists leave "their readers and themselves inconsolable" (Ramazani 1994: 1–4). Schenck goes as far as to label modern elegiac poetry "elegies manquees". (Schenck, 1986: 108). The phrase, originally used by Potts to describe Shalley's *Alastor* (Kennedy 2007: 7) refers to writing which "offers no new light or new life" as it is purely melancholic in its nature (Potts 1967: 224). Such poetry, Kennedy argues, reflects a wider trend in literature which involves an acknowledgement of the issue discussed by Slavoj Žižek and Giorgio Agamben, namely, that "we live in a profoundly melancholic age and that melancholy involves not only an attachment to loss but also pleasurable anticipation of loss" (Žižek 2000: 657–663). However, the ambivalent stance towards that which is lost or threatened with extinction and prevailing mood of "desolation and rage which accompany grief" (Kennedy 2007: 56) do not necessarily determine the melancholic character of an elegy. On the contrary, in accordance with Clewell's interpretation of Freud's theory, the ambivalent attitude can result in the "self-strengthening" and the Wordsworthian "self-obssession" of the speaker, which occur in contemporary elegy not as a certainty but as a possibility, an ongoing task (Clewell 2004: 46–67). This fact is acknowledged by Ramazani, who recognises the generally anti-consolatory character of the twentieth century elegy, as well as its negation of traditional conventions; however, he asserts that contemporary

181 In his widely acclaimed study *The English Elegy Studies in the Genre from Spencer to Yeats*, Peter Sacks distinguishes the following primary and secondary conventions of elegy:

a. Primary: A pastoral context; the use of repetitions, refrains and repeated questions, outbursts of anger and cursing, a procession of mourners, a movement from grief to consolation, concluding images of resurrection.
b. Secondary: Division of mourning between several voices, questions of reward, contest and inheritance between elegist and subject, the elegist's reluctant submission to language and accompanying protestation of incapacity and his need to draw attention to his own surviving powers (Sacks 1985: 2).

elegiac poetry is "far from [being] uniformly melancholic" (Ramazani 1994: 30). On the contrary, it evokes "multiple kinds of grief" (Ramazani, 1994: 30) and different ways of confronting the conflict between repudiation and internalisation of the lost object. To examine this topic, the following close analysis of selected poems investigates several conventions of traditional elegy, whose transformed versions can be observed in Harrison's *The School of Eloquence.*

One of the most characteristic elegiac conventions according to Sacks is the movement from grief to consolation, understood as an idea which "has underwritten both: psychoanalytical discussion of mourning and literary criticism of elegy" (Kennedy 2007: 35–36), that "loss leads individuals from initial confusion to regained self-possession" (Kennedy 2007: 36). In *The School of Eloquence*, mourning does not have a typically consolatory character tantamount to the full acceptance of loss and reconciliation with fate. Despite the wide and acute distance existing between the mourner and that which is mourned, ultimate detachment from the lost object never comes and mourning does not end. Instead, it becomes an ongoing process, constructive, not destructive in its nature, which maintains continuity of memory and ensures the possibility of inheritance. Unlike melancholy, a state of mind tantamount to a "death-like loss of identity," to use Sacks' words (1985: 17), the work of mourning offers the possibility to maintain the development of the poetic "I" of the speaker. It is important to stress that the continuous effort of writing elegies is presented in Harrison's poems as an ongoing project of Trauerarbeit. A close reading of the elegiac sonnets reveals that for Harrison, there is no consolation that can be achieved once and for all, it is not an attainable aim; there is, however, a suggestion that by creating a poem, a concrete structure, the feeling of grief may be sustained and turned into a constructive material from which the poem is woven.[182] Consequently, the work of mourning must be seen as the creative work of the poet, his craft, which decides his identity, continuously constructed by the power of inheritance and in relation to a given moment in history.

The creative task the poet undertakes is closely combined with the dramatic relationship between loss and figuration exemplified in *The English Elegy* by the story of Apollo and Daphne (Sacks 1985: 4). In Ovid's *Metamorphoses*, Daphne, pursued by Apollo, changes into a laurel tree to avoid his reach. Apollo, suffering from

182 "There is an experience of loss. Language both emerges from it and acts upon it. Language becomes the poem that works through the originating experience." (Kennedy 2007: 50)

unrequited love, embraces the tree but cannot be consoled.[183] Then he decides to "refer to the nymph … by focusing on a detached part of the tree, the fragmentary sign [i.e. the laurel wreath[184]]" (Sacks 1985: 4) and projects it into the future as a "consoling substitute" (Sacks 1985: 4) for Daphne, the lost object of desire. Whereas transformation of the nymph into the tree can be termed "organic metamorphoses" the second "alteration," (Sacks 1985: 4) transformation of the part of the tree into the wreath, seems to imply, according to Sacks:

> A move from organic nature to the item of an unnatural, societal code [and] to enforce and confirm that Apollo's consoling sign can never enjoy a purely organic relation to the object that it signifies, or for which it substitutes … Daphne is thus eventually transformed into something very much like a consolation prize … and a sign of poethood.… a consoling sign that carries in itself a reminder of loss on which it has been founded. (Sacks 1985: 4)

In Harrison's poems there is no consolation offered by the possibility of metamorphoses; the most often repeated transformation is of the body undergoing cremation which consequently results in the annihilation of the body, turned into dust and smoke.[185] What the poet creates seems to be rather a fearful image of *vanitas* than of consoling hope. But everyday objects, sometimes very intimate ones that survive the parents and represent them play a similar role to that of a consolation prize. The father's cap, an Eccles cake, the product of the baker's work, Kensington Cigarettes and, most noticeably, a wedding ring which survives the fire of cremation; each object carries in itself a remainder of loss, the loss of the loved ones and the loss of the working-class culture. There are, however, a few poems in which through the working of the metaphor Harrison's parents are transformed into something else,[186] a new entity, just as Daphne transforms into a laurel in Ovid's

---

183 "Refugit tamen oscula signum" 'But even the wood shrank from his kisses' (Metamorphoses 1.556).

184 "Since thou canst not be my bride, thou shalt at least be my tree. My hair, my lyre, my quiver shall always be entwined with thee, O laurel. With thee shall Roman generals wreathe their heads …" (Metamorphoses 1.557–1.560)

'… at, quoniam coniux mea non potes esse,
Arbor eris certe' dixit 'mea! Simper habebunt
Te coma, te citharae, te nostrae, laure, pharetrae:
Tu duci bus Latiis aderis, … ' (Metamorphoses 1.557–1.560)

185 "Gold survives the fire that's hot enough/ to make you ashes in a standard urn" (Timer 1–2).

186 In "Marked with D."—father becomes a loaf of bread, in "A Good Read"—the father becomes Harrison's writing, a poem he writes. In "Background Material"—parents turn to photographic images of themselves.

Metamorphoses. Not only is "loss ... followed by the figurative ... compensation" (Sacks 1985: 4) but it also becomes a source of poetry, and poetry in turn becomes an attempt to recreate and continue that which is lost.

The structural question that emerges of how to "figure[187] and represent loss" (Kennedy 2007: 21) is, according to Kennedy, one of the most important issues for contemporary elegists, who display a broad scepticism about the possibility of figuration and strong doubt in the creative power of language (Kennedy 2007: 21). The elegist, Kennedy observes:

> Starts from a negative position. Positives made into negatives by death must somehow be made into positives again or have that transformation compensated for. [Elegist's] love or perhaps more properly, ... desire for the deceased[188], must be narrated as loss, as dispossession .... [he/she is] always faced with unsatisfactory resurrections, unfinished and unfinishable conversations ... Words and image are insubstantial in comparison with the previous corporeal existence of the deceased[189]. (Kennedy 2007: 21)

The figuration of loss, its poetic representation, demands that "impotence and inactivity" (Kennedy 2007: 23) are transformed into power. In order to forge this transformation the poet must turn lack into poetic recourse, and this Harrison does in his family sonnets with an undeniable force and conviction. It must be stressed that in *The School of Eloquence* "lack" is a very broad-ranging concept, encompassing everything the speaker mourns: loss of loved ones, but also the lack of a sense of belonging of the individual to a particular community, the lack of language, and of culture which is becoming extinct, and consequently the lack of possibility of expression caused by the cultural hegemony of the privileged classes. In Harrison's sequence lack becomes "a means of gaining control" (Kennedy 2007: 29). This can be observed, for example, in the movement of numerous poems from the lack of voice to the gain of voice, although it is never an uninterrupted process but a broken and an uncertain one, underpinned by constant threat of failure and suppression (Sacks 1985: 4). The following analysis[190] of selected elegiac sonnets investigates the issue of mourning and its relationship to

187 Kennedy stresses the key role of the word "figure" which "combines senses of representation, of making estimates and of working out in order to achieve understanding" (2007: 21).

188 Or as in the case of Harrison's poems, ambivalent feelings towards the lost object, not only positive but also negative.

189 Or in a wider sense of that which is mourned, of the lost object.

190 *The School of Eloquence* is analyzed here in the form the sequence obtained in its most recent publication i.e. Tony Harrison *Collected Poems*. London: VIKING *an imprint of* Penguin Books. 2007.

the theme of constructing identity, and shows how, through the adaptation of traditional elegiac conventions, the continuity of mourning is being sustained and universalized as the speaker reaches beyond private despair and individual loss into the social and historical context.

In his poem "Postscript: The Panel", Thom Gunn expresses an opinion that the dead, whose presence we cannot deny, become part of us. By saying, "Their story, being part of mine, refuses to reach the end" (Gunn 2000: 16). Gunn does not only stress the existence of a lasting bond between the dead and the living but also suggests the inevitability of the internalisation of the lost object, whose story weaves into the story of the elegist. An unwillingness to abandon his dead (Kennedy 2007: 145) is equally characteristic of the speaker of Harrison's poems, who expresses a strong tendency towards internalisation of the lost object, but at the same time acknowledges a painful distance between the dead working-class parents and himself, their estranged son who "makes up"[191] for his faults in poetry.

The *ambivalence of distance*, a theme of many of the elegiac sonnets, is introduced in the first poem of the sequence i.e. "Book Ends." The poem presents the first of many images of the family circle which, despite the deaths of both parents, is being continuously sustained, as the subsequent poems will prove, by the literary effort of their son.[192]

> Baked the day she suddenly dropped dead
> we chew it slowly that last apple pie.

---

191 We had a bitter quarrel in our cups
and there were words between us, yes,
I'm guilty, and the way I make it up's
in poetry, and that much I confess. (Confessional Poetry 13–16)

192 In the poem entitled "Illuminations II", the speaker asserts:
the family circle, one continuous US!
....
Two dead, but current still flows through us three
though the circle takes forever to complete
eternity, annihilation, me
that small bright charge of life where they both meet. (7, 13–16)
The powerful line "One continues US!" becomes a poetic task whose approximate time cannot be determined, since "the circle takes forever to complete" (14). The fact of loss is recognized and acknowledged by the speaker. The consequence is the necessity of continuous effort of transforming loss into poetic resource through the work of mourning. The poem stresses the internalization of the lost object, as the dead meet in the one who is alive, the son, the elegist; he becomes the link between the parents, the one which makes the continuation of the family chain possible.

…
You're like book ends, the pair of you, she'd say,
Hog that grate, say nothing, sit, sleep, stare …
…
A night you need my company to pass
and she not here to tell us we're alike!
…
Back in our silences and sullen looks,
for all the Scotch we drink, what's still between's
not the thirty or so years, but books, books, books.
(Book Ends 1–2, 5–6, 11–12, 14–16)

"Book Ends" depicts the moment of sudden disruption of that circle by the death of the mother "the agent of connection" whose "absence removes the binding, disconnects the 'book ends'" (Byrne 1998: 16–17). The first two lines of the poem, "with no simile, metaphor, or other poetic device" (Byrne 1998: 16–17), communicate the mother's absence in a straightforward way. However, as Byrne suggests, their syntax is far from ordinary:

> We don't usually substitute the pronoun 'it' for a noun-phrase (such as "apple pie") before we have introduced the noun-phrase. The word choice imposes a grammatical structure; the sentence is divided into two clauses: 'Baked the day she suddenly dropped dead' and 'We chew it slowly that last apple pie' The first poetic line leads us to expect the subject—the thing that has been baked—but postpones fulfilling the expectation by moving to the protagonists of the poem 'we' … 'we chew it slowly' again defers giving us the information we expect: what is 'it'? … So the whole weight of … stress is therefore on 'the last apple pie.' (Byrne 1998: 16)

This deferral to give information illustrates the reluctance to finish the process of eating and thus appears to be the moment of final separation from the loved one, a final disconnection. The absence of the mother materializes itself in the object, which "carries in itself the remainder of loss," brings the retrospective image of the "immediate past of the poem, before the death" (Byrne 1998: 16–17), the image of the mother baking. In the light of Abraham and Torok, the sharing of food could be read as a figurative indication of the process of introjection and the acceptance of loss. As was stated above, such "communion" i.e. sharing of food can mean, according to Abraham and Torok, "that rather than the person of the deceased, it is our mutual presence that we are taking into our bodies in the form of assimilable food; as for the deceased, we shall deposit him in the earth and not in ourselves" (1980: 8). However, as the following poems show, the distance between the lost object and the elegist is not sustained but constantly changes through the sequence. The speaker of the poems frequently internalizes the lost object but in the same time feels estranged from it, assuming at times a position of an outcast, external observer or/and critic.

In "Book Ends," the "books, books, books" which come between the father and the son, are not only books Harrison read[193] but also the ones he has written and continues to write in an attempt to save the working class culture from extinction, the books his parents did not approve of and did not understand. In the poem entitled "Bringing Up" the speaker recalls a comment made by his mother, now dead, after she has read *The Loiners* and flung the book in the fire in disgust: "*You weren't brought up to write such mucky books!*" (Bringing Up 16). The gesture of committing the book to the flames is later repeated by the son, who imagines putting his book of poems into his mother's coffin before cremation. The emotional distance between the son and the mother, who would have been embarrassed to meet her God with a "mucky book" in her hand (Bringing Up 8–9), is contrasted in the poem with the image of physical proximity:

> And there together in the well wrought urn,
> what's left of you, the poems of your child,
> devoured by one flame, unreconciled,
> like soots on washing, black on bone-ash white. (Bringing Up 10–13)

The second line of the above-quoted stanza describes the posthumous union of the body of the mother and the volume of poems, but can be also read as the speaker's assertion that what is left of the mother whose body has irreversibly turned into dust is her son's book, whose continual presence is suggested in the poem by the existence of many copies. In the light of the reference from the Book of Genesis "Dust thou art, and onto dust thou shalt return" (Genesis 3: 19) the volume of poems and the mother's body are reduced to what they essentially are and, as it turns out, they are made of the same material, compared in the poem to soot, black particles, a by-product of coal combustion. The familiarity of the image of washing stained by soot introduces the working-class context of the industrial north and suggests the ground from which Harrison's poetry stems. Though the gulf between the poet and his working-class mother divides them

193 The line gives the poem a strong political stance. As Blake Morrison states: "Harrison's poems about his parents are more than simple elegies, ... to praise them for being 'moving' (as most reviewers and critics have done) is to emasculate them of their hard political edge. "Book Ends," Morrison continues "is an elegy, but it shows that the elegy need not to be an apolitical form .... the son 'a scholar', the father 'worn out on poor pay', they have been forced apart not by the passing of time but by a system which assimilates bright working-class boys into the middle-class" (1991: 55).

even after her death, the genealogical link between the pair of them (Rowland 1998: 13) is recognised and sustained. The urn with the ashes, the product of transformation, like the apple pie in "Book Ends," plays the role of "consolation prize," an object that carries in itself a reminder of the loss on which it has been founded (Sacks 1985: 4). In Ovid's *Metamorphoses*, the leaves of the tree become artificially entwined (Sacks 1985: 5) to create a new object bearing a socially recognizable meaning. The transformation of Daphne into the tree results in the creation of the laurel wreath, the sign of poethood (Sacks 1985: 5). A parallel turn occurs in Harrison's poem, in which the urn becomes a sign denoting poetry, or more generally, art, by means of an intertextual allusion to John Donne's "Canonization" and indirectly to Keats's "Ode on a Grecian Urn." In both poems, an urn is depicted as an embodiment of art, which gives fixity to forms impermanent in life (Brooks 1949: 146). In Donne's poem,[194] "a well-wrought urn" (Canonization 33) becomes a metaphorical representation of a sonnet. Though it is humble in comparison to more magnificent tombs, the urn is fit for holding the ashes of the great, and the sonnet too is an appropriate form to immortalize the "legend" (Canonization 30) of the lovers. The "legend," as Louthan Doniphan says, is given numerous layers of meaning in the poem:

> If the life-story is considered that of saints—a valid meaning of *legend*—we have an anticipation of the secular-sacred imagery which follows. As their inscribed epitaph, the legend is too insignificant for tombs. As their eulogy, it is too commonplace for hearses. (... *hearse* in Donne's time might refer to 'A temple-shaped structure of wood used in royal and noble funerals .... It was decorated with banners, heraldic devices, and lighted candles; and it was customary for friends to pin short poems or epitaphs upon it.') (1951: 114–15)

The intertextual allusion asks the reader to see "the well wrought urn" (Bringing Up 10) from Harrison's poem as sign of poethood, a vessel which, in "Bringing Up" quite literally, contains within its "rooms" (Canonization 32) a "legend" (Canonization 30) of the lost object, the story of the citizens of Leeds. According

---

194 We can die by it, if not live by love,
And if unfit for tomb or hearse
Our legend be, it will be fit for verse;
And if no piece of chronicle we prove,
We'll build in sonnets pretty rooms;
As well a well-wrought urn becomes
The greatest ashes, as half-acre tombs,
And by these hymns, all shall approve
Us canonized for love; (Canonization 28–36)

to Sacks, "Daphne's 'turning' into the tree matches Apollo's 'turning' from the object of his love to the sign of her" (1985: 5). And this is "an act of troping that any mourner must perform" (1985: 5) in order to attain consolation. Nevertheless, for Harrison, the acknowledgement of loss, and the transformation of the lost object into a consoling sign, is not tantamount to consolation understood as a relief and letting go of the lost object. The ashes remain unreconciled, and it is the voice of the weeping mother whose "proletarian puritanism could never stomach her son's 'mucky' treatment of sexuality" (Spencer 1994: 83), which constitutes the ultimate ending of the poem.

The situation is further complicated by the second literary allusion, to Keats's *Ode on a Grecian Urn*, which introduces an unsettling ambiguity of the role of art: it defies death but at the same time petrifies the immortalized object. The action portrayed on the urn:

> Goes on though the actors are motionless; the song will not cease; the lover cannot leave his song; the maiden, always to be kissed, never actually kissed, will remain changelessly beautiful. The maiden is, indeed, like the urn itself, a "still unravished bride of quietness"—not even ravished by a kiss; and it is implied, perhaps, that her changeless beauty, like that of the urn, springs from this fact. (Brooks 1949: 145)

Paradoxically, that which is deathless is also lifeless, and that fact, powerfully stated by Keats, is used by Harrison to ask a question about the possibility of figuration. How can an elegist represent loss in his verse, if the representation only appears to revive the lost object and only seemingly maintains its existence. This resurrection must always be unsatisfactory (Kennedy 2007: 21) since it is never fully accomplished, it is always a possibility, an attempt limited by nature of art and time. Harrison's attitude to writing elegiac verse may be compared to that of Matthew Arnold, who metaphorically presents writing poetry as a quest[195] (Kennedy 2007: 30), undertaken by previous generations of poets: a quest which contemporary poets choose to continue even if the outcome of poetic enterprise will always remain questionable and uncertain. Harrison refers to the words of his literary antecedents, Donne and Keats (Kennedy 2007: 30) but also the words of

195 Thyrsis! in reach of sheep-bells is my home.
-Then through the great town's harsh, heart-wearying roar,
Let in thy voice a whisper often come,
To chase fatigue and fear:
Why faintest thou! I wander'd till I died.
Roam on! The light we sought is shining still.
Dost thou ask proof? Our tree yet crowns the hill,
Our Scholar travels yet the loved hill-side. (Thyrsis 232–240)

his working-class mother, asserting his place in the pantheon of British literature and in his ancestry line and as a consequence, drawing attention to his own surviving powers (Sacks 1985: 2), his "unreconciled" (Bringing Up 12) identity as poet and Loiner. This fact is relevant since the problem of figuring loss in "family sonnets" has an important, socially-tinged dimension particular to Harrison, a poet detached from his roots by the education he received. H. G. Widdowson notices that the recurring theme in *The School of Eloquence* is:

> One of disparity of values and guilt that … [Harrison's] scholarship has estranged him from … [his parents] and their working-class ways. Even his portrayal of them is betrayal of a kind, since it can only be based on the dissociation of his experience and expressed in a poetic idiom they cannot understand. He cannot talk about his parents in the way he talked to them. (1993: 22)

This fact makes the poetic representation of the dead parents and of the working-class culture they represent an ambiguous task, one that poses a question about the relationship between the elegist and the lost object. The elegiac sonnets are expressive not only of grief and need for continuity of working-class experience but most importantly of the "dilemma of identity" (Widdowson 1993: 22). The speaker of the poems is simultaneously "intellectually detached" (Widdowson 1993: 22), describes the lost object from a distance, in the third person, and, deeply "involved in the first person, a part of it all as well" (Widdowson 1993: 22).

One of the poems exploring this dichotomy is "Long Distance II," a sonnet about the loss of communication and an attempt at continuity. In the poem, the speaker ventures retrospectively back to the moment two years after his mother's death to observe his father "incapable [or unwilling] of recognizing the loss of the loved object" (Rowland 1998: 14):

> Though my mother was already two years dead
> Dad kept her slippers warming by the gas,
> put hot water bottles her side of bed
> and still went to renew her transport pass.
>
> You couldn't just drop in. You had to phone.
> He'd put you off an hour to give him time
> to clear away her things and look alone
> as though his still raw love were such a crime. (Long Distance II 1–8)

The shifting distance between the speaker and his parents is described in the poem through the use of first-, second-, and third-person pronouns and terms of reference denoting Harrison's parents.

In *The School of Eloquence*, Harrison uses three sets of terms of reference (my mother/my father; mi mam/mi dad [dialect versions; mam/dad] and each set suggests a slightly different affective involvement (Widdowson 1993: 24): *my mother/my father* having the strongest distancing effect, and *mom/dad* bearing a strong overtone of familiarity. *Mi dad/mi mam* prove to be more problematic as frequent use of dialect forms in Harrison's poetry or, more precisely, the variation in their representation[196] is one of the poetic strategies which illustrate the ambivalent attitude of the speaker towards the lost object, understood as the speaker's dead parents and more generally, as the working-class culture of the North. As Widdowson asserts, the use of dialect can suggest identification with northern culture and values but can also serve as an "ironic distancing of the self" (1993: 30), a form of "mockery" (1993: 30). The ambivalence may be read as an "uncertainty of position" (1993: 30) by the speaker, who is unable to identify unambiguously with the place of his origin, but also as a prerequisite for successful mourning if interpreted in the light of Freud's *The Ego and the Id*.

Although the poem under discussion does not contain the latter set of terms (mi dad/mi mam), the ambivalent position of the mourner is established by means of a complicated interplay of relations described in the poem and shifts in distance between poetic personas. The first stanza establishes three relationships (father and son, mother and son, father and mother) but the distance is different in each case. The use of the informal, "affectively marked" (Widdowson 1993: 24) expression "dad" (Long Distance II 2) gives an impression of proximity, in contrast to the expression "my mother," (Long Distance II 1) which suggests long distance, not only resulting from her physical absence, but also from the passing of time as she is "already two years dead" (Long Distance II 1). The distance between the parents is on the one hand, confirmed by the fact of the mother's death, but on the other, called into question by the actions of the father, who behaves as if she was still present. After the initial introduction of the personas "interacting" in the poem, the mother and father are further referred to as "he" and "she." In this part of the chapter, the first-, and second-person pronouns ('I' and 'you') are discussed as "terms of address" and third-person pronouns as "terms of reference", as proposed by Widdowson (1993: 23), as the relationships between personal pronouns allow a greater understanding of the poem under discussion:

> It is through the categories of person … that we make a connection between self and others and establish positions of identity.… The first- and second-person pronouns …

196 They occur as direct speech (written in italics): "*Carrots choke us wi'out your mam's white sauce!*" (Long Distance I 4), unmarked: "Mi aunty's baby's still. The dumbstruck mother" (Study 9) or in single inverted commas: "All the 'old lot' left gave her the same" (Next Door 11).

> identify participants and provide the necessary terminals so to speak, whereby people are connected in communicative interaction. They coexist in the same plane of involvement. Thus they are in principle interchangeable in the turn-taking of thought: the second person is potential first person, and each presupposes the existence of the other. The same person shifts roles into … addresser and addressee. And these pronouns are … independent and self-contained. They are terms of address rather than reference. The third-person pronouns … indicate a non-participant role; they are terms of reference rather than address. (1993: 23)

The second stanza begins with the use of the second-person pronoun (you), which despite having no participant role, serves as a substitute for the third-person impersonal pronoun "one" (Widdowson 1993: 25), and suggests a distanced attitude by the speaker, who refrains from using the first-person pronoun "I." After listing "a series of objective statements of observable facts" (Widdowson 1993: 25) about the father's behaviour in the first stanza, the speaker goes on to report the reasons for that behaviour and then attributes "feelings and attitudes to the first person which cannot possibly be," according to Widdowson, "accessible to observation" (1993: 26) in the following two stanzas:

> He couldn't risk my blight of disbelief
> Though sure that very soon he'd hear her key
> Scrape in the rusted lock and end his grief.
> He knew she'd just popped out to get the tea. (Long Distance II 9–12)

It seems that the speaker manifests a growing involvement in the situation since he is able to empathetically articulate his father's feelings. Consequently, the distance between the two men gradually shortens until the opening of the final stanza, which begins with a blunt statement of disbelief or, as Widdowson calls it "a definite assertion of separate and independent identity" (1993: 26): "I believe life ends with death and that is all" (Long Distance II 13). The speaker establishes his position in contrast to the melancholic attitude of the father, unwilling to acknowledge the undeniable fact of death, but the actions he undertakes undermine his own statement. In the following lines, the second person pronoun is used in a fully participant sense as the speaker addresses his dead parents: "You haven't both gone shopping; just the same, / in my new leather phone book there's your name / and the disconnected number I still call" (Long Distance II 14–16). Although death is proclaimed in the first line of the last stanza as the ultimate act of discontinuity, the speaker continues to call the disconnected number, regardless of the obvious futility and perhaps absurdity of his attempts at communication. But his persistence is not merely a sign of a deeply rooted habit (Poster 1997: 91) but an "acknowledgement of the twin spectres of death and silence" (Poster 1997: 91), the extinction and the absence of voice which marked the lives of his parents and their ancestors. And so the act of calling the disconnected number can be read as a form of protest against class hegemony and class discrimination which deprived people like Harrison's father of their voice and made them yearn for "release from mortal speech" (Marked with D. 11), that "kept … [them] down" (Marked with D. 12), on the bottom rung of the social ladder. The "historical silencing of the working-class" (Roberts 1999: 159) overlaps with the more intimate silence (Roberts 1999: 159) that fell between the speaker and his parents when they were alive and can be still "heard" after their death. The metaphor of the disconnected number repeatedly dialled by the speaker transforms lack, in this case lack of voice, into poetic resource. Characteristically for the elegiac mode, negative is changed into positive (Kennedy 2007: 23) since despite the fact that "life ends with death and that is all" (Long Distance II 13), the poem continues. The final three lines "significantly qualify the blank finality of that negative credo" (Poster 1997: 91) as if in answer to the advice given by Heine in *Gorgon*: "Gaze and create" (Harrison 1992: 62) which defines the "continual enterprise" (Haffenden 1991: 228) of writing as an act of defiance against death and silence.

Numerous elegies "canonical and otherwise, are founded" according to Kennedy "on historical reconstruction of the relationship between the elegist and elegized subject" (2007: 49). "Long Distance II" belongs to the group mentioned above, as it presents a certain net of family relations in a given moment of time, reconstructs the relationships as they were two years after the mother's death and then confronts them with now, in an attempt to establish the connection between the past and the present visible in the mirror image of the father and son. The speaker repeats his father's actions, identifies with his father's mode of mourning, showing a certain degree of "resistance to the reality of severed relationship" (Widdowson 1993: 27). Consequently, the suggestion that the father's behaviour, his "raw love" (Long Distance II 8) is socially unaccepted, is equally true about the behaviour of the speaker, who still calls and probably will not cease to call, the disconnected number. Observing the actions of the father (and by way of analogy the actions of the son) the reader is put in the position of a voyeur gazing at a private life turned into a spectacle. The fact that the father's display of affection can be potentially seen as a "crime" (Long Distance II 8) against a socially accepted form of experiencing loss, can be read as a subtle comment about the issue of in/decent "male mourning"[197] (Kennedy 2007: 28),

---

197 For a discussion about the distinct features of male and female elegiac poetry see: Celeste M. Schenck (1986) "Feminism and Deconstruction: Re-Constructing the Elegy', Tulsa Studies in Women's Literature, vol. 5, no. 1: 13–27 and Melissa F. Zeiger

which according to Kennedy is "necessarily associated with self-absorption, with self-watchfulness under the gaze of others .... [and with] culturally and socially enforced suppression" (2007: 28). Sacks' concept of elegiac mourning sheds light on this issue. The activities of the father are an example of unsuccessful, futile mourning since, unlike Apollo, he is not able to "turn away from or to trope the dead" (Sacks 1985: 72), in Freudian terms "to find a new attachment" (Kennedy 2007: 94). As Ramazani writes, Sacks' model of "healthy" mourning assumes that the mourner must redress "loss and overcomes grief by installing a substitute for the lost person" (1994: xi). One may argue that in the poem under discussion, "the substitutive ... act of troping" (Sacks 1985: 5) occurs. The mother is replaced by signs that carry in themselves a remainder of loss such as the slippers and hot water bottles, but they signify the presence, rather than absence of the lost object (Rowland 1998: 15) and denote continuity rather than change. The fact that the speaker stays faithful to his father's mode of mourning, even to the point of adopting an object denoting his dead parents' presence, a "new black leather phone book" ("Long Distance II" 15) with their names inside, suggests an attempt at the continuity of experience, "shared interiority" (Kennedy 2007: 87) of the elegist and the lost object or even a "potential of achieving identity by preserving ... [the] relations in a kind of continuous present" (Schenck 1986: 24).

According to Kennedy, the male mourner who wants to express his grief traditionally has to find a suitable method of performance so as not to be accused of feminine meekness and lack of self-control (2007: 28). As George Puttenham writes in *The Arte of English Poesie*:

> To weep for any sorrow ... is not so decent in a man: and therefore all high minded persons, when they cannot chose but shed tears, will turne away their face as a countenance indecent for a man to shew, and so will standers by till they have supprest such passion, thinking it nothing decent to behold such an uncomely countenance. (1589/1909: 296–297)

Harrison's ambivalent attitude to the tradition of male mourning manifests itself in the fact that he does not refrain from emotionally charged images, references to tears[198] and tearful reaction to loss.[199] Apart from "invoking previous elegists as respectable role models; and ... occupying the literary space that they have

(1997) *Beyond Consolation: Death, Sexuality and the Changing Shapes of Elegy*, Ithaca and London: Cornell University Press.

198 For example in "Still," "An Old Score," "Blocks," "Bringing Up," "Changing at York".

199 For example in "Isolation".

made respectable," (Kennedy 2007: 28) Harrison invokes the ghost of his father who becomes for him an ambivalent role model in the art of mourning. There is something sentimental or even unmanly if seen in the light of Puttenham's comment, about the father's melancholic attachment to everyday objects, but also in mundane activities and intimate gestures which characterize the way of mourning the elegist chooses to adopt.

In "Isolation" the speaker is moved to tears not by the memories of childhood moments with his now dead mother, not by her fresh grave, but by the sight of the father looking for a private piece of garment, his long johns. The poem covers a relatively long stretch of time as it starts with a remembered moment from the past when the speaker "cried … as a boy" (Isolation 1) and takes the reader through a journey on the day of his mother's funeral, when he is an adult man. The change that occurred somewhere between "now" and "then," on the way from childhood to adulthood, is marked by the fact that then he cried, and now he doesn't. The present simple tense[200] suggests that it is a more permanent feature of his, now mature, manner of behaviour, rather than a description of a momentary state of emotions. On the contrary, the past event is remembered as an isolated, concrete incident "I cried once as a boy when I'd to leave her," (Isolation 1) which stresses the importance of the particular episode of separation. The poem moves forward in time, towards the moment after the funeral while simultaneously journeying through the familiar sites of Leeds, which serve as catalysts for the childhood memories of the speaker. As the poem unfolds, it becomes clear that the memories of the speaker have their roots in a distant past, stemming from the childhood memories of his mother:

> but I don't cry now …
> ….
> and don't, though I notice by the same railtrack
> hawthorns laden with red berries as they'd been
> when we'd seen them the day that we returned
> from the hospital on this same train together
> and she taught me a country saying that she'd learned
> as a child: *Berries bode bad winter weather!* (Isolation 4, 7–12)

The way in which objects-remainders of loss function in Harrison's poetry can be compared to the role of objects in the poetry of Douglas Dunn, as described by Jerzy Jarniewicz in *The Uses of the Commonplace in Contemporary British Poetry: Larkin, Dunn and Raine*. According to Jarniewicz:

---

200 "but I don't cry now" (Isolation 1).

> What the poet is interested in is the relation between the object and man … the relation, or the position a given object occupies in the world-within-a poem becomes Dunn's real concern … the use of the mere name of a thing is expected to bring about a definite set of values and provide an implicit comment on a scene or situation of which that thing is an element. (1994: 124)

In Harrison's poem the hawthorn berries (Isolation 8) carry in themselves a remainder of loss as they evoke in the speaker the memory of the lost object, and additionally, by functioning in a given context, in the world-within-a-poem, they serve as metaphorical links holding together the family history Harrison reconstructs. They function similarly to the Eccles cake (Currents I 1), described by Harrison in the poem "Currents," whose taste, in a truly Proustian fashion, brings back the world long time gone. The poem starts with an apostrophe. "An Eccles cake's my *petite madeleine*!" (Currents I 1) and the characteristically northern biscuit becomes a central image around which the poem unfolds. Similarly, the image of berries highlights the connection between the present and the past, as it appears on different time levels of the story told: the mother, who as a child learns a country saying *Berries bode bad winter weather!* (Isolation 12), repeats it to her son on a train; he remembers her words as an adult man and repeats them once more in his poem, letting his mother's voice continually resonate even after her death.

As an element of the northern landscape which for the speaker looks unchanged and familiar,[201] the berries symbolize an abstract permanent quality and a fleeting possibility of continuity which is to be questioned in the concluding lines. The spiritual presence of the mother denoted by the images of "hawthorns laden with red barriers" (Isolation 8) and of the familiar sights of Leeds is contrasted in the poem with her physical absence suggested by the final image: the father preoccupied with a frantic search for his long johns. Paradoxically, it is this common object that introduces the theme of grief and despair, not by any particular features it may possess, but by the fact that it represents the vulnerability of the father in the face of loss. The name of the object Harrison uses ("long johns") has a slightly comical tinge. Its triviality is highlighted by the fact that like "grapefruit" from Dunn's *Port Logan and a Vision of Live Maps*, it has no literary tradition (Jarniewicz 1994: 123) as opposed to "hawthorn," which has frequently reappeared in English verse throughout the ages.[202] The name of the father's undergarment belongs to world of the concrete, the physical and the

---

201 … though I notice by the same railtrack / hawthorns laden with red berries as they'd been / when we'd seen them… (Isolation 7–9).

202 See for example: Edmund Spenser *The Shepherd's Calender*, William Howitt "Forest Minstrel," Siegfried Sassoon "A Hawthorn Berry," William Shakespeare "Sonnet 18."

ordinary, but despite its seemingly unpoetic character it is used to talk about universal issues: death, separation and grief.

Poems such as "Long Distance II" and more indirectly "Isolation" hint at "the question of inheritance" (Kennedy 2007: 30), which reoccurs in *The School of Eloquence* and is closely connected with the issue of constructing the identity of the speaker, who sees his working-class legacy as a force which determines the poetry he creates.[203] It should be noted that "the question of contests, rewards and inheritance" (Sacks 1985: 2) is counted by Sacks among the most characteristic elegiac conventions and confirmed by Kennedy to occupy an important place in contemporary elegiac verse[204] where, in the context of male mourning, it is often evoked within the frame of "father-son relationships" (Kennedy 2007: 31). Sacks' explanation of the origin of the relation between inheritance and mourning provides a useful context for a discussion on Harrison's usage of the convention:

> Originally … in the vegetation rites and their successors, the act of mourning quite simply included the act of inheritance, for the participant ingested the god or its symbol (to take the wafer and the wine is still an act of repeated inheritance.) The connection between mourning and inheritance has remained a close one throughout history … in Greece the right to mourn was from the earliest times legally connected to the right to inherit. (Sacks 1985: 37)

A reoccurring idea in Harrison's poetry, as the following analysis of selected poems will show, is that the working-class legacy to which the poet claims a right, can only be accepted and assimilated by means of continuous mourning. The ancient rule of law according to which those who did not mourn their dead were deprived from the right to inherit[205] (Sacks 1985: 37) echoes in Harrison's family

---

203 See discussion on "Heredity" in the first chapter.

204 Kennedy writes:

> Seamus Heaney's elegies 'Casualty'and 'In Memory of Sean O'Riada'… portray their subjects as bestowers on the elegist of special powers and perceptions: 'a rhythm/ Working you' and 'trusting the gift' that produced mackerel 'like a conjured retinue'. In 'A Postcard from North Antrim' Heaney makes Sean Armstrong exemplify the speech of Ulster that he has turned into poetry (Heaney 1979: 24, 29, 20). John Forbes's elegy for fellow Australian poet Martin Johnson 'Lassu in cielo' mocks inheritance by having its subject justify excessive use of garlic by invoking classical authorities (Forbes 1998: 50).… In the words of Douglas Dunn's triple elegy for Norman MacCaig, Sorley MacLean and George Mackay Brown, the relationship between the elegist and elegized is always that of 'those whom we succeed' (Dunn 2000: 35). (2007: 31)

205 Margaret Alexiou, the author of *The Ritual Lament in Greek Tradition* quotes Isaios (c. 420–350 BC), one of the ten Attic Orators, the author of speeches regarding the

poems, in which mourning is often presented as containing an element of a task: as stated above, the speaker says in "Confessional Poetry," that he is writing to make up for his estrangement from his parents and the working-class background, or to use Sacks' words, to prove "his proximity to the dead" (1985: 37). However what is especially important for the understanding of the dynamics of Harrison's elegiac verse, is the fact that in the majority of family poems from Part II of the sequence, the main purpose of mourning does not lie in the final acceptance of loss or the commemoration of the lost object, and so the development of the poem is not a straightforward movement from grief to consolation. Instead, mourning takes the form of a trial which has to be undertaken by the speaker in order to "wrest … [the] inheritance from the dead," (Sacks 1985: 37) presented in the poems as a difficult but unavoidable task. And it is the acceptance and assimilation of the legacy by the one who succeeds which becomes the primary purpose of mourning.

Before the analysis of the poem entitled "Fire-Eater," which is a metaphorical illustration of this process, attention should be drawn to the poems which correspond to the "Fire-Eater," by means of repetitive patterns: they contain fire imagery and the symbol of a ring which "serves to epitomise what is permanent in the parents' legacy to their son" (Spencer 1994: 83). Rowland notices that the repetitive "tropes of annihilation in the sequence" form a net of dense interrelations to the point where they become "untenable" (Rowland 1998: 13), and the same can be said about the tropes of inheritance. As Stantner points out, "repetition is an inherent part of elegiac tradition: the subject returns again and again to the site of mourning in order to attain a transformed structure of identity" (1990: 59). In Harrison's poems, the return to the site of cremation (and burial)[206] but also recurrence of the same motifs and symbols regarding burial and inheritance, remain in accordance with one of the roles of repetition in traditional elegy, as distinguished by Sacks. It creates "a sense of continuity, of an unbroken pattern such as one may oppose to the extreme discontinuity of death" (1985: 23) and serves to illustrate the concern with "faithfulness of genealogy" (Rowland 1998: 14) which underpins the fabric of many of the family sonnets. Creating a sense of continuity, by which "time itself is thereby structured to appear as familiar … medium, rather than as an open-ended source of possible catastrophe" (Sacks 1985: 23) is one of

---

issue of inheritance: "Is it not the most unholy thing if a man without having done any of the customary rites due to the dead, yet expects to take the inheritance of the dead man's property?" (Isaios quoted in Alexiou 1974: 21).

206 See for example: "Book Ends II," "Long Distance II," "Isolation," "Marked with D.," "Under the Clock."

several reasons for repetitious character of the elegy genre. Additionally: "Repetition of words and refrains and creation of certain rhythm … have the effect of controlling the expression of grief while also keeping that expression in motion" (Sacks 1985: 24) and serve as a method of asserting the "recognition of loss" since the mourner is confronted with fact of death over and over again (Sacks 1985: 24). Repetition is also used to "create the sense of ceremony" during which "the unique death is absorbed into the … cycle of repeated occasions" (Sacks 1985: 24), which on one hand serves as a reminder that "the time has not been arrested" (Sacks 1985: 24) by the fact of loss and the survivors must "move on in time"[207] (Sacks 1985: 24), but on the other indicates the necessity of continual mourning and the importance of remembrance.

In the poems "Timer" and "Continuous", the image of a ring, which appears also in "Under the Clock" and "Punchline," is an example of a recurring motif, which can be read as a symbolic representation of inheritance and continuity of working-class experience. One of the reasons why "Timer" and "Continuous" can be discussed together, apart from the fact that they both "describe the process of cremation and repeat the maxim that rings survive intense heat" (Rowland 1998: 14), is the fact that "Continuous" chronologically succeeds "Timer". As Rowland states, the former can be termed "a companion piece" (1998: 14) to the latter, as it was published in the *Times Literary Supplement* five days after the appearance of the award-winning poem (Rowland 1998: 14). "Continuous" develops further the theme of cremation developed in "Timer".[208] The speaker assists in the ceremonial disposal of the body,[209] repeating the same structure of a familiar event, but since he bids farewell to a different person[210] the trajectory of the theme

207 Sacks gives as an example of the end of Bion's *Lament for Adonis* in which Aphrodite is being called to restrain herself from despair: "Cease thy lamentations this day, Cytherea; refrain from beating thy breast. Thou must weep for him again, thou must bewail him again in another year" and a line from Whitman's "When Lilacs Last in the Dooryard Bloom'd": "I mourned and yet shall mourn with ever returning spring." (1985: 24)

208 This can be read as a part of a more general theme of gradual departure of the lost object from the world of the living. Poems of the sequence describe different stages of that departure, with different moments succeeding loss. The speaker recognizes the loss which is not necessarily tantamount, as it was stated in the former part of the chapter, to the detachment of the speaker from the lost object.

209 Or possibly imagines doing so as we read in another poem from the sequence (i.e. "Punchline") that he missed his father's cremation.

210 "Timer" refers to cremation of the mother's body whereas "Continuous" evokes the cremation of the body of the speaker's father.

can be metaphorically compared to a spiral rather than a circle. The repetition involves an element of alteration and so the reader comes back continually to the same point but at a different level of the theme, which progresses and evolves. The relationship between the poems concerned with the cremation theme exemplifies a structural feature of the entire sequence in which, as Roberts aptly points out, "everything forms part of an inter-relating oeuvre, and poems derive meaning from each other in an unusually direct way" (1999: 158).

"Timer" introduces an opposition between "institutional defacement" (Ramazani 1994: 18) of the dead indicated by mention of the mortuary institution organising the cremation, personified by the clerk and represented by an anonymous buff envelope and "poetic individuation" (Ramazani 1994: 18) characteristic, according to Ramazani, of modern elegy. In the poem under discussion cremation, as a means of disposal of the body, seems to be strongly inscribed within the context contemporary depersonalization and objectification of the dead and dying,[211] sustained by "'funeral home' memorial park and a hospital freer than their predecessors from ... emotional and kinship ties" (Ramazani 1994: 18). They can be termed "neutral social spaces" (Ramazani 1994: 18) since:

> They cut through local chains of affiliation, impose bureaucratic order on the disruptive chaos of death ... and discipline unpredictable eruption of mourning. In the modern elegy, the often idiosyncratic and intimate representations of mourning and the dead could be seen as resisting the increasingly impersonal ... propensities of modern mortuary institutions ... The encompassing trend in elegy is from what Long calls "... universalistic portrayals of individuals" toward "participatory, particularistic portrayals of individuals".... the elegy is assuming ever more of "the rich particularizing details that flash out people and events.... And while obituaries become "the person empty cenotaphs of rationalizing society," elegies become a person-filled counterforce against it. (Ramazani 1994: 19)

In the "Timer" the individuation of the dead mother is achieved in part by the use of a dialect word "cardy," which identifies her (and the speaker) as coming from

---

211 In "Poetry of Mourning" Ramazani cites the research concerning cremation practices in Great Britain:

> Throughout the Twentieth Century, changes in mortuary practice have instanced the disappearance of death and the dead. In England, the growing popularity of cremation reflected an ever more scientific, secular and privatistic attitude toward the dead, although it was also a response to real problems of space, cost and sanitation. From the first English cremation in 1882, the numbers rose to ten thousand in 1936, and to more than half the dead by 1968. (1994: 16)

Geoffrey Gorer claims that "at least in some cases cremation is chosen because it is felt to get rid of the dead more completely and finally than does burial" (1965: 39).

a working-class background. As Roberts claims, there is something intimate or even "transgressive" (1999: 161) in the speaker's coming into possession of the garments of the mother, which have been taken off her body before cremation. Taken out of the package, they constitute just another set of clothing which remains after their owner turns into ashes, but in the elegy, the itemizing of the garments is mirrored in the final stanza by the itemizing of the mother's bodily parts, and this endows "cardy, apron, pants, bra, dress" (Timer 10) with a particularistic and highly emotional charge. According to Rowland, as the speaker imagines intimate parts of his mother's body sifting slowly through the ring, which survived the heat of the incinerator, "he reconstructs rather that dismembers the images of the loved object" (1998: 13):

> It's on my warm palm now, your burnished ring!
>
> I feel your ashes, head, arms, breasts, womb, legs,
> sift through its circle slowly, like that thing
> you used to let me watch to time the eggs. (Timer 13–16)

For the speaker, the ashes which fit a "standard urn" (Timer 2) have a particular form and can be identified not only with a given person by the whole background she represents, with the time and place which shaped the speaker's identity as both "a poet and a biographical individual" (Roberts 1999: 161). This fact is illustrated by the metaphorical rendering of the mother's ashes as sand trickling from the top to the bottom of the egg-timer the poet used to watch as a child in his mother's kitchen. A similar, purely personal, memory is evoked in "Continuous" by the ring of the dead father, which glinted on his finger while he used to take his young son to James Cagney films—the only art they ever shared (Continuous 2). The inherited ring the speaker of the poem wears and the looped tape playing organ music at the father's funeral are "figures for the inescapable continuities" of working class "life, memory and habit" that run "across three generations" (Spencer 1994: 82):

> The hand that glinted with the ring he wore,
> *his* father's, tipped the cold bar into mine
> …
> He's on the platform lowered out of sight
> to organ music, this time on looped tape,
> into a furnace with a blinding light
> here only his father's ring will keep its shape.
>
> I wear it now to Cagneys on my own (Continuous 6–7, 9–13)

The influence of the working-class culture which fuels his verse upon Harrison's poetic identity is often metaphorically depicted in his poems by images of the blackness of coal (or soot), which becomes his physical, inherent feature and defines his individuality: for example in "On Not Being Milton," where the speaker has to first grow black enough (On Not Being Milton 4) in order to reconnect with his background, or in *Newcastle is Peru*, where coal lines his fingerprints, and makes him smudge everything he touches (Newcastle is Peru 153–160). Sometimes, blackening is closely associated with the destructive force of fire and occurs as a result of scorching, as in the poem from Part II of *The School of Eloquence* titled "Fire-Eater" where the working class identity is inherited with difficulty and pain, and the mere act of accepting it demands both courage and the skill of a conjuror:

> My father speaking was like conjurors I'd seen
> pulling bright silk hankies, scarves, a flag
> up out of their innards, red, blue, green,
> so many colours it would make me gag.
>
> Dad's eldest brother had a shocking stammer.
> Dad punctuated sentence ends with but …
> Coarser stuff than silk they hauled up grammar
> knotted together deep down in their gut.
>
> Theirs are the acts I nerve myself to follow.
> I'm the clown sent to clear the ring.
> Theirs are the tongues of fire I'm forced to swallow
> then bring back knotted, one continuous string. (Fire-Eater 1–12)

The swallowing of the pentacostal "tongues of fire,"[212] which the speaker recognizes as belonging to his dead father and uncle Joe,[213] is an act of maintaining continuity (now he, as his father did, will draw flame-like words from his innards) and a form of trial in accordance with the elegiac formula that inheritance has to be achieved with difficulty and effort (Kennedy 2007: 29–34, Sacks 1985: 36–37). The poem describes the process of going back to the roots foreshadowed in "On Not Being Milton" and understood as creation of poetry whose origins

---

212 1. And when the day of Pentecost was fully come, they were all with one accord in one place. 2. And suddenly there came a sound from heaven as of a rushing mighty wind, and it filled the entire house where they were sitting. 3. And there appeared unto them cloven tongues like as of fire, and it sat upon each of them. 4. And they were all filled with the Holy Ghost, and began to speak with other tongues, as the Spirit gave them utterance. (NT Apostles Acts 2:3 *King James Version*).

213 The uncle is first mentioned in the sequence in the poem entitled "Heredity" discussed in the previous chapter and then reappears in "Fire-Eater" and "Study."

lie in the the native land. By writing poetry, the speaker "proves his proximity to the dead" (Sacks 1985: 37) as he constructs his verse by internalizing the lost object, represented by his father's and his uncle's working-class speech. The internalization is metaphorically described in the poem by the act of swallowing the tongues of fire—an image which correlates with Sacks's description of ancient forms of inheritance, which involved ingesting the symbol of God (Sacks 1985: 37). And although the attitude of the speaker towards the lost object remains ambivalent, since he recognizes the lack of eloquence and crudeness of the way his father and uncle spoke, he follows their acts (Fire-Eater 9).

What is most important, the task of following the speaker undertakes does not imply a simple imitation. As Spencer notes, "the ties of filiation require the son to fashion the string of his own that will both continue the family 'line' and supersede earlier speech acts by retying the grammatical knots and virtually *reinventing*[214] the vocabulary to express the family's often unarticulated experience" (1994: 83). Spencer draws attention to the fact that the act of inheritance presented in the poem involves an element of transformation of the legacy. The speaker modifies it to serve his own purpose since, as Sacks explains, the act of inheritance cannot comprise of mere "ingestion" (1985: 37), what must occur is and additional element "of alteration or surpassal … some device whereby the legacy may be seen to have entered a new successor" (1985: 37). The ability to create poetry is a skill which the speaker's ancestors did not posses and so the public manifestation of that skill (the action of the poem is set in a circus ring) can be read as this act of surpassal and consequently as "an assertion of … power," (Kennedy 2007: 30) the surviving power of the one who succeeds.[215] Kennedy points out that the idea of an elegy as a "heroic performance can be traced back to the contest in Theocritus and other ancient pastoral poems" (2007: 29) where "beneath an apparently innocent singing match, a poet asserts his position as true hair to a poetic legacy" (Sacks 1985: 36). Although in "Fire-Eater" there is no contest, and the only heir to the working-class legacy is the speaker himself, both "surpassal" (Sacks 1985: 37) of the ancestors in art of speaking and "alteration" (Sacks 1985: 37) of the legacy occur. Consequently, the succeeding release of the song is the result of a skilful transformation of the awkward and coarse working-class diction into poetry

214 Emphasis added by the author of this book.

215 As Kennedy notices "the heroic assertion of his own power has a surprising consequence: the elegist often places himself in a superior relation to his subject" (2007: 30). The author gives three examples of the poems where such an attitude of the elegist towards the subject of the elegy occurs: Shelley's "Adonais," Matthew Arnold's "Thyrsis" and W.H. Auden's "In Memory of W. B. Yeats."

which has the power of making order out of chaos and which, unlike the voice of Harrison's father and his stammering uncle, will be heard on the public arena, denoted in the poem by the circus ring. By taking part in the act of inheritance, accepting and transforming his legacy, the speaker proves himself to be able not only to "turn profit from his grief" (Kennedy 2007: 34) but also to "extract what can be termed a use value from the deceased, which can be returned to the community of the living" (Kennedy 2007: 34) in the form of poetry. The concluding lines contain a recurring motif in Harrison's poetry: an assertion of continual and inviolable poetic effort, and indicate that the working-class legacy has left a permanent mark on his poetic identity. His song is a product of black vocal cords, (Fire-Eater 15) "scorched" (Fire-Eater 15) by the "tongues of fire," (Fire-Eater 11) the awkward diction of his predecessors.

The poem which closes Part II of the sequence continues the theme of legacy and the inter-relation between the poet and his origin. In "Background Material," the background of two photographs metaphorically represents the disappearing working-class culture and although it is not made explicit in the poem, the origin of the speaker, which constitutes, as the title suggests, the material from which his poetry is made. His ghost, like his presence in the pictures, is suggested by the shadow he casts and a reflection of his figure in the father's eye, and so is simultaneously a part of the photographed world and an onlooker who creates the image. The role of the photographer reflects his role of an elegist who tries to preserve the image of his dead parents and sustain the continuity of the working-class experience of his predecessors. His shadow and his reflection—in other words his inexplicit presence in both pictures—is their shared feature and a link that joins the family circle, but at the same time, it constitutes a flaw which casts doubt on whether what we observe can be called art. This carefully constructed image can be read as an instance of the author's critique of his own filial poetry, labelled by some critics as overtly intimate and sentimental, and simultaneously as an ever-present question of the possibility of figuration of loss through art, the possibility of retrieving the images of the lost object from the realm of shadows. It seems obvious that the answer must be negative, as both parents and their working class background represented in the poem by a local pub are gone. What is more, the speaker's parents are represented in the poem by still images, which function as remainders of the loss and permanent absence of the lost object. Consequently, the distance between the poet and his parents, constituted by the medium of photography, is strongly suggested. However, the recognition and permanence of loss is counterbalanced in the poem by the assertion that the past evolves into the present, that "then" and "now" create a continuum which can be sustained by the medium of poetry. The fact that the shadow visible in the mother's photograph seems to be cast by the speaker not years ago but at moment of writing the poem[216] suddenly reduces the distance between the two time planes and suggests that the past can be entered and continued. "Background Material" repeats the idea prefigured in "A Good Read," a poem which, as Byrne writes, metaphorically defines "the father as an uncompleted text rather than a finished publication" (Byrne 1997: 89). As a representative of the working-class culture which constitutes a living tissue of Harrison's poetic identity, the figure of the father cannot be either "laid aside" or satisfactorily "captured in words" (Byrne 1997: 89), or definitively "put down in poems" (A Good Read 13). The inconclusiveness of Harrison's poetic enterprise expressed in the final line "Once I'm writing I can't put you down" (A Good Read 16) is a confirmation of the indissoluble bond between father and son, based on the idea of mutual containment, which is illustrated in "Background Material" by the penultimate couplet: "in his, if you look close, the gleam, the light, / me in his blind right eye, but minute size" (Background Material 13–14) which seems a distant echo of the motif of reflections in eyes and tears characteristic for John Donne and other English metaphysical poets.[217] As Harrison said in an interview, he is his mother and his father and simultaneously his parents "meet" (Illuminations II, 16) and survive in him since he takes over their legacy and "returns it to the community of the living" (Kennedy 2007: 34).

216 "in hers, as though just cast from where I write, / a shadow holding something to its eyes" (Background Material 15–16).

217 See for example John Donne's "The Good Morrow" and "Ecstasy" where the act of looking into each other's eyes and seeing each-other's reflections in the pupils, symbolizes love understood as self-contained whole, a complete and perfect microcosm.

Chapter Four
"Half versus half, the enemies within"

Changing Patterns of Revolt in *v.*

> We know of no people without names, no languages or cultures in which some manner of distinctions between self and other, *we and they*,[218] are not made ...
> Self-knowledge—always a construction no matter how much it feels like a discovery—is never altogether separable from claims to be known in specific ways by others.
> (Calhoun 1994: 9–10)

Calhoun's comment proves relevant for the discussion on *conformity vs rebellion*[219] and their role in identity construction, since both components of this opposition refer to the strategy adopted by a "social actor" (Castells 2000: 6) and because they can be analyzed as two distinct forms of relationship between the "social actor" (Castells 2000: 6), an individual or a group, and the social world, in other words between "self and other, we and they" and consequently also between, as Harrison puts it in one of his most acclaimed poems, "them and [uz]". According to Bokszański, characteristic features of a given identity, when seen in the light of the *conformity vs rebellion* opposition, must be discussed in relation to the constitutive values characteristic of a given social order in which an individual or a group operates[220] (2007: 39). Consequently, the *conformity vs rebellion* opposition

218 Emphasis added by the author of this book.

219 The opposition constitutes one of the three dimensions of the notion of identity analyzed by Bokszański in *Tożsamości zbiorowe* Warszawa: Wydawnictwo Naukowe PWN, 2007. For more detailed explanation of their role in identity construction see the introduction to the book. The terms: *conformity* and *rebellion* have been used here in accordance with Bokszański's choice of register ('konformizm' 'conformity;' 'rebellion' 'bunt'). Bokszański refers at this point in his study to the typology developed by Robert K. Merton (Bokszański 2007: 43) presented below.

220 In the case of Harrison's poetry discussed in this chapter, it will be, generally speaking, the social order characteristic of the British politics of the 1980s. However a closer reading reveals that what Harrison is most interested in is the confrontation of different social orders characteristic of various communities, removed in time and space: for example, the working class community of 1980s Leeds, mining communities of the past centuries, speakers of RP, football supporters, etc. All these communities differ from each other in the scope and the level of influence they can exert and are characterized by different sets of values.

is often analyzed in relation to the issues of collective identities and diverse processes of social change which take place within the sphere of social movements (Bokszański 2007: 39). For example, Bokszański refers to a typology of collective identities proposed by Manuel Castells:

> Legitimizing identity: introduced by the dominant institutions of society to extend and rationalize their domination vis-à-vis social actors, a theme that is at the heart of Sennett's theory of authority and domination, but also fits with various theories of nationalism.
>
> Resistance identity: generated by those actors who are in positions/conditions devalued and/or stigmatized by the logic of domination, thus building trenches of resistance and survival on the basis of principles different from, or opposed to, those permeating the institutions of society.
>
> Project identity: when social actors, on the basis of whichever cultural materials are available to them, build a new identity that redefines their position in society and, by so doing, seek the transformation of overall social structure. (2000: 8)

This "distinction between three forms and origins of identity building" (Castells 2000: 7) is relevant for a reading of Harrison's work. It is created on the assumption, to which Harrison persistently returns throughout his poetic career, that the "construction of identity always takes place in a context marked by power relationships" (Castells 2000: 7) and as such it is never free from the political and the social turbulences of the modern world.

Bokszański suggests that the *conformity vs rebellion* opposition and its relevance for the process of identity construction can be seen as closely related to the "types of individual adaptation" developed by Robert K. Merton (1968: 195). The author of *Social Theory and Social Structure* proposes the following five modes of behaviour (Merton 1968: 195), which can be adopted interchangeably by a given social actor: conformity, innovation, ritualism, retreatism and rebellion

Ways of adjustment	Cultural goals	Institutionalized recourses
Conformity	+	+
Innovation	+	-
Ritualism	-	+
Retreatism	-	-
Rebellion	+/-	+/-

(+) denotes "acceptance" (-) denotes "rejection"
(Merton 1986: 205)

For the sake of the following discussion, it is important to focus on the final type of adaptation. It differs from the first four, as it constitutes a reaction, aimed at institutionalization of new goals and methods and "which presupposes alienation from reigning … standards" (Merton 1968: 210). As the table shows, *rebellion*, a process triggered by the assumption that change is necessary, is characterized by the rejection of a current set of values and the subsequent acceptance of a new set,[221] and as such it remains in opposition to *conformity*, which assures the stability of the prevailing social and cultural order (Bokszański 2007: 38). Nevertheless, what is important for the sake of the subsequent discussion of Harrison's poems, and of *v.* in particular, is not so much the difference between conformity and rebellion but between rebellion and *ressentiment,* a notion introduced "in a special technical sense" by Nietzsche and developed in the field of Sociology by Max Scheler.[222] *Ressentiment* as Merton explains, referring to Scheler's study, although seemingly similar to *rebellion*, is essentially a completely different phenomenon:

> This complex sentiment has three interlocking elements. First, diffuse feelings of hate, envy and hostility; second, a sense of being powerless to express these feelings actively against the person or social stratum evoking them; and third, a continual re-experiencing of this impotent hostility. (1968: 210–211)

However, the most important fact, according to Merton, which distinguishes *ressentiment* from *rebellion* is that the former does not involve the authentic transformation of the value system (Merton 1968: 211). Its goals do not represent any particular values which would be cherished by the person or group who resents, since the one who resents condemns the very thing he/she secretly desires (Merton 1968: 211). This opposition (i.e. *rebellion* vs *ressentiment*) plays an important role in Harrison's poetry and is reflected most visibly in the ambiguous characters of his protagonists—"ambivalent heroes" as Sandie Byrne calls them (1997: 22), whose "oppositional identities" (Byrne 1997: 23) fall outside any straightforward

---

221 It has to be stressed that the acceptance of the new set of values is a possibility, not a certainty. While the process takes place, it functions as a future goal, more or less likely to be achieved.

222 See: M. Scheler *Vom Umsturz der Werte* Leipzig, Der Neue Geist, 1919. As Merton points out Scheler's book is a highly influential and at the same time widely criticised work discussed among others by: V. J. McGill in his article "Scheler's theory of sympathy and love" published in *Philosophy and Phenomenological Research* (1942, 2: 273–291) and S. Ranulf in *Moral Indignation and Middle-Class Psychology: A Sociological Study* (Copenhagen 1938, s. 199–204).

definitions. They are the ones in between, the men of "conflicting interests" and "divided loyalties" (Byrne 1997: 23)—agents of *agon*.[223]

Merton uses the term "rebellion," Bokszański, who as he himself admits, refers to Merton's classification, uses in his study the Polish word "bunt," which can be translated into English as both "rebellion" and "revolt". The term "revolt," which today evokes specifically political connotations, "widely used, if not banal" (Kristeva 2000: 2) holds, however, "a few surprises" (Kristeva 2000: 2), and if we take into consideration its etymology, proves to be more than adequate for describing the attitude of Harrison's characters. Kristeva, who conducts an etymological analysis of the word in *Sense and Non-sense of Revolt*, suggests that "two semantic shifts mark the evolution of the word: the first implies the notion of movement, the second, that of space and time" (2000: 1).

> The Latin verb *volvere*, which is at the origin of revolt, was initially far removed from politics. It produced derivatives with meanings—semes—such as "curve" … "turn," "*return*" … under Italian influence in the fifteenth and sixteenth centuries, volutas, voluta—in French volute … as well as volta and voltare suggest the idea of *circular movement* and by extension, *temporal return*. Volta also means "time"—as in "one time" or "once"—hence, "*turning back*."[224] (Kristeva 2000: 2)

The idea of revolt in Harrison's poetry, understood as a type of attitude towards the surrounding social world and an identity-shaping force, cannot be discussed in separation from the phenomenon of return. The return, understood metaphorically, as the return to one's roots through writing[225] and literally as the journey back to Leeds which the speaker undertakes in numerous poems, constitutes for Harrison the prerequisite for revolt. It is the place of origin, the native land which influences to a great extent the particular political and social stance the poet takes when he speaks in defence of the forgotten history of the working class and its silenced voices. The facts that he chooses a pen as his weapon, speaks of "*inky* digit of defiance,"[226] and decides consciously to become a public poet, who as O'Brien suggests takes a side[227] (1998: 59) make the following observation made

223 For further discussion of the issue see Chapter II of the book.

224 Emphasis added by the author of this book.

225 See for example: "On Not Being Milton".

226 Emphasis added by the author of this book. See: Tony Harrison *The Inky Digit of Defiance* The PEN/Pinter Lecture 2009, privately Printed for Faber and Faber p. 8.

227 However, the identification with that side i.e. with the northern working-class people, may be only partly successful and is, as the following analysis will prove, highly problematic.

by Kristeva an interesting point of reference. Kristeva's research clearly demonstrates that the word "revolt" bears kinship to the word "book":

> Another direct derivative from Latin belongs to this lineage [which began with "volvere"], the adjective *volubilis*, "that which turns with ease," as in *volubilitas linguae;* the French equivalent is volubile (voluble). And volumen, sheets of paper scrolled around the stick, with the spatial meaning of "wrapping" or "covering," results in "volume," which comes to mean book in the thirteenth century. (2000: 2)

The metaphor of the "inky digit of defiance," (Harrison 2009: 8) links the issue of revolt and the problem of eloquence represented in several of Harrison's poems by books or lexicon.[228] Harrison took the phrase (i.e. "inky digit of defiance") from a BBC World Service programme which covered an election in Afghanistan. The reporter described women leaving the polling booth, raising their hands towards the public, their fingers marked with "indelible ink" (Harrison 2009: 8) that proved they had just voted. In his lecture, Harrison compares their "inky digits of defiance" (Harrison 2009: 8) as the reporter called them, with the fingers of his uncle Harry, the protagonist of "Heredity,"[229] who being deaf and dumb, "wielded a thick … dictionary in one hand, pointing to the word he wanted with the other" (Harrison 2009: 7) to communicate with those (including Harrison) who were not fluent in sign language. As "he licked his fingers … so as to be able to flick through the pages … ink of the lexicon darkened his defiant digit" Harrison acknowledges that his uncle's "maniac lexical need" (Harrison 2009: 7) was one of those forces which influenced his poetic identity, as it evoked in him "the passion for language and languages, and for what is still [for him] supreme articulacy and eloquence of poetry" (Harrison 2009: 8). There is irony in the fact that Harrison's poetic enterprise has for its basis inarticulacy and silence. What is interesting, however, is that the inky digits of the inarticulate Afghan women and of Harrison's uncle Harry defying against "what he called with two jabs at the brandished dictionary: 'Tory error' (Harrison 2009: 7), become in Harrison's writing, a distinctive feature of poets who acquire their inky digits through their own form of defiance, by means of the "power to master words,"[230] and most literally smudging their fingers with ink (Harrison 2009: 8). A parallel image to the one referred to by Harrison in the lecture in 2009 can be found in *Newcastle is Peru*, a poem he wrote much earlier:

---

228 See for example: "Book Ends," "Aqua Mortis," "Bringing Up," "Me Tarzan".

229 For the discussion of the poem see chapter II of the book.

230 A quotation form Arthur Scargill's comment printed in *Sunday Times*, 10 January 1982, used by Harrison as an epigraph to *v.*

My fingerprints still lined with coal
send cold shudders through my soul.
Each whorl, my love-, my long life-line,
mine, inalienably mine,
lead off my body as they press
onwards into nothingness.
I see my grimy fingers smudge
everything they feel or touch. (153–160)

Here, coal, a geological element of the landscape and a symbol of political conflicts, stands for Harrison's historical and personal inheritance. Coal stains the fingers like "indelible ink," soaks deep into Harrison's identity, filters through his imagination and pervades the soul to assume the shape of "grimy" or rather, "inky" fingerprints, which he leaves on everything he touches. The two "inkiest digits," according to Harrison "are those of the V-sign (turned the wrong way around) or the 'Fuck you!' single middle digit" (Harrison 2009: 8). In the quotation above, "inkiest" means the most defiant, rebellious, revolutionary but also provocative and offensive. The link between defiance and ink, revolt and book, rebellion and writing which Harrison establishes by means of the "inky digits" metaphor can be traced in many of Harrison's poems and finds an especially interesting rendering in his most controversial and perhaps his most rebellious work.

The prominent example of the rebellious and/or revolutionary attitude of the speaker/s[231] of Harrison's poems towards the social and political reality of contemporary Britain can be found in his in/famous, "deliberately public" (O'Brien 1998: 51), elegy, entitled *v.*—whose reading, broadcast by Channel Four on November 4th 1987 caused a considerable stir among the audience. The reception of the poem, and the discussion, or as some critics put it "an outrage" (Eyre 1991: 365, Spencer 1994: 91) it evoked at the time of its appearance, relate closely to the question of the identity of a "public poet" (Eyre 1991: 365), to which Harrison persistently returns in his work from *The Loiners* onwards. At this point it is important to state that the political and the social lie at the very core of "the world—within—a poem" (Jarniewicz 1994: 124) and that this fact is made explicit already by the poem's epigraph: a quotation from Arthur Scargill, the defeated leader of the NUM in the miners' strike of 1984: "My father still reads the dictionary every day. He says your life depends on your power to master words" (Harrison 1987: 235).

231 The use of the plural form seems to be justifiable here since Harrison introduces multiple voices in his poetry. In the case of *v.*, the two voices which come to the foreground are that of the poet and his adversary/alter ego—the skin.

By quoting Scargill, Harrison confirms his ongoing fascinations with the issues he tackled in *The School of Eloquence*. As Spencer points out, "It is not difficult to see the appeal of the Scargill's quotation for Harrison.... it testifies to a continuity of commitment from one generation to the next" and "speaks of an interest in language as passionate and persistent as Harrison's own" (1994: 92). The "power" to which Scargill refers is the "mastery of language as such,"[232] (Spencer 1994: 91) nevertheless, the figure of the speaker links it with the "mining community resistance" and "to Ian MacGregor's programme of pit closures" (Spencer 1994: 91) and it is the mining community[233] which becomes the collective protagonist of the poem. Its often oblique but unsettling presence evokes such issues as "the trauma of urban-industrial change" (Spencer 1994: 91), the problem of communal solidarity[234] and the will to defy the oppressor which permeates the history of this particular working-class group from the beginnings of its existence. Due to its strong tradition of militancy and resilience (Gaventa 1980: 37), it is possible to associate the mining community with the second type of identity-building proposed by Castells, which "constructs forms of collective resistance against ... oppression" (2000: 7) and which may be accompanied by what Castells calls *the exclusion of the excluders by the excluded*[235] (2000: 7). What makes this method of

---

232 It seems that Spencer's comment should be further specified as it is the language of the privileged classes, whose mastery is being referred to in the quotation. Jerzy Jarniewicz comments on Harrison's use of Scargill's words in *W brzuchu wieloryba: Szkice o dwudziestowiecznej poezji brytyjskiej i irlandzkiej*:

> Adequate language becomes a guarantor of success. Its acquisition is strictly connected with the range of power one possesses. Words acquire additional value, giving access to the space closed before. Especially in England, where, not so long ago, it was possible to detect, based on pronunciation, which elite school the speaker graduated from. (2001: 91 My translation)
>
> Właściwy język staje się gwarantem powodzenia. Jego przyswojenie jest ściśle związane z zakresem posiadanej władzy. Słowa nabierają dodatkowych wartości, dając dostęp do rejonów dotychczas zamkniętych. Zwłaszcza w Anglii, gdzie jeszcze do niedawna można było po wymowie rozpoznać, którą z elitarnych szkół mówiący ukończył. (2001: 91)

233 Mining community is understood in this chapter as an example of a *community of life and fate* (Bauman 2007: 11) defined in the second chapter of the book.

234 For the further discussion on the issue of solidarity among the British miners see the following chapters in Richard's *Miners on Strike: Class, Solidarity and Divisions in Britain*: "The Basis of Solidarity" (1996: 16–32), "The Limits of Solidarity" (1996: 39–54), "The Union and the Problems of Solidarity" (1996: 58–79).

235 A process defined by Castells as "building of the defensive identity in terms of dominant institutions/ideologies, reversing the value judgment while reinforcing the boundary" (2000: 7).

identity construction possible is the combination of historical and geographical conditions in which a given community came into being and which characterized its further development (Castells 2000: 7).

The introduction of the mining community as a "collective character" and the problems represented in the poem by the mine/coal metaphor deserve to be discussed in detail in order to explain the various dimensions of revolt described by Harrison which form the individual poetic identity of the speaker and function as a major driving force of the British working class, shaping its collective identity. Why does Harrison choose this particular "occupational group of workers" (Richards 1996: 15) and their story to represent the fate of British working-class in general, and furthermore, why does he develop the metaphorical structure of the poem on the basis of the mine/coal imagery? The most important reason may well be the mere fact that Leeds, like other northern cities, had a long mining tradition and that the mining industry has been largely responsible for both the prosperity and the later decline of the region. What is more, coal—a product of geological forces, the "black gold" of the north—acquires in Harrison's poetry a role comparable to the one which turf, "valuable fuel" and "building material" (Jarniewicz 2011: 63), plays in the poetry of Seamus Heaney:

> The large territories of Ireland, reaching once seventeen percent of the whole surface, are boggy. They cannot be cultivated but give the Irish a different resource—turf. It is cut with a special spade having a long handle and sharp edge, often with blades at both sides. It is cut out of the bog in May, most usually, and then it is dried in the sun and wind. It is usually done collectively in the group of neighbours and friends who selflessly come to help—it is an old Irish custom called *meitheal*, which creates the sense of community and solidarity, strengthening tribal bonds among the village dwellers.[236] (Jarniewicz 2011: 63)

The words used by Jarniewicz to describe the meaning of digging turf in the Irish context could be used to define the way in which Harrison sees extracting coal in the context of the English industrial north. It is a type of work connected symbolically with the fate of the place of the poet's origin (Jarniewicz 2011: 63), an activity

---

236 My translation of: Całe obszary Irlandii, dochodzące ongiś do siedemnastu procent jej powierzchni, to tereny podmokłe. Nie nadają się pod uprawę, ale dają Irlandczykom inne bogactwo—torf. Tnie się go specjalnym szpadlem, o długim trzonku i ostrym ostrzu, często ze skrzydełkiem po obu stronach. Wycina się go z bagien najczęściej w maju, po czym suszy na słońcu i wietrze. Czynność tę wykonuje się zazwyczaj zespołowo, w gronie sąsiadów i przyjaciół, którzy przychodzą z bezinteresowną pomocą w pracy—to stary irlandzki obyczaj zwany *meitheal*, współtworzący poczucie wspólnoty i solidarności, wzmacniający plemienne więzi między mieszkańcami wioski (Jarniewicz 2011: 63).

opening the door to the past (Jarniewicz 2011: 64) inscribed in the history and culture of the place and its community (Jarniewicz 2011: 64). It is also a community-building activity (Jarniewicz 2011: 63) which demands solidarity and mutual trust from the people undertaking it. In the case of mining, a strong but, as the following discussion will show, an ambiguous communal bond is reinforced by numerous factors, the reality of a specific working environment being one of them:

> You see, what folks don't understand … is the bond of the miner. I work in a place … where … we're working against the atmosphere that's *highly explosive*,[237] I trust you not to take a match, a cigarette, to ignite and blow us to smithereens. I trust you do set the pit prop, to hold the roofs up, when you've been on shift before me, secure. I trust you … and it gets a bond between you, because you are both in the same conditions—it's a great leveller down in pit—it doesn't matter if you've got a mansion [or] … a shanty hut—because you are all the same—you are all black, sweaty, mucky, and wear rags, and you are on your hands and knees—it doesn't matter what you've got up there—it's a great *leveller*. (Anonymous miner qtd in Richards 1996: 18)

This and the other comments of miners quoted in this chapter represent part of a study conducted by Andrew Richards and presented in his book *Miners on Strike: Class Solidarity and Division in Britain* (all the interviews were carried between 1989–1990). As Richards explains:

> One hundred-and-seventy-three members of the NUM … and forty seven of UDM … were interviewed … The principal qualification for an interviewee was that he worked in the coal industry during the period covering the 1972, 1974 and 1984–1985 strikes …. interviewees were drawn mainly from those pits which had survived the contraction of the industry between 1985–1989. However, the process of contraction itself (whereby miners had transferred to pits in existence in 1989–1990), and the use of 'snowballing' technique of making contacts, ensured that interviews were also conducted with miners from pits which had closed since 1985. (1996: 241)

The choice of the interviewees and the issues tackled in the interviews make them an especially interesting illustration of the social/cultural context in which Harrison's *v.* was created and in which it functioned on a public arena at the time of its first publication and TV broadcast. Additionally, they offer a chance to see the nature of work in the mining industry, as well as the outcomes of the spectacular defeat of the 1984 strike from the perspective of the insiders. One intriguing feature of this perspective, reflected in Harrison's poetry, is the way in which the speakers perceive their own living environment, a division of the space they inhabit into two realities: the one "above" and the one "below" the ground. Those two realities

---

237 Emphasis added by the author of this book.

which make up their everyday existence, although connected, are nevertheless characterized by a different hierarchies of values and gathered by different sets of rules, adherence to which proves necessary for human survival.

Harrison adopts this perspective in his poetry to "tell us of a history from below" (O'Brien 1998: 59), as he sees it as part of his working-class legacy. It is first and foremost the history of "working-turned-*under*class"[238] (O'Brien 1998: 64). Nevertheless, Harrison takes the above/below opposition to a different level giving it a multilayered, metaphorical meaning. The mine and its "lowest worked-out seem" (v. 16) are inscribed into the frame of a larger "archaeological metaphor" (Kristeva 2000: 15) according to which "the past," accumulated like coal, below the ground, "exerts a geological pressure on the present" (Spencer 1994: 93). Harrison retells in *v.* a story from the underworld which entails the experience of the miners who worked down the pit through the centuries. It is essentially the story of the forgotten, individual and communal past and as the following analysis will demonstrate, bringing it back is not possible without confrontation with the Other, which is both strangely familiar and dangerously alien. It is interesting that a similar metaphorical rendering, "a series of archaeological metaphors" (Kristeva 2000: 15), is used by Sigmund Freud in a letter he wrote in 1936 to the Swiss philosopher and psychoanalyst Ludwig Binswanger (1881–1966), quoted by Kristeva in *The Sense and Non-sense of Revolt*:

> "I have always dwelt only in the ground floor and basement of the building .... In that you are the conservative I am the revolutionary. Had I only another life of work before me I should dare to offer even those highly born people a home in my lowly dwelling" (Translation: you are highly placed; I would like to offer people like you who deign to accord me some attention a place in this basement where I am trying to develop a revolutionary spirit.) (2000: 15)

For the sake of the subsequent analysis, that which is below, either because it is excluded on the basis of its degraded status or because it is hidden, is also regarded as that which is different, the one in opposition. In *v.*, that which is below is additionally "highly explosive" (Anonymous miner qtd in Richards 1996: 18) or potentially violent[239]; it is that which undermines, seethes just below the surface. One of the problems discussed in the subsequent part of this chapter is how in *v.*, the division into "above" and "below" goes beyond the experience of the English miner and

238 Emphasis added by the author of this book.

239 Violence and resentment are embodied in the poem most vividly in the character of the skin—the representative of the working under-class.

becomes the feature of the human condition, and that how the adoption of this perspective by the poet shapes his perception and consequently his poetic identity.

"This graveyard stands above a worked-out pit" (v. 29) says Harrison in *v.* setting the poem within the context of a mining culture characterized for centuries by an "unending violence of US and THEM," (v. 70) which in 1984 manifested itself as "revolt" (Richards 1996: 229) against governmental policy of pit closures.[240] The problem of "us" versus "them" opposition which reappears in Harrison's poetry as an important factor influencing his poetic identity[241] is considered by Lockwood one of the most important forces operating within the mining culture. Lockwood states that the mining industry "concentrate[s] workers together in solitary communities and ... isolate[s] them from the influences of the wider society" (1975: 17). It is, according to him a "distinctive occupational culture" (1975: 17) characterized by "shared work experiences" (1975: 18) and "centered on an awareness of 'us' in contradistinction to 'them' who are not a part of 'us.' 'Them' are bosses, managers ... and ultimately, the public authorities of the larger society"[242] (1975: 18). Richards describes mining communities as "more militant than other segments of [the] working population" (1996: 16) and the nature of their "history and development ... [as] underpinned [by] a tradition of resilience, solidarity and militancy" (1996: 16). The "position of mining as a highly strike-prone industry" mentioned earlier in this chapter (Richards 1996: 17) has often

---

240 As David P. Cristopher explains

> [t]he late 1970s were times of strikes and confrontation .... in the early 1980s Britain economic crisis worsened. Manufacturing declined and the shipbuilding, mining and steel industries practically disappeared .... Unemployment rose to over 13 per cent, and with more than 3 million people out of work the government became deeply unpopular. There was civil and industrial conflict in most areas, and in April 1981 rioting broke out in the streets of Brixton, south London, and in other cities around the country .... The crisis seemed to deepen when [in] ... 1982, Thatcher led Britain into war with Argentina ... [but] in spite of record unemployment, riots and war, the Conservatives emerged victorious in the general election in 1983 .... [their] economic and political ideas ... included an even greater reduction of public spending ... [and] privatis[ing] industries in public sector. The measures were highly unpopular with the working class ... and resulted in more violent industrial disputes .... The most notorious confrontation was the miner's strike of 1984–1985 (2010: 11).

241 See: discussion on "Them and [uz]" in Chapter II of the book.

242 For further discussion upon the "them" versus "us" opposition and its role in the working-class culture see Richard Hoggart's *The Uses of Literacy: Aspects of Working-class Life, with Special References to Publications and Entertainments.* London: Chato and Windus, 1957, p. 62.

been associated with the "isolation and insularity"[243] (Richards 1996: 17) of miners who were regarded through centuries as a "breed apart,"[244] (1996: 17) strange and potentially dangerous. Richards provides two examples of the way mining communities were perceived by outsiders. The first comes from Daniel Defoe's *A Tour through the Whole Island of Great Britain*, published in 1726, the second from M. Benney's *The Legacy of Mining* which appeared more than two hundred years later, in 1978. Despite the long span of time stretching between the two accounts, they both share a similar view of miners as separated from the rest of the society by their customs and physical appearance:

> What with the dejected countenances of the men, occasioned by their poverty and hard labour, and what with the colour or discolour which comes from the coal, both to their

243 The "position of mining as a highly strike-prone industry" (Richards 1996: 17) can be explained by the so-called isolated mass hypothesis, developed by Kerr and Siegel, according to which" [e]mployees form a largely homogenous undifferentiated mass" (1954: 191–192). As Richards argues "constant contact between individuals created cohesion and as consequence good environment for the development of permanent organizations (like trade unions)…. So, as the mining communities were cohesive, homogenous and relatively isolated, they were as a result highly strike-prone" (1996: 17).

244 It should be noted that this perception of the mining community has been developing in parallel to the more general perception of the North, which especially after the Industrial Revolution has been always associated with coal and coal extraction. As Katie Wales writes:

> The Industrial Revolution merely compounded images of the Northern alienation: the wilderness of nature was replaced by the wastelands of slagheaps, which continued to evoke well into the twentieth century the Other Worlds of either the lunar or post-Holocaust landscapes. Grime was added to the grit. The iconography of the North became strongly associated with mine, mill and factory, with … working class …. The late twentieth century aftermath of the Industrial Revolution, with the dereliction of factories and mills leading to widespread unemployment, did little to alter such … perceptions (2006: 27).

The accounts of writers and journalist such as Beatrix Campbell and Charles Jennings who wrote about the North confirm Wale's point of view:

> London experiences the 'provinces' as if they were up the Amazon, up a mysterious not say jungle path (Campbell 1984: 33).
>
> Pig-ignorant southerners like me … generally fail to distinguish between Yorkshire and Lancashire. We can't tell the accents apart … And if in doubt, we tend to lump everything north of Birmingham up to say, Sunderland, into Yorkshire. Lancashire is the forgotten country (Jennings 1995: 62).

clothes and complexions … they are, indeed *frightful*[245] fellows at first sight. (Defoe qtd in Richards 16)

Here encamped on a vast raft of coal … was a *tribe*[246] of Englishmen so distinct in their way of life that, had they been situated on a remote island in the South Seas, they would have been a subject of a dozen ethnographic monographs. (Benney qtd in Richards 16)

The culture of mining communities, which for Harrison functions as a synecdoche of the more generally understood working-class culture, possesses other characteristics (related to isolation and insularity) that may be seen as responsible for the fact that mining is a highly strike-prone industry (Bulmer 1975: 85–88). The conditions in which miners have to function under the ground deserve a more detailed analysis, firstly, in order to understand the nature of the values which perish with the death of working-class culture and secondly, to determine how the mining metaphor relates to the theme of revolt and hence to the issue of the miners' strike. One aspect of mining culture which is responsible for the development of a rebellious spirit amongst miners and "generates the possibilities for collective action" (Richards 1996: 18) is the "working environment" (Richards 1996: 18) i.e. the mine itself, mentioned in this chapter as a source of miners' solidarity and a "great *leveller*" (anonymous miner quoted in Richards 1996: 18). The connection between the place (here the mine) and readiness to rebel against the oppressive system indicates that the theme of revolt as presented in *v.* can be discussed in relation to the locodescriptive character of the poem and its central image of the graveyard undermined by the subsiding pit.

Next Millenium you'll have to search quite hard
to find my slab behind the family dead,
butcher, publican, and baker now me bard
adding to their beef, beer and bread.

With Byron three graves on I'll not go short
of company, and Wordsworth's opposite.
That's two peers already, of a sort,
and we'll all be thrown together if the pit

whose galleries once ran beneath this plot
causes the distinguished dead to drop
into the rabblement of bone and rot,
shored slack, crushed shale, smashed prop. (v. 1–12)

245 Emphasis added by the author of this book.
246 Emphasis added by the author of this book.

Harrison begins *v.* by recognizing his affiliation with the dead artisans of his family and class. He establishes his own origins. On one hand, he asserts his connection with the baker and the butcher, and on the other with Byron and Wordsworth. Reading further, we are reminded that art and craft are two sides of the same coin since Byron was a tanner and Wordsworth an organ builder. Harrison's future grave-neighbours are local tradesmen, the namesakes of Romantic poets known for their non-conformist attitude—"the aristocratic rebel, radical and exile, and his … compatriot, the youthful revolutionary who came home in the end of Toryism" (O'Brien 1998: 62). Now Byron and Wordsworth are part of the landscape as their ashes mix with the coal dust of the old worked-out pit above which the cemetery stands. This image is inscribed with a powerful sense of history as the poem goes back to the times when "with no man here at all" (v. 311) the coal began "as 300 million-year-old plant debris" (v. 312). But before readers are reminded of the role of "vast, slow" (v. 433) geological forces in the creation of the mining industry, they are presented with a more recent history of the pit, which is today merely a "worked-out black hollow" (v. 308) but was once the "centre of the community"[247] (Richards 1996: 21) and "loomed large over every activity" of its members (Bulmer 1978: 28). The "life of Leeds," as the poet ironically notices, is "supported by the dead" (v. 300) because the pit which "ranges over the churches used as warehouses, the boarded-up shops, the football ground which has become a cockpit for displaced aggression" (Byrne 1997: 70) contains literally and metaphorically the remains of the city's industrial past. Since "the individual miner's life, and that of preceding generations" has been always "entwined with the fortunes of the local colliery" (Richards 1996: 32) it is not surprising that the

247 As Richards explains since "historically the presence of coal determined the location of mines … the mine became the centre of the community that subsequently emerged in its vicinity" (1996: 20). This is the reason why the decision to sink the pit had such serious consequences, it was practically synonymous with the destruction of the entire community. "Pit was the village" Marshall writes "paying its wages, supporting its shops …. There is little other industry …. The pit is the reason for the village and if the pit dies the village dies too" (1984: 39). The account of one of the miners interviewed by Richards clearly shows the way in which mining communities were structured around collieries:

> When a pit is sunk … the village … come[s] second. The village is built around the colliery and … all the social life is directly connected to the colliery … and when the pit … dies, you lose the community of the villager and the surrounding area … where every pit is, there's a village attached to it … you've your miners' welfare halls, where you had your snooker and your chess clubs, your llibraries … it was all built around the colliery. (Anonymous miner qtd in Richards 1996: 20).

"impetus for collective action amongst the miners ... was historically driven" (Richards 1996: 32). The "sense of [ones] own history" (Francis 1985: 267), which underpins the necessity for defiance against the oppressive system (Richards 1996: 32) is what Harrison alludes to by means of mining imagery. The remembrance of past struggles and continuity of working-class experience is what triggers "the resistance put up by miners when their livelihoods and communities are threatened" (Richards 1996: 32) and the resistance of a poet who decides to "occupy ... /Poetry" (Them and [uz]" II, 1–2) and rebel against the prevailing social order established by the users of the Queen's English. And it is precisely the locus of the poem's action which becomes the instance of rebellion foreshadowed in "Them and [uz]". The graveyard undermined by the pit has as its "source of dissent and resistance" (Byrne 1997: 67) a country churchyard depicted by Gray in his "Elegy Written in a Country Churchyard" Pastoral image becomes for Harrison a "model of difference" (Byrne 1997: 67), which at the same time inspires and irritates. As Byrne suggests, characteristically for the locodescriptive poems the place in both Gray's elegy and Harrison's *v.*:

> Generates a narrative structure within a more or less static meditation through introduction of the scene before the poet, survey of that scene, contemplation of associations arising from the scene, and departure, while the associations arising from the scene extend the subject-matter beyond the immediately apparent objects. (1997: 67)

Just as in the case of Gray's "Elegy Written in a Country Churchyard", the immediate setting in *v.* triggers reflection on universal issues, the speaker moving beyond his private experience to gain a wider, social perspective. Harrison consciously refers to the tradition of British poetry endowed with "a special sense of importance in human experience of the interaction between the human spirit and the spirit of place" (Byrne 1997: 70), but he appropriates this tradition to serve his own purpose. His Beeston Hill Cemetery is not an archetypal place like Gray's churchyard (Byrne 1997: 67) but a concrete, recognizable and emotionally charged one, as it is a place where the speaker's parents are buried and where he hopes to rest when his time comes. Harrison takes the burial ground from a rural to an urban context and gives it the disturbing character of post-industrial Limbo, substituting the peaceful atmosphere of "picturesque Arcadia" (Byrne 1997: 67) with images of unrest and potential chaos caused by the subsiding pit. While Gray writes, "Each in his narrow cell forever laid, / The rude forefathers of the hamlet sleep" (Elegy 15–16) creating an impression of harmony and eternal order, Harrison unearths the foundations of the Beeston Hill Cemetery and replaces an image of neat and clean cells with the disturbing image of a massive grave where the equality of the forefathers is assured by the process of decay. The subsidence of the worked-out seam causes the distinguished dead to lose their dignity but also their individuality. They become impossible to distinguish as they fall into a "rabblement of bone and rot" (v. 11), losing their place in the hierarchy of the buried dead. Sean O'Brien in The *Deregulated Muse* highlights the double meaning of the word "rabblement" used in the third line of the stanza. According to *The Shorter Oxford English Dictionary*, "rabblement" is encountered in 1545, meaning "rabble … in various senses" but also, from 1590, "riotous conduct". The second meaning is especially interesting in the context of Harrison's subject. Beeston Hill Cemetery stands on the old worked-out pit of a coalmine—a symbol of social unrest in the history of the industrial North. The bodies of the distinguished forefathers merge with the bodies of the "pit's lost casualties" (O'Brien 1998: 62)—whose lot was linked with the lot of the mine since they once belonged to the working class of Leeds. The image of the worked-out seam stands for the destructive power of geological force which operates beneath the graveyard, and the power of history which undermines and influences the present condition of the city. The riotous conduct is suggestive of the personification of the bone and rot, which fits well when we consider that the decomposition of human tissue once belonged to the living bodies of the miners rising against the oppression by the more privileged classes.

The rebellious character of Harrison's method becomes evident when one takes into consideration the cultural aesthetic which stands behind Gray's Elegy (Byrne 1997: 70), the aesthetic which implies the "imposition of order upon nature" (Byrne 1997: 70):

> The career of … landscape gardeners or estate-planners … depends upon the same social evaluation of 'landscape' one finds in the painting and locodescriptive poetry of the period … [and] upon the transformation of the traditional 'common' into private property as result of a long process of … agricultural 'improvement'. The invisible grid of property makes possible the reconstruction of the land as 'landscape'. (Byrne 1997: 70)

Byrne further suggests that "representations of eighteenth-century landscape reinforce a representation of the national social order as a harmonious totality" (1997: 70). Harrison begins *v.* in the manner in which his predecessor begins his *Elegy*: with a landscape which, as Byrne describes, "'fades' into a reflection on the entire social order" (1997: 70) but the social order of 1980s Britain proves to be "grounded on a worked-out pit" (Byrne 1997: 70), unsettled by violent social "versuses," pervaded by the anger and resentment of the dispossessed. It is difficult not to agree with O'Brien, who suggests that the image of the collapsing graveyard raises "the whole tradition of equality and similarity in death … for ironical consideration … plays an elaborate joke on Gray's vision of order and permanence" (1998: 62). The departure from the classical model and its values is even more visible in Harrison's "politics of form" (Spencer 1994: 92) which manifests itself in the "assault" of the iambic line (O'Brien 1998: 60), which disrupts the traditional rhythm of its beat. The second line[248] of the first stanza preserves it but already the third and fourth lines[249] lack on regularity or as O'Brien says, "at least approach the limits of metrical acceptability"[250] (1998: 61). Critics generally agree (O'Brien, Spencer, Byrne) that the disruption is not an accident but a conscious decision of the author, "a strategic feature … [and] a continuation of the dramatic practice of the sonnets" (O'Brien 1998: 61). The final line of the third stanza is an interesting example of a structure which works on different levels and delivers the message by means of its visual and aural qualities. Byrne deconstructs the line into five patterns:

> The visual pattern comes from the apparent arrangement of words in a pattern of two syllables followed by one-syllable, though 'shored', 'crushed' and 'smashed' are spoken as one syllable. The temporal pattern consists of the alternation of (conceptually, if not actually) longer and shorter words. The grammatical arrangement is an alternation of adjective and noun. Aurally, the line is patterned by alliteration and assonance, and the opposition of long/short vowels and alveolar/paleto-alveolar fricatives. Metrically, the three feet are almost spondees. (1997: 69)

Harrison's infringement of decorum (O'Brien 1998: 61) often draws attention to the aural qualities of the poem and demands that the poem be read aloud. The "spondaic piledriver blows" (O'Brien 1998: 61) of "shored slack, crushed shale, smashed prop" (v. 12) constitute an onomatopoeic illustration of the mine caving-in but also confirm the fact that those lines "*exist* to be spoken" (O'Brien 1998: 61) and probably to be spoken in a full voice to express their "insistently physical" (O'Brien 1998: 61) and "bluntly concrete" (O'Brien 1998: 61) character. As the following example shows, the effort the poet makes to highlight the aural qualities of his verse plays an important role in constructing his rebellious poetic identity. In "Book Ends", Harrison proves that as much as a mine is a "battlefield," language is "a *place*[251] of struggle" (Kennedy 1996: 39).

---

248 "to find my slab behind the family dead" (v. 2).

249 "butcher, publican, and baker now me bard/ adding to their beef, beer and bread" (v. 3–4).

250 The fact is also noticed by Spencer who states that the third line of the first stanza is "irregular to the point of quantum difference from anything Gray would have countenanced or been capable of." (1994: 92).

251 Emphasis added by the author of this book. Harrison's resorts often to the usage of spatial metaphor when talking about language, speech or literature, see for example: "Them and [uz]". This method illustrates the poet`s conviction that there is a direct

you said you'd always be a clumsy talker

...

but not too clumsy that you can't still cut:

You're supposed to be the bright boy at description
and you can't tell them what the fuck to put! (Book Ends II, 7, 10–12)

An angry father scorning his son who cannot write an epitaph for his mother's gravestone, an image which echoes later in *v.* when the poet reads the Latin and Greek inscriptions on the graves of his parents, contains a rhyme which shows the tension between RP and dialect and demonstrates that the choice of words is a political act, a strategic move in the battle for power and control. If the reader pronounces the words "cut" and "put" in Received Pronunciation, he violates the requirements of traditional form (the poem is a sonnet) however, they rhyme when pronounced in dialect and the rigid form is preserved. Harrison shows how the barbarian speech can "occupy" the "vehicle of bourgeois culture," (Helie 2000: 170) the sonnet can only remain a sonnet in its traditional form if it is read in dialect. The "language of the oppressors [and] ... the language of the oppressed" (Helie 2000: 170) continuously collide since every instance of reading demands a conscious or unconscious (Helie 2000: 170) decision to choose between the two. One reason why the spoken language is of such concern to Harrison[252] is its characteristic "to be perpetually in a state of change," (Milroy and Milroy 2005: 47)which also means it is much more ephemeral and prone to suppression and extinction than written language (Milroy and Milroy 2005: 47). As Milroy and Milroy write:

> The most fully described and codified forms of language are those appropriate to public, formal and especially, written usage. One effect of this has been a neglect of the structure and social dynamic of spoken forms and hence a tendency (in the absence of adequate descriptions of speech) to evaluate spoken usage on the model of written usage. (Milroy and Milroy 2005: 47)

---

relationship between loosing one's language or freedom of expression and loosing one's land, becoming homeless. See: "National Trust": The dumb go down in history and disappear/ and not one gentleman's been brought to book:/ *Mes den hep tavas a-gollas y dyr/* (Cornish) – 'the tongueless man gets his land took' (National Trust 13–16).

252 The opposition between spoken and written form of language in Harrison's writing was mentioned in the second chapter of the book, other aspects of the issue should be brought to light here in order to explain the importance of the opposition in reference to the theme of revolt.

The seemingly weaker position of the spoken language resulting from its relatively poor description,[253] which reduced the possibility of its further codification (this is especially true in the case of colloquial English grammar), meant that it could not have formed an apt tool for enforcement of standardization (Milroy and Milroy 2005: 51). As mainly in "the writing system … a high degree of uniformity has been achieved … [t]he ideology of standardization has been less successfully applied to spoken language" (Milroy and Milroy 2005: 51), so in the opposition of written vs. spoken form, it is the latter that remains more "free," unbound, prone to variation and change (Milroy and Milroy 2005: 51) and, as it seems when we consider Harrison's approach to speech, it can become a successful language of revolt.

If Harrison uses dialect in his poems, because it is the private voice of his family and class he was born into, the question of "a praxis of voicing dialect" (Helie 2000: 164) must arise. This is directly related the phenomenon of poetry readings, whose place in working-class tradition has been discussed in Chapter II of the book. As Helie points out, voicing dialect means making the private voice take part in a creation of the "public discourse" (Helie 2000: 164) which in the case of Harrison's poetry becomes an act of revolt: an act proclaiming the "marginalized, indigenous voices" to be fit for the "public sphere"[254] (Helie 2000: 164). According to Helie poets like Harrison:[255]

> Even if they have internalised the depreciative discourse held against their place [i.e. North] in their childhood, … they offer, as mature poets, *private* versions of the North in order to respond to the *public* discourses … they can assert the centrality of *their* North in the national imagination. By using dialect they create a poetic space in which their voice stands for silenced voices. (Helie 2000: 165)

However, by reading aloud, becoming speakers in front of the public, they have continuously made the choice mentioned above: whether to read in the "northern accent or use Received Pronunciation" (Helie 2000: 164). The first, probably rather obvious, paradox which the choice to read in dialect entails is the fact that although RP is "elitist" and "prestigious" (Helie 2000: 164) whereas dialect is "a popular means of expression," (Helie 2000: 164) RP reaches a wider audience and in that sense it may be considered more "democratic" (Helie 2000: 164). The

253 According to Milroy and Milroy, this did not change until the 1960s (2005: 51).

254 An example of such a rebellious act could be the controversial televised reading of *v.* broadcast in channel Four.

255 In her article, Helie speaks of Ted Hughes, Basil Bunting and Tony Harrison as three poets who, although very different, share the preoccupation with their northern legacy and use northern dialect in their verse.

second paradox, which seems to be much more important in the context of *v.* and the theme of revolt, is connected with the situation in which Harrison found himself: he is a poet writing and reading his poems in dialect to an almost exclusively well-educated, middle-class audience. His protest against linguistic exclusion his "revenge," (Kennedy 1996: 39) not only "leaves the revenger as remote from those he loves as from his opponents" (O'Brien 1998: 52) but also governs an audience formed primarily out of the "enemies" (O'Brien 1998: 52). In *v.* the poet attempts to claim affiliation with the dead by establishing his working-class identity and furthermore, claims the right to speak in the name of the dispossessed as their successor. This claim is made explicit already in the first stanza, where the poetic "I" sets himself in the line with his working-class ancestors: "butcher, publican, and baker, now me bard/ adding poetry to their beef, beer and bread" (v. 3–4). According to Spencer the image of urban landscape is divided into two: the space below and the space above the ground confirms the act of belonging:

> *v.* opens with images of vertical and horizontal ancestry. On the vertical axis are the occupants of the cemetery poised above the empty galleries of a long disused pit. The narrator is positioned horizontally in relation to the community of decent people whose graves lie around him. Both planes converge in the image of the hypothetical, ultimate levelling down that will collapse the graveyard into the lowest worked-out seam of the mine. (1994: 93)

This implies the concept of identification and belonging, which becomes more and more evident as the poem develops. They can only be fully achieved in death, metaphorically rendered by ultimate levelling. Identification and belonging are reflected in the idea of unity, which is represented in the twenty-first stanza by the word "UNITED" (v. 84) graffitied on the grave stone.

> Though I don't believe in afterlife at all
> and know it's cheating it's hard *not* to make
> a sort of furtive prayer from the skin's scrawl
> ...
> and make the thoughtless spraying of his team
> apply to higher things and to the nation. (v. 125–127, 131–132)

All the "players" as Shakespeare would have it, the poet, his ancestors, the striking miners "are united in being equally subject to geological forces," (Spencer 1994: 98) just as the tombstones with Latin and graffitied verses are subject to gradual subsidence of the cemetery ground. Harrison takes a broader perspective and puts Beeston Hill cemetery in the context of geomorphologic history. Three million years ago, the primeval forests began to be converted into coal seams that lie beneath the graves (Spencer 1994: 98). The same will happen to the baker, to the bard, and to working-class youth vandalizing the burial ground. The poet in whom, by virtue of his profession, the place provokes the reflection of a universal issue, believes that the skin's "UNITED" (v. 84) may fade in time but the promise of unity in death that lies in wait underneath the graveyard is permanent. He looks at the language of anger inscribed into the landscape of the graveyard in the form of sprayed obscenities that cover the religious references and names of the dead generations, creating strange palimpsests, and he tries to understand the reasons behind the act of vandalism, "sympathize" (Byrne 1997: 72) with its authors:

> This graveyard stands above the worked out pit
> Subsidence makes the obelisks all list
> One leaning left's marked FUCK, one right's marked SHIT
> sprayed by some peeved supporter who was pissed.[256] (v. 29–32)

---

256 The scope of the book does not allow for a detailed analysis of the theme of football club rivalry, however, it seems important for the sake of understanding of the character of the skin, to stress the specific role of football in the cultural life of northern England and in the everyday life of working-class men. As Peter Davidson explains in the *The Idea of North* "Football and boxing were two legitimate means by which the working-class man of the 1930s could rise to a position of esteem, if not affluence" (2005: 203) Football is a recurring motif in visual arts and literature about the North (Davidson 2005: 203) and is one example of the "cultural artifacts," as Wales calls them, which form the public image of the entire region (2008: 29). A famous photo by Humphrey Spender, an artist whose images of Tyneside taken in 1938 influenced, according to Davidson, all "subsequent photographers of northern England" (2005: 202), is a good example of the embodiment of the football ethos inscribed in the identity of the northerner. The photograph, *Newcastle United Football Club Changing Rooms, Tyneside, 1938*, is essentially a static, tranquil image of a footballer, smoking a cigarette after the match has ended. According to Davidson:

> It is an essay in urban pastoral: a moment of stillness, even of mastery in which the quotidian is frozen into the appearance of high art. It is also a heroic image, monumental sculpture, expressing the sense in which—to the spectators who have been standing for two hours in the cold—the player is a heroic figure indeed …. It is a translation … into the terms of high art of the expectations and hopes that the figure of the footballer carries for the anonymous crowd who embody, for the duration of Saturday afternoon, the City. (2005: 203)

The image brings to mind a poem by Simon Armitage:

> In the freezing cold with both teams snorting
> like flogged horses, with captains and coaches
> effing and jeffing at backs and forwards,
> talking steam, screaming exhausting orders
> that's not breath coming from my bloke, it's smoke. (Goalkeeper with a Cigarette 27–31)

The football supporter is angry not only because of his team's defeat mentioned in the preceding lines. The subsiding landscape of the graveyard mirrors the declining condition of the Leeds working class, which lacks a solid basis for future existence. The *v.* sprayed on the tombstones stands for "versus," expressing rivalry between football teams but also for numerous strains in Leeds society[257] and culture that constantly clash leading to the disruption and deconstruction of the place. The poet is aware of the fact that the prospects for the citizens of Leeds are rather slim and this awareness consolidates his decision to take upon himself the role of representative, not only of his working-class ancestors but also of the working-class unemployed of 1984 England. The occupation of poetry foreshadowed in "Them and [uz]" is a means to fulfill this role by "taking up tenancy and ownership to make a better job, to restore what the buggers, the speakers of RP, have edited out or suppressed" (Kennedy 1996: 40). The echo of the "inky digits

---

The images depict fleeting moments and embody the impermanence of life, its smoke-like fragility, but also bring to life working-class everyday rituals like going to football matches and smoking, which made up the texture of northern culture. Cigarette smoke, associated here with the communal feeling of belonging ("my bloke") brings to mind the "smoke-whitened air" in paintings by Lowry and carries overtones of nostalgia of the time long gone. In Harrison's *v.* these memories which bring to life an image of the "heroic age of the working-class between the wars" (Davidson 2005: 204), meet head on with 1980s reality where football rivalry is associated with aggression and vandalism. The contrast between past and present, one of the "versuses of life," symbolically depicts the degradation of the culture of working-class England and adds to the elegiac tone of the poem.

257 class v. class as bitter as before
....
Hindu/Sikh, soul/body, heart v. mind,
East/West, male/female, and the ground
these fixtures are fought out on's Man, resigned
to hope from his future what his past never found. (v. 69, 73–76)

The "v" sign "can be associated with affirmation in solidarity in victory, the national unity embodied in war time by … Churchill … and Biblical and general abbreviation for 'verse.'" (O'Brien, 1998: 60). According to O'Brien, the fact that "so many significant social features and conflicts should congregate under the one-letter sign provides … and example of the polysemantic scope of language" (1998: 60) and creates a conception of universal interdependence. It is also important to notice that in British culture, within the sphere of body language, the "v" sign with the palm turned to the other means victory whereas the same sign made with a palm turned to oneself is an offensive gesture. This distinction can also be treated as a context for further analysis of the possible meanings of the sign in Harrison's text.

of defiance" metaphor comes back in line in which the poet admits: "This pen's all I have of a magic wand" (v. 121). It seems that the act of eloquence can in a miraculous way "give some higher meaning to […] the scrawl (v. 127)" intended as "a mere desecration" (v. 130) and raise them to the higher level above the grim reality of the worked-out pit and degenerated city.

But the poet's liberal stance meets with absolutely no respect from the side of the local character who appears suddenly and out of nowhere. The entrance of the skinhead interlocutor makes the estrangement of the poet distinctively clear and seriously undermines his attempt at identification with the revolutionary working class tradition. The "poet [is] denied" both "contiguity" (Kennedy 1996: 71) and continuity and consequently also the right to identify with the "working-class need … to affirm … collective existence" (Byrne 1997: 74). His knowledge of Latin and Greek works as a stigma that determines his exclusion. The skin who, belongs to a Leeds social reality into which the poet does not fit, directs his anger against the poet's sophisticated lexicon, treating it as a rejection of social and linguistic solidarity. And from the outflow of aggression, emerges the question of family loyalty and class betrayal:

> *So what's* a cri-de-coeur, *cunt? Can't you speak*
> *the language that yer mam spoke. Think of 'er!*
> *Can yer only get yer tongue round fucking Greek!*
> *Go and fuck yourself with* cri-de-coeur!
>
> 'She didn't talk like you do for a start!'
> I shouted, turning where I thought the voice had been.
> *She didn't understand yer fucking 'art'!*
> *She thought yer poetry obscene!*
> ….
> *Don't talk to me of fucking representing*
> *the class yer were born into any more*
> *Yer going to get' urt and start resenting*
> *It's not poetry we need in this class war.* (v. 165–172, 265–268)

The difference between the learned language and the Loiner is traditionally marked in the poem by the use of italic. This method, according to Hargreaves, creates the impression "that the language of dominance provides a context for words spoken by those who have gone under and are at the bottom of the social pile"[258]

258 Helie comments upon the use of italics in a broader context of the use of dialect: Harrison uses dialect not only as an antiquarian bent on preserving old forms of language but also as dissident intent on questioning the structure of power. The poems are like forums in which different voices can be heard, a phenomenon made

(Hargreaves 1995: 240). The skinhead conducts as Spencer puts it an, "anti-intellectual tirade directed against educated language" (1994: 95). However, it is difficult to dismiss his torrent of abuse as a product of a "lumpen-ploretarian" (1994: 95) mind since he is presented rather as "a tough-minded class warrior" (1994: 95) than an under-class racist. One may argue that he is both and as such he occupies an "uncomfortably problematical" position (Spencer 1994: 95) like the poet, who represents on one hand the power of eloquence employed to revolt in the name of those marginalized by the oppressive system and on the other the oppressive system itself. From the point of view of the skinhead, he is after all an embourgeoised (Spencer 1994: 95) working class member, who has compromised his class position for the benefits of education. This fact casts serious doubt on the possible success of his revolutionary poetic enterprise.

Byrne calls the skinhead an "effective concrete poet" who "sees his words made instantly manifest" (Byrne 1998: 55). Despite the fact they are vulgar they are sharp, fierce, pertinent, uncompromising.

> While the sprayed messages bring about no political change, they do succeed in leaving a permanent, or at least long-lasting, record of the skin's existence; they do succeed in recording the anger of working-class Leeds youths (if not its causes); they effect a change, in Harrison's attitude—as he chooses not to erase them. (Byrne 1998: 55)

The poet who is torn between ambivalent feelings of "outrage and relish for the skin's language" (Byrne 1998: 55) and at one point decides to enter the skin's linguistic territory and adopts his way of speaking: "Listen, cunt! I said" (v. 205). As Byrne concludes the skinhead's behaviour enrages the poet, "bringing out profanity (the skin beneath the skin) which reaffirms the common roots of the two personae" (Byrne 1997: 72). Nevertheless, the gulf between them widens and the poet tries to level with his interlocutor to demonstrate his solidarity with "the skinhead's sense of oppression" (Byrne 1998: 55) by recalling an "act of vandalism committed by [his] younger avatar" (Byrne 1998: 55). Angered by the hollow promises made by an MP, Hugh Gaitskell, and "wobbly soprano warbling" (v. 226) of Herman Darewski's band, the young poet resorts to aggression in a semi-sexual act of "ejaculating" (Byrne 1998: 54) over the crowd "with a fire extinguisher" (Byrne 1998: 54):

> And I hit the fire extinguisher ON knob
> and covered orchestra and audience with spray.

> clear by the typography: the voice of the working-class is inscribed in italics and there are many attempts at linguistic realism; the voice of the middle-class is quoted in inverted commas; the rest of the poem is the poet's own voice, torn between the other public voices. (2000: 160)

I could run as fast as you then. A good job!
They yelled 'damned vandal' after me that day. (v. 241–244)

The recurring attempts at identification are relevant in reference to the question of the "resistance identity" (Castells 2000: 7) of the speaker, who claims his loyalty to a particular, underprivileged social group but is being continuously rejected. What may appear surprising is that the sources of the skin's imagery seem to be similar to Harrison's and so his sneering could be taken for a distorted mirror image or "a parody of all that Harrison desires to convey in his poetic register" (Byrne 1998: 55). The skin, like the poet, refers to coal and mining "*'ave got about as much scope to aspire / above the shit they're dumped in, cunt, as coal / aspires to be chucked on t'fucking fire*" (v. 178–80), working-class occupational tradition "*Ah'll tell yer then what really riles a bloke. / It's reading on their graves the jobs they did- / butcher, publican and baker. Me, I'll croak / doing t'same nowt ah do as a kid.*" (v. 185–88) and the idea of writing public verse "*Yer've given yourself toffee, cunt. Who needs / yer fucking poufy words. Ah write mi own. / Ah've got mi work on show all over Leeds / like this UNITED' ere on some sod's stone*" (v. 269–72). The skin appropriates themes and language which he sees as rightfully and inherently his own and indirectly questions the poet's right to use "badges of manual labour" such as "grime, sweat, spittle, grease" as emblems of his "*working*-classness"[259] (Byrne 1998: 53) or to compare slaving at nuances (Social Mobility 3) of language to any working-class struggle. Harrison's attempt at identification is doomed to fail since the skinhead sees the poet as one of "them" not "us," which means that there can be no parallel between manual labour and poetic effort.[260] Poetry cannot be added (v. 4) to bread; baker and bard share no common ground. The right to revolt, seen here, as Castells would have it, as "a form and origin … of identity building" (2000: 7), is being constantly undermined by the question of betrayal and so the poet becomes the man of conflicting interest, one of the ambivalent heroes which populate Harrison's verse.

The conflict between poet and the skin which evokes an important question of the poet's right to inherit and use in his poetic enterprise working-class tropes, themes, histories,[261] is essentially the conflict between two kinds of revolt: poetic revolt and "*class war*" (v. 268) underpinned by the idea of aggression and physical

259 Harrison often compares writing to physical labour, referring to indications of physical exhaustion and to dirt which accompany manual work, despite the fact that he recalls the time where they "offended his fastidiousness" (Byrne 1997: 53) see "Currents I" and "Still".

260 See for example "Social Mobility".

261 The question of inheritance has been discussed in Chapter III.

violence. This conflict manifests itself in the poem primarily through language: the language of aggression (symbolized by the sprayed obscenities) collides and interacts with the languages of so-called "high culture" (symbolized by the Latin engravings). It is important to stress the fact that the skin voices resentment and rejection in a working-class dialect, and so the conflict between two kinds of revolt can be also seen as the conflict between dialect and the language of eloquence which become different tools of revolutionary action. To understand the nature of this conflict, it is necessary to refer to the working-class experience, since the skin/skald confrontation is deeply grounded in the social context and the reality of working class existence. The conflict between two kinds of language can be seen as an instance of a broader concept of the so-called "Pygmalion" narrative (or trope) (Wales 2008: 142) which is reflected in the phenomenon of crossing the 'boundary' between classes "by going to grammar school, or leaving North [for] … personal betterment and higher social status" (Wales 2008: 142). This process had great influence on Northern discourses and became a source of recurring themes in Northern literature[262]. As Wales states, issues of language were central to it:

> In changing status, school-educated or self educated Northerners have had to face the prospect of crossing particular sociolinguistic and also psycholinguistic boundaries in addition to the dialectal in order to meet the expected norms of the "Received Standard" and "Received Pronunciation". In anthropological terms this can be seen as a "rite of passage", a movement from one role or stage of life to another, with not only associated "rituals," but psychological states of tension, anxiety and friction and feeling of being in social limbo: also termed generally as liminality (Martin 1981: 50 following Turner 1967). As its Latin root suggest, is the stage or state of being "on the threshold," between clear social identities, "between two worlds" as academic Richard Hoggart … describes it, born in Leeds in 1918 and raised, an orphan, in a working-class household. (2008: 143)

The "seminal moment of transition to grammar school in the 1940s when … [the poet] became conscious of the schism between his own dialect and the written word" (Wales 2008: 147) became a theme of many poems of *The School of Eloquence* such as "Them and [uz]" or "Me Tarzan". Other poems such as *v.* and "Wordlists" describe the consequences of the act of transition which influence the adult Harrison, who feels he loses the ability to speak in dialect: "the tongue that once I used to know / but can't bone it up on now, and that's mi mam's" (Wordlists

262 It should be noted that "the majority of these discourses have been [produced] by male writers, and the majority of these journeys themselves [made] by men … opportunities for women were severely limited until well into the twentieth century (outside domestic service or the music hall) and aspirations traditionally less highly held" (Wales 2008: 142).

15–16). His skinhead alter-ego accuses the poet of abandoning the "the solidarity and rituals of *communitas*" (Wales 2008: 143) by changing his speech habits, and represents the common *resentment* (Wales 2008: 143) of working-class people felt towards those speaking "posh" or "la-di-la," those who sounded "throssen up" or "knack" (Wales 2008: 143). The poet "acquired Standard English through education" (Helie 2000: 169) but decided to return to his "own tongue" (Kennedy 1996: 41), "*the language*" his "*mam spoke*" (v. 166), and this, as Kennedy puts it, "becomes a revolutionary act in an unresolved, never-ending struggle … a linguistic luta continua" (1996: 41). Difficulties lie in the nature of the external context, in the lack of social acceptance but also in the nature of the internal conflict:

> For if Harrison's project is to "occupy" or inhabit various discourses or voices then he is equally, occupied or inhabited by them … individual's relation to and position in culture is always precarious, always renegotiable. … Language is simultaneously the place in which one's status is located and the means by which it is constantly being redefined, brutally or subtly upgraded or downgraded. To appropriate may also involve being appropriated. … Harrison's own identity and status are a continuing process of adaptation. (Kennedy 1996: 41)

As O'Brien writes, "the skinhead is the poet's other half … the one who did not get away, who can't tell Greek from French, whose fury rejects the evasions of poetry" (1998: 63). Looking at the poet versus the skin we catch a glimpse of who Harrison is and who he might have been if he had chosen to stay in Leeds. After all, the poet can identify with such working-class members as Edwin Waugh (1817–1890), Thomas Wilson (1773–1858) and others who chose to try their luck in the London entertainment business or taught themselves to read and left to become teachers, printers or booksellers[263] (Wales 2008: 141). The skin is a descendant of those who remained in the North and his character is constructed (Roberts 2007: 164) from familiar motifs such as "football," "lager," "obscenity," and "vandalism," stereotypically associated with the working-class gone under. On one level he embodies a clichéd representation of the region which is recognized in the social consciousness by, as Wales puts it, "metonyms of the North and Northerners," including "poverty, factories, football—to which are opposed mental images of the

263 Leaving the North has a long tradition in the history of the working-classes: "Escaping the mine or factory by becoming a professional singer or entertainer was certainly a common way from the nineteenth century onwards" (Wales 2008: 141). Harrison refers to this part of working-class experience in one of his poems: "For the kids who never made it through the school / the Northern working-class escaped the grind / as boxers or comedians, or won the pools" (Punchline 2–4).

South—the bowler hat, the thatched cottage, cricket" (2008: 28–31). Assuming that the skin/skald conflict is internalized, the skinhead represents this part of the poetic identity of the speaker, which stands for the North seen by the Southerners as provincial, "idiotic brother" but also dangerous and unpredictable, "radical Other" (Helie 2000: 162).

> He took the can, contemptuous, unhurried
> ...
> He aerosolled his name. And it was mine.
> ....
> Half versus half, the enemies within
> the heart that can't be whole till they unite. (v. 277, 280, 285–286)

The internalized conflict analyzed above reveals the complicated nature of revolt as described in the poem under discussion and points to the important role which revolutionary attitude plays in the construction of the liminal identity of the poetic "I" in Harrison's verse. Although they seem mutually exclusive, both attitudes, those of the skin and of the skald, are necessary to forge the creative tension which maintains the continuity of poetic enterprise. Eloquence and anger do not exclude each other, similarly to delight and horror which just like "blossoms and dangerous political bullshit ... exist in us all" (Harrison 2009: 12). Revolt is not merely a matter of choice for Harrison, it is a necessity, an attitude inherent in the nature of a poet since as Brecht writes:

> Inside me contend
> Delight at the apple tree in blossom
> And horror at the house-painter's speaches.
> But only the second
> Drives me to my desk. (Bad Time for Poetry 17–21)

The belief that a poet's anger is as important for his/her poetry as the tender emotions and delightful experiences is unquestionably a source of the strength and diversity of Harrison's verse, which can be delicate and careful but also abrasive and militant (Harrison 2009: 11). Nevertheless, it is a belief which proves risky especially in the light of Merton's theory for which *rebellion* and *ressentiment* are two sides of the same coin. In *v.* the process of social stigmatization is reversed: in the skin/skald conflict, it is the skin, the seeming underdog, the victim of the abusive system who denies the poet the freedom of speech. And it is the skin who reminds the poet of the possibility to fall into the trap of *ressentiment* which is often born out of social injustice. The question of the fine line between revolutionary attitude and the one of hate and hostility lures in between the lines and is never finally answered. The poem makes it clear that it is as hard to judge when rebellion becomes a riot as to determine when the act of representation of the suppressed becomes patronizing and consequently offensive to those represented. Nevertheless those dangers should not, says Harrison, stop poets from writing, they should press on with the "fury of … [their] polemic" (Harrison 2009: 9) even if what they write may stir up anger among the public, cause offence, even at the risk that the "laser-focused rage" may become, according to some, "detrimental to … [their] verse" (Harrison 2009: 9). The task of the poet is not to write likeable poetry but to write poetry which does not shrink from danger, which does not fall silent in an act of avoidance of dark or controversial topics. In his PEN/Pinter Prize Lecture Harrison "summons" the true revolutionaries, the poets "persecuted, silenced, killed in previous centuries and in our own" (Harrison 2009: 20). One of them is Geo Milev, a Bulgarian poet brutally murdered by the police in 1925. After his body was burned, all that was left of him was the blue glass eye, which becomes a symbolic image of vigilance in the poem by Yannis Ritsos, whose words quoted by Harrison serve as a metaphorical image of revolutionary poetic attitude:

> His eye is being kept in the Museum of Revolution
> like seeing stone of the struggle. I saw his eye.
> In his pupil there was the full story of the Revolution, blue scenes
> of blood-stained years
> blue scenes with red flags
> with dead who carry in their raised hands a blue day.
> His eyes never closes,
> this eye keeps vigil over Sofia.
> This eye sees, illuminates and judges.
> Whoever looks at this eye wins back his eyes.
> Whoever looks at this eye sees the world. (Ritsos qtd in Harrison 2009: 20)

In the heart of poetic revolt lies the "unswerving and unflinching gaze" (Harrison 2009: 20) and the subsequent creative effort, constant "shuffling through the pages" which gives the poet an inky digit. The metaphor of the inky digit of defiance referred to in the preface to this chapter echoes the famous Shakespearian image of an "artificer 'branned' in the very process of working with the caustic materials of his trade"[264] (Valbuena 339). Harrison's poetic identity is of a "dyer who works in ink" (Valbuena 339), his inky digits which remain "indelibly stained … will always mean he has cast his vote in favour of the dumb or the silenced being given a voice, of totally free speech" (Harrison 2009: 20–30).

---

264 Thence comes it that my name receives a brand,
And almost thence my nature is subdued
To what it works in, like the dyer's hand. (Sonnet 111, 5–7)

Chapter Five
"This frightening mask"

Continuity of Poetic Gaze in Selected War Poems

In her lecture "Precarious Life and the Obligations of Cohabitation" delivered in May 2011 at the Nobel Museum in Stockholm, Judith Butler discussed the problem of ethical response to suffering and the special role of images and accounts of war, which are imposed upon the viewer/reader "from the outside, from elsewhere, from the life of others" (Butler 2011: 3), sometimes as an "imposition," "without ... consent" (Butler 2011: 2), and that constitute a "particular form of ethical solicitation" (Butler 2011: 3). Butler puts forward the thesis that "ethical demands that emerge through the global circuits" in today's world of polyphonic communication "depend on the reversibility of the proximity and distance" (Butler 2011: 4) and further widens the scope of possible analysis, suggesting that "*certain bonds are actually wrought through this reversibility*" (Butler 2011: 4). To "register an ethical demand ... that is reducible neither to consent nor to established agreement and takes place outside of established community bonds" (Butler 2011: 5) she refers to Arendt and Levinas, whose theories treat complicated relations of "ethics, proximity, and distance" (Butler 2011: 5). In the case of the latter it is the frequently discussed (Butler 2004: 131) notion of the "face" of the Other, the one different from the "self," that proves to be particularly interesting in the context of Harrison's poetry. The notion of the "face" developed by Levinas and analyzed by Butler in the abovementioned lecture, and in her acclaimed book *Precarious Life: The Powers of Mourning and Violence*, is multilayered and complicated. On the linguistic level, it is already possible to notice that associations with what in English is called "face" are numerous and must differ considerably from culture to culture:

> Let us take the language Levinas spoke. The French word *visage*, like the German *Gesicht*, refers to seeing and being seen. The Hebrew expression *panim*, not unlike German *Angesicht* or *Antlitz*, emphasizes the face facing us or our mutual facing. The Russian term *lico* means face, cheek, but also person, similar to the Greek *prosopon* which literally refers to the act of 'looking at' and which stands not only for the face but also for masks and roles, rendered in Latin by *persona*. In general, we may distinguish a narrow, rather common view from a wider more emphatic meaning. (Waldenfels 2004: 64)

It seems necessary to consider the fact that from Levinas's perspective, the face of the Other is not simply what "it seems to be, and it is much more than that," since it introduces "the hungering, thirsting, enjoying, suffering, working, loving, murdering human being in all its corporeality" and otherness (Waldenfels 2004: 64). Butler begins her discussion of the issue by connecting the notion of the "face" with the problem of the proximity/distance anithesis:

> There are two dissonant dimensions of Levinas's ethical philosophy. On the one hand, there is the importance of the category of proximity.... Indeed, it seems that the ways that others act upon us, without our will, constitutes the occasion of an ethical appeal or solicitation. This means we are acted upon and solicitated prior to any clear sense of choice. To be impinged upon another assumes a bodily proximity ... we are to some extend affected and claimed by the "face" that acts upon us .... On the other hand, our ethical obligations extend to those who are not proximate. (Butler 2011: 6)

The "face," as Butler points out, makes an ethical claim upon us but not "because of its sameness," not because there are any similarities between the Self and the Other; actually, "Levinas insisted we are bound to those we don't know" and those who do not share with as a given community, nationality or culture (Butler 2011: 7) and so are distant even though they may live in considerable spatial proximity. This is the condition of every self, to be "born into this situation of being compelled to honour the life of the other ... whose claim on life comes before our own" (Butler 2011: 7). It should be noted that, as Butler says, the face in Levinas' interpretation "conveys the commandment without necessarily speaking it" (Butler 2004: 133). Levinas writes:

> The approach to the face is the most basic mode of responsibility ... the face is not in front of me (en face de moi), but above me; it is the other before death, looking through and exposing death. Secondly, the face is the other who asks me not to let him die alone as if to do so were to become an accomplice of death. Thus the face says to me: you shall not kill .... My ethical relation of love for the other stems from the fact that the self cannot survive by itself alone, cannot find meaning within its own being-in-the world (1986: 22–23).

Consequently, the face cannot be understood strictly as a mouth or reduced to the mouth (Butler 2004: 133). To explain the idea that the "face" is "not exclusively a human *face*"[265] Butler refers to (2004: 133) Vassili Grossman's *Life and Fate*, evoked by Levinas in "Peace and Proximity." Levinas comments on Grossman's image in the following fragment:

> [T]he story ... of the families, wives, and parents of political detainees travelling to Lubyanka in Moscow for the latest news. A line is formed at the counter, a line where one can see only the backs of others. A woman awaits her turn: [She] had never thought

265 Emphasis added by the author of this book.

> that the human back could be so expressive, and could convey states of mind in such a penetrating way. Persons approaching the counter had a particular way of craning their neck and their back, they seemed to cry, sob, and scream. (1996: 167)

According to Butler, the face in Grossman's imagery functions as a catachresis: it "describes the human back, the craning of the neck, the rising of the shoulder blades like 'springs'" (Butler 2004: 133). Various parts of the body are then said to utter a cry as if they were a mouth. Waldenfels associates it with the way the face expresses the Other. "The otherness," writes Waldenfels, "does not lie behind the surface of somebody we see, hear, touch or violate.... It is the other as such and not some aspect of him or her that is condensed in the face" (2004: 65). And consequently "the whole body expresses, our hands and shoulders do it as well as our face taken in its narrow sense"[266] (Waldenfels 2004: 65). Returning to Butler's comment on Grossman's work, the face according to Butler is conceptualized here as "a series of displacements" (2004: 133) and then in turn, figured as a "scene of agonizing vocalization" (2004: 133); the utterance brought to the Self by the face of the Other is "the utterance which is not, strictly speaking, linguistic," it is the figure for "what cannot be named" (Butler 2004: 133), or as Anne Whitehead puts it, "a figure for something else" which "makes visible a cry of human suffering that cannot be directly represented" (2005: 369). According to Butler, it seems that this "wordless vocalisation of suffering that marks the limits of linguistic translation" (Butler 2004: 133) evoked by the catachresis of "face as back" may lead to an assumption that "the face, if we are to put words to its meaning will be that for which no words really work" (Butler 2004: 133). It is true that Levinas comments upon the face, in an apparent act of seeming

---

266 Waldenfels discusses the two basic meanings of the word "face":

> In general we can distinguish a narrow, rather common meaning, from a wider, more emphatic meaning. To the ordinary meaning belongs the frontal view, the face-to face or even the facade of a building. The face itself constitutes the central zone of the body where our eyes and our mouth are located and the play of features takes place. We cannot close our face as we close our eyes, we can only protect it by visible or invisible masks. The emphatic sense of the word comes forth when a face is understood not simply as something present, but as the other's corporeal self-presence, performed by the gaze or appeal we are exposed to. What we call 'face' is culturally overdetermined, marked by certain aesthetic, moral and sacred features. We are living in the face of the other, seeking or fleeting it, running the risk of losing our own face. In connection with our body the face is subjected to... face restoring and face making ... At the same time the face plays its part in acts of facing another, performed on the stage of life. (2004: 64–65)

explanation, though he does not tell the reader what the face actually *is*[267]. He talks of "The face as the extreme precariousness of the other" (Levinas 1996: 167). Butler further develops this thought, suggesting that "to respond to the 'face', to understand its meaning, means to be alert to what is precarious[268] in another life" (2004: 134). In many of his poems, Harrison is concerned with the following question: In what ways is the self connected to the Other and what are the possibilities of identification or perhaps communication with the Other in the face of various raptures and "versuses" which remain between the two? Butler suggests that the relationship is actually inherent to the human condition and in a way precedes social bonds, so it exists above (although stays very closely related to) the level of class relations, territorial co-habitation or nationality:

> I want to insist upon a certain intertwinement between that other life, all those other lives, and my own—one that is irreducible to national belonging or communitarian affiliation. In my view (which is surely not mine alone) the life of the other, the life that is not our own, is also our life, since whatever sense "our" life has is derived precisely from this sociality, this being already, and from the start, dependent on a world of others ... we are, however distinct, also bound to one another. And this is not always happy or felicitous experience. To find that one's life is also the life of others, even as this life is distinct, means that one's boundary is at once a limit and a site of adjacency, a mode of spatial and temporal nearness or even boundedness. (Butler 2011: 9)

A similar idea is formulated by Wenger who, as Ming Lim suggests, "engages the Other in a mutual exchange of experience and identity" (Lim 2007: 255) which is unavoidable, which means that the self is inextricably linked with the Other and consequently that identity is to large extent constructed through the constant interaction with the Other:

> And so, identity is incomplete. It requires the approach of the Other but also my active participation in the Other's identity-structure. Participation desires reification. Reification does not simply mean giving thingness to abstraction; it also refers, in Wenger's

267 According to Waldenfels, who speaks about Levinas' notion of the face, "we are able to say only what ... [the face] is not ... the list of negations is long and sometimes tiresome" as it seems capable of an ongoing expansion. "We are told" Waldenfels continues "that the face is not something we can see or touch, while moving within open horizons ... it has no plastic form to be transformed in images; it has no eidos, no 'adequate idea' by which we could represent and grasp it .... 'the face speaks'" (2004: 66–67).

268 For a detailed discussion on the issue of precariousness of the Other see Butler's book entitled *Precarious Life: The Powers of Mourning and Violence*. London and New York: Verso, 2004: 128–151.

> terms, to a process of naming, encoding, describing, interpreting and so on—in other words it is a form of language, a language in, and of, the world of lived relations. It is the interplay of participation and 'reification' that makes up identity. (Lim 2007: 255)

What is important for Wenger, and what can be seen in Harrison's verse, is the belief that identity is essentially a historical construction—it is a process written into the "history of practices" developed by the Self engaging with others (Lim 2007: 256). There is a possibility to engage in a dialogue with the Other in the "dynamic nexus of difference—without—violence" relations since one can make a choice, hence a conscious decision, as Lim asserts, to "reconcile, displace or overshadow divergent ... meanings without necessarily restricting the Other's freedom," (Lim 2007: 255). Although in Wenger's work, discussed by Lim, this idea is developed around the issue of learning practices, its core, the "complementarity between Self and Other" (Lim 2007: 255) remains a very interesting point of reference in the context of Harrison's poems, which discuss, among other things, different dimensions of the complementarity between opposites and the problem of divided, ambiguous identity in which the Self and the Other remain in constant, sometimes turbulent, interplay. One of the questions that the following chapter attempts to answer, concentrating chiefly upon three more recent poems by Harrison, namely, "A Cold Coming," "Cornet and Cartridge" and "Shrapnel," closely follows Butler's inquiry: How does the fact that "we are solicited by images of distant suffering in ways that compel our concern and move us to .... voice our objection" (Butler 2011: 2) influence the role of a poet and particularly the poet who has chosen "public poetry"[269] as his craft? If he/she "registers ... resistance to

269 It is important to stress the fact that the abovementioned activity of writing, "public poetry" can be discussed in reference to the emblem of the mask which covers/ replaces/ becomes a face. Both (i.e. the idea of public poetry and the emblem of the mask) can be found in the context of Greek theatre, which made a specific use of the mask and which, according to Harrison, was inherently public, that is, entailed reciprocity born out of the unifying nature of the place itself. Harrison explains his interest in the Greek tradition as follows:

> I think that the move for me towards public poetry came from some of the dilemmas I had when having left a working-class background and started learning Latin and Greek at grammar school, I wanted to write a poetry which did some kind of honour to what I was learning, but also would reach people like my parents, and use what I think of as a common language. And it seemed to me that the common language was used in the theatre. It has to be in the theatre, the common bond of the theatre, especially in Greek theatre where the audience and the actor where lit by the common light of the sun, that this was ideal conditions to create a common language. And, so that out of that need I think, I was moved

violence through concrete … means" (Butler 2011: 2) available to him/her, that is, through writing, how does this fact pertain to his/her poetic identity and what form can his/her ethical response to suffering take in the face of the words uttered by George Steiner and Theodor Adorno? Their statements echo in some of Harrison's lines, which seem to express similar doubt in the force of the poetic enterprise, announcing its perhaps slow but unavoidable twilight:

> In the Theogony Hesiod describes the flow of sweetness of the Muses as 'inexhaustible' but nearer our time Byron called the Muses 'the weary nine' and Keats had looked to Helicon and found that: … all is dark / Around thine aged top … [Endymion] 'The sun of poetry is set' he said … how much wearier the Nine will be … in the latter end of the twentieth century, how much darker the summit of the Muses' haunt. This weariness of the nine, this erosion of affirmative spirit … this darkness, this *nephos* on Helicon has been made darker by two World Wars, the terrors of Nazism in fearful conflagrations unleashed on Hiroshima and Nagasaki in 1945. (Harrison 1991: 435)

In "The Inkwell of Dr Agrippa" Harrison recalls Pablo Neruda's story about two boys who develop a silent way of communication (Harrison 1991: 32):

> One time, investigating in the backyard of our house in Temuco the tiny objects and minuscule beings of my world, I came upon a hole in one of the boards of the fence. I looked through the hole and saw a landscape like that behind our house, uncared for, and wild. I moved back a few steps, because I sensed vaguely that something was about to happen. All of a sudden a hand appeared, a tiny hand of a boy about my own age. By the time I came close again, the hand was gone, and in its place there was a marvelous white sheep. The sheep's wool was faded. Its wheels had escaped. All of this only made it more authentic. I had never seen such a wonderful sheep. I looked back through the hole but the boy had disappeared. I went into the house and brought out a treasure of my own: a pinecone, opened, full of odor and resin, which I adored. I set it down in the same spot and went off with the sheep. (Neruda 1993: 339–40)

Neruda was driven to poetry by "exchange"[270] and "silence"[271] and so was Harrison. Although "blessing" (Rylance 1997: 135), the other word Rick Rylance uses to denote that which triggered in both authors the need to write, is perhaps not the word Harrison would use to describe his writing experience, he can at least partly relate to Neruda's reflection upon the source of poetic inspiration:

---

into theatre, and in the theatre I was able to find a language which I hope would address more than the kind of people I found read poetry and books. (Harrison interviewed by John Tusa)

270 See for example: "Fire-Eater".

271 See for example: "Heredity".

> When I search my childhood for something to explain what drove me to poetry, something like Pablo Neruda's story of the silent exchange of a toy lamb and a pine cone through a hole in the fence I can think of nothing so significantly beautiful, but there are things which brought me … the same precious idea 'that affection that comes here from those unknown to us who are watching over our sleep and solitude … widens out the boundaries of our being and unites all living things!' My images are all to do with the War. (Harrison 1991: 32)

Rick Rylance is intrigued by "the sudden transition from the Wordsworthian register, which cradles the quotation from Neruda, to the abrupt sentence which announces memories of war" (1997: 136). Harrison's recollections of the earliest memories which come back in his poems are similarly constructed. They combine the familiar and commonplace with the political and violent and so they resemble the above-quoted passage where the image of intimacy, the silent exchange between children, co-exists with the image of war, "alluring neighbourliness" (Rylance 1997: 139) stands side by side with atrocity and extermination. Harrison writes:

> One of my earliest memories is of bombs falling … myself and my mother crouching in the cellar, me begging to be allowed to rush out into the lit-up streets, the whistlings sounded so festive. The next morning I found the overgrown tennis courts in the local park pitted with bomb craters…. Another is the contact I had with German prisoners of war in a work party near our street. I remember only children talked to them much …. Another is a street party with a bonfire …. As I grew up …. I came to realise that the cause of celebration was Hiroshima. Another is the dazed feeling of being led by the hand from the cinema into the sunlit City Square after seeing films of Belsen 1945. (Harrison 1991: 32)

For Neruda, the exchange brought home an assertion "that all of humanity is somehow together" and made him think of writing as a form of communication with those remaining "elsewhere" (Butler 2011: 3). His story which has "at one level … alluring neighbourliness" but at another level evokes feelings of strangeness and mystery (Rylance 1997: 139) is essentially a story about an exchange of a gift which remained inside the poet as a source of inspiration and poetic drive. The image of children exchanging objects entails, like the images recalled and poetically retold by Harrison, an interplay of distance and proximity, different from but akin to the one described by Judith Butler. This interplay allows the Other in. The Other may be remote in space or remote by being unknown, benign or angry, sometimes betrayed, sometimes suffering, but always distant and close at the same time. Present in Harrison's earlier poetry, the interplay of distance and proximity assumes numerous forms in his more recent poems, which can be ambiguous and sometimes deeply disturbing. The closeness and remoteness of the Other's face—which may be unveiled or hidden from the poetic "I" like the face of Neruda's young interlocutor presses upon the poet a demand to persistently look for words, evokes in him "the need to speak beyond the fence" (Rylance 1997: 139).

A powerful example of a poem which describes a face-to-face encounter with the Other is Harrison's "A Cold Coming" printed on 14 February 2003[272] in *The Guardian*, which devoted sixteen pages of its special edition (edited by Don McCullin) to photographic images of the 1991 Gulf War. Harrison's poem appeared next to Kenneth Jarecke's famous photograph of an Iraqi soldier whose charred body remains in a sitting position inside a vehicle burned on the Basra road. As Whitehead notes, "the image was widely suppressed in the USA, and in Britain it appeared only in the Observer on Sunday 10 March 1991," (2005: 349) the reason being its upsetting content but also its anti-war character:

> [It] clearly demolished the propaganda that this was a 'clean' and 'bloodless' war. It showed the death of an Iraqi soldier incinerated in his truck ... He was one of thousands of Iraqi troops who were bombed from the air by the allies as they fled north from Kuwait city, on foot or in tanks, armoured vehicles and trucks, at the end of the war. This slaughter, notoriously described by one American officer as a 'turkey shoot', took place on 27 February 1991. (Whitehead 2005: 349)

McCullin comments in a special edition of *The Guardian* on the type of images promoted by the US government, which gave mainly an aerial view of events, an impression of a casualty free techno-war, which cannot touch the viewer directly as it is distant and abstract, devoid of the bodies of the dead, reducible to "light traces from missiles and shells" and an occasional parade "of military hardware" (Whitehead 2005: 350). He considers it an obligation of a war photographer to "see and tell" as it is his/her "job to show some of that horror, to say: this is the real war, this is what it's like on the ground, this is what war does to you." (qtd in Whitehead 2005: 350) or to use Sontag's words, to show that "war tears, rends ... rips open, eviscerates ... scorches ... dismembers ... ruins" (Sontag 2004: 7). Jarecke's photograph fulfils this obligation, positions the viewer face to face with the horror of war, with the aftermath of ultimate violence. The photograph was reprinted in 2003 in a book titled *The Eye of War* edited by Philip Knightley, Sarah Jackson and Annabel Merullo, where it is accompanied by a short commentary by Jarecke, who focuses on the life vs. death dichotomy, and the thin line which separates both. His words prove to be interesting in the context of Harrison's poem,

---

272 The poem was first published on the main editorial pages of the Guardian on 5 and 18 March 1991 together with "initial Illumination"—both poems where comissioned by the newspaper (Whitehead 2005: 349).

which essentially animates the charred corpse of the soldier. It seems that by giving voice to the Iraqi, the poet responds to the quality of the picture commented upon by the photographer:

> I'd seen a couple of casualties here and there in Kuwait but the first serious bodies were on Highway 8 .... This picture has become well known, but I didn't think it was just one of many photographs there. I think the reason it stands out is that *you can imagine the driver alive*[273] .... He is fighting to get out of his burning vehicle, and anyone looking at the photograph can understand *how powerful the desire to live is.*[274] (Jarecke qtd in Knightley 2003: 150)

An article by McCullin published together with the Cold War photographs may suggest, as Whitehead writes, that photographs like Jarecke's which make "atrocity ... visible," which shorten the distance between the Self and the suffering Others are also "straightforwardly readable," (Whitehead 2005: 351) i.e. they are a voice of protest, they speak for the those who can no longer speak, "for the Iraqis incinerated in the American ambush on the Basra road" (McCullin qtd in Whitehead 2005: 351). John Berger[275] and Susan Sontag put this assumption into question and suggest that the image captured by the eye of the camera may be interpreted in numerous ways by the viewer. Berger warns against a possible depoliticization (Berger 2009: 44) of war, caused by images depicting "moments of agony" (Berger 2009: 43) which may universalize violence and veil reality. It should be always remembered that "wars we are being shown are being fought directly or indirectly in 'our' name" (Berger 2009: 45). Sontag focuses on the way in which the identity of the victims, often revealed by the caption, affects the way photographs will be construed:

> To the militant, identity is everything. And all photographs wait to be explained or falsified by their captions. During the fighting between Serbs and Croats at the beginning of the recent Balkan wars, the same photographs of children killed in the shelling of a village were passed around at both Serb and Croat propaganda briefings. Alter the caption,

---

273 Emphasis added by the author of this book. Compare with the following lines: "Though fire has flayed off half my features / they once were like my fellow creatures'". (A Cold Coming 101–102)

274 Emphasis added by the author of this book. Compare with the following lines: "He heard my thoughts and stopped the spool: / 'I never thought life futile, fool! / Though all Hell began to drop / I never wanted life to stop. / I was filled with such a yearning / to stay in life as I was burning." (A Cold Coming 85–90)

275 For Berger's discussion of this subject see: John Berger 'Photographs of Agony', in *About Looking*. London: Bloomsbury, 2009. pp. 41–44.

and the children's deaths could be used and reused.... Photographs of an atrocity may give rise to opposing responses. A call for peace. A cry for revenge. (Sontag 2004: 9)

Both Berger and Sontag stress that the act of the viewer looking at the photograph is essentially equivalent to looking at a reality filtered through someone else's gaze, or as Jerzy Jarniewicz describes it: "we are observing an observation" 'patrzymy na patrzenie' (Jarniewicz 2011: 156). Additionally, a photograph "is always an image that someone chose, to photograph is to frame and to frame is to exclude" (Sontag 2004: 41).

Whitehead proposes that "Harrison's poem can be read as an extended 'caption,' which suggests that the meaning of the photograph is not self evident; although the poem may also have a life away from the image in Harrison's publications, the photograph nevertheless remains its referent." (Whitehead 2005: 352). If the poem is to be understood as an extended caption, it may perform a similar function to the one performed by captions of Goya's famous sequence of etchings *The Disasters of War* which "depicts the atrocities perpetrated by Napoleon's soldiers who invaded Spain in 1808 to quell the insurrection against French rule" (Sontag 2004: 39). The captions are added to authenticate presented situations; after all, they are handmade images always considered to be less believable than photographs but this is not their only role (Sontag 2004: 41). As Sontag explains:

While the image like every other image is an invitation to look, the caption ... insists on the difficulty of doing just that. A voice, presumably the artist's, badgers the viewer: Can you bear to look at this? One caption declares: One can't look ... Another says: This is bad ... Another retorts: This is worse ... Another declaims: Barbarians! ... What madness!, cries another. And another: This is too much! (Sontag 2004: 40)

It is important to stress that Harrison does not deny the fact that as an author of "A Cold Coming" he was inspired by a photograph (the poem was published next to the image), that he did not see the corpse "live" and that consequently, he is like an average newspaper reader to whom the suffering of the Other comes mediated through someone else's gaze. However, the speaker of the poem actually meets the corpse of the Iraqi, and the fact that he is asked to face the horror of the mutilated body directly in a face to face confrontation is stressed several times: "So I held the microphone / closer to the crumbling bone /.... / Don't look away! I know it's hard / to keep regarding one so charred, /..../ I gazed at him and he gazed back" (A Cold Coming 19–20, 97–98, 165). And so if the poem is to be read as an extended caption, its message will be similar to the message sent by Goya's commentary: the atrocities of war are so dreadful it is difficult to fix one's gaze upon them. The question the poem asks is whether one has a right or perhaps even an obligation to look or whether one should turn one's head away as the poet/journalist at one point tries to do? According to Sontag it is possible that "the only people with the right to look at the images of suffering of the extreme order are those who could do something to alleviate it … the rest of us are *voyeurs*, whether or not we mean to be" (Sontag 2004: 38). An interesting context for this problem, i.e., of a supposed voyeurism, can be supplied here by a reference to Jarniewicz's analysis on Heaney's work. Jarniewicz comments on Seamus Heaney's bog poems which, like Harrison's "A Cold Coming," were written in response to a photographic image, more precisely, they were inspired by a series of photographs published in an archaeological study of the bog bodies written in 1971 by P. V. Glob, titled *The Bog People: Iron Age Man Preserved*. Jarniewicz stresses that Heaney is essentially looking at a mediated image of agony, an interpretation of death (Jarniewicz 2011: 154).

The photographed bodies of ritually murdered victims are not only already explained and invested with historical and cultural significance, but are also frozen in time, like the figures carved on the Keatsian urn, untouched by temporal change. They "turn into a one-dimensional and immutable being" 'zamieniają się w byt jednowymiarowy i niezmienny' Jarniewicz states and stand in contrast to reality which is "open, changing and which cannot be unambiguously defined" 'otwartą zmienną i niepoddającą się jednoznacznej definicji rzeczywistością' (Jarniewicz 2011: 155). John Berger develops this issue, stressing the unique character of the "sudden moments of agony" which do not follow a linear time pattern, do not fall into the historical sequence of human experience:

> These moments are in reality utterly discontinuous with normal time. It is the knowledge that such moments are probable and the anticipation of them that makes "time" in the front line unlike all other experiences of time. The camera which isolates a moment of agony isolates no more violently that the experience of that moment isolates itself.… The image seized by the camera is doubly violent and both violences reinforce the same contrast: the contrast between the photographed moment and all others …. Such moments … are discontinuous with all other moments. They exist by themselves. (Berger 2009: 43)

Harrison acknowledges this fact: in his poem, life and death coexist, "held in suspension" as Whitehead writes "in the … 'frozen' present" (Whitehead 2005: 358), a poignant confirmation of Baudrillard's contention that the Gulf conflict is essentially "the dead war" (Baudrillard 1995: 62) and the reminder of the fact that a photograph is a "memory freeze-frame …. its basic unit is a single [motionless] image" (Sontag 2004: 19). The theme of death is developed further on the basis of intertextual references to "Journey of the Magi", voiding Eliot's poem of transcendental meaning (Whitehead 2005: 358) and regenerative potential: after all "the birth of Christ has been reduced" in Harrison's rendering "to the bathos of cold spunk" (Whitehead 2005: 358). Whitehead suggests that in "Journey of the

Magi" Eliot "revisits and sanctifies the landscape of The Waste Land" (Whitehead 2005: 357): the signs of the miracle exist even if the speaker of the poem cannot decipher them. Harrison strips the landscape back to its barren condition, offering a cruel perspective of a "frozen phial of waste" remaining unchanged in "the chilled suspension of the present" (A Cold Coming 168, 172), outside the temporal sequence of events as if a "Medusa-like countenance of frenzy and despair" (Macneile Dixon qtd in Harrison 1991: 435) had turned on this landscape and petrified it.

In light of the fact that the poem was published in 1992 in *The Gaze of the Gorgon*, a collection which revolves around the darkest moments of the twentieth century, the possible relationship between the character of the dead Iraqi soldier and the figure of the gorgon, "the petrifying face of modern warfare" (Whitehead 2005: 359), cannot pass unnoticed. Whitehead dwells on the different interpretations of the character, stating that one possible interpretation is to read him as a gorgon—a figure whose gaze cannot be directly met:

> Harrison transposes the Perseus story on to modern history to suggest that the poet's art acts as a mirror-shield and with this he can reflect (on) the horror of modern warfare and not be frozen into silence. The poet opposes the war by reflecting its horrors in his poetry, which he catches and gives back .... Perseus' heroism simultaneously involves both looking and looking away. Harrison's poem .... offers an 'indirect gaze' at the photograph of the dead Iraqi, enabling us to ... engage with the horror of the death the image reveals. Much of the 'indirection' in the poem comes through the 'I' of the persona, who substitutes his gaze for our own. (Whitehead 2005: 360)

Nevertheless, the Iraqi can be also regarded as victim, turned into stone by the gorgon's gaze, the one who looked directly into the horror, the "complete witness,"[276] and so the meeting which takes place is essentially an encounter with the dead, reminiscent of the tradition going back to Dante and Vergil. What the speaker confronts is the dead soldier's suffering countenance; paradoxically, a face which is no longer a face, since it has been deformed, turned into Eliotean waste by the "unfriendly fire," petrified into a "mask" (A Cold Coming 14). The confrontation is direct since it takes place in the "full light of day" (Harrison, Facing Up to the Muses, 1991: 441) like in the Greek *theatron*, "this place for seeing" (Harrison,

276 Primo Levi uses this expression *In The Drowned and the Saved* (and Whitehead quotes it after him In "Tony Harrison, The Gulf War and the Poetry of Protest"). Levi states:

> [W]e, the survivors, are not the true witnesses .... We are those who by prevarication or good luck did not touch bottom. Those who did so, those who saw the Gorgon, have not returned to tell about it or have returned mute, but they are the ... complete witnesses .... We speak in their stead, by proxy. (1988: 63–64)

Facing Up to the Muses, 1991: 441) as Harrison calls it, where the terror was "not only shared but also seen to be shared" (Harrison, Facing Up to the Muses, 1991: 441) and where the audience stood face to face with the actors and with each other.

The situation created in the poem is a parallel attempt at "communal endurance" (Harrison, Facing Up to the Muses, 1991: 441); the terror of war embodied by the mutilated human shape is confronted by the speaker and the confrontation is "seen" (Harrison, Facing Up to the Muses, 1991: 441) by the reader. Harrison quotes Nietzsche's *The Birth of Tragedy* to illustrate his stance, namely, that he is not abandoning the word as a tool of resistance despite being aware of its limitations, its ambiguous and misleading character, since it is language and especially the language of tragedy that allows the witness to face the agony and the horror without being turned into stone. This thought is not new in Harrison's poetry, but "A Cold Coming" strongly emphasizes especially both intimations in the power of the word and persistent acknowledgement of its importance, suggesting that the role of the contemporary poet whose work will always remain overshadowed by the twentieth "century's terrible events" (Harrison, Facing Up to the Muses, 1991: 436) can be explained in reference to Greek tragedy. The idea enters the poem indirectly with the words of the Iraqi Soldier addressing the poet/journalist for the first time:

> 'Don't be afraid I've picked on you
> for this exclusive interview.
>
> Isn't it your sort of poet's task
> to find words for this *frightening mask*?[277]
>
> If that gadget that you've got records,
> words from such scorched vocal chords,
>
> press RECORD before some dog
> devours me mid-monologue.' (A Cold Coming 11–18)

Whitehead associates the Iraqi's mask with the one mentioned by Derrida in *Memoires of the Blind: The Self-Portrait and Other Ruins* (1993: 72) and consequently attributes fright to the mask as its inherent feature as the mask always stands for "death or blindness" (Derrida 1993: 72). If, as Derrida writes "every mask announces mortuary mask" (1993: 72). The Iraqi's disfigured face becomes a memento mori, it is "a movement towards silence" (Whitehead 2005: 263) which

277 Emphasis added by the author of this book.

would explain Harrison's description of the "mask" as "dumb." (A Cold Coming 156) However, the dumbness of the mask seems to be only an initial phase in the poem: the "skull" (A Cold Coming 37) is dumb as long as the words are not found for it by the poet, as with the mask in Greek tragedy, which depends on the actors' ability to speak and the author's ability to write. The skull's "gaping rictus" (A Cold Coming 159) again brings forth the Greek mask since it is "designed with an open mouth" in order "[t]o go on speaking even at critical moments" (Harrison, Facing Up to the Muses, 1991: 445). Harrison juxtaposes the "naked human face" with a "tragic mask" (Harrison, Facing Up to the Muses, 1991: 445) and comes to the following conclusion:

1. What does the human face do when we are presented with .... blood, death, violence and terror? We tend to close our eyes.
2. What does the human face do, what we do, when we gaze on such violence? We become silent. 'There can be no poetry after Auschwitz' ... The word is dead .... The mask facing up the Muses, refuses to surrender *emphasis*.
3. What does the head do when it suffers or witnesses suffering? It tends to bow down. .... If a mask gazes on the same horrors, the same terrors, it goes on gazing. It is created with open eyes .... Words never fail it. It goes on speaking .... It is created to stay upright ... to present itself. (Harrison, Facing Up to the Muses, 1991: 446)

Harrison continues his analysis of the mask by referring to the tragedy of Oedipus, who enters the stage, his bloody eye sockets displayed for the audience's gaze. "Words" Harrison says "have not failed the mask of the Oedipus" and his head "stays unbound for us to see the terrible sockets" (Harrison, Facing Up to the Muses, 1991: 446). The face/mask of the Iraqi soldier resembles that of the King of Thebes: it presents itself to its interlocutor and to the reader with all its horror. Even more importantly it goes on speaking despite belonging to the man who looked into the eyes of the Gorgon and turned into a stone. As Whitehead notices, Harrison's analysis attributes a sense of independence to the Greek mask[278] (2005: 363)—a feature which likens it to the human face despite the fact that the juxtaposition offered by Harrison aims at foregrounding the differences between mask and face rather than their similarities. The fact that they are in a dichotomous relationship separates the mask and the face and binds them at the same time:

278 "Harrison's discussion of the mask is notable for conceiving of it in isolation, as if it is the mask itself that speaks and looks. In rhetorical performance, however, it is the actor behind the mask who looks and speaks the words of the poet" (Whitehead 2005: 363).

they complement each other like other "versuses of life" (v. 65) enumerated in Harrison's working-class elegy. In the poem the Iraqi's countenance is a disfigured face which has turned into a mask but also a mask[279] which bares resemblance to the face it once was[280]. It is described as an "unfleshed skull" (A Cold Coming 57) which speaks and gazes, which bears witness to the atrocities of war, which continuously looks at the "phial of waste" (A Cold Coming 168) with eyes wide open, and like the mask of Greek Tragedy, it "refuses to surrender emphasis," "it stays upright", "it presents itself" (Harrison, Facing Up to the Muses, 1991: 446).

It cannot be forgotten that it is the author of a tragedy who gives the Greek mask its voice, just like it is the poet who finds words for the frightening mask of the Iraqi, which becomes evident when seen in the context of the "rhetorical gesture of the poem" analyzed here (Whitehead 2005: 361). The choice of prosopopeia is not accidental; it is directly connected to the process of identity construction of both the persona of the poet who responds to the image of suffering and the persona of his charred interlocutor, the "complete witness" (Levi 1988: 64) of war atrocities. Prosopopeia has, in the core of its meaning, an idea of figuration, and more precisely the creation of a face, an emblem of human identity which carries the notion of distinctiveness but also the notion of identification with others, with the human race. In a study of Wordsworth's *Essays upon Epitaphs*, Paul de Man defines prosopopeia as:

> [T]he fiction of an apostrophe to an absent, deceased, or voiceless entity, which posits the possibility of the latter's reply and confers upon it the power of speech. Voice assumes mouth, eye, and finally face, a chain that is manifested in the etymology of the trope's name, *prosopon poien*, to confer a mask or a face (prosopon). (1984: 75–76)

The line which announces the task of the poet, "Finding words for the frightening mask" (A Cold Coming 14) echoes the idea of the restoration of identity based upon the "rhetorical function of prosopopeia," which can be defined as "positing voice or face by means of language" (de Man 1984: 81). In other words, the language and the ability to be heard are the means, as Mcquillan writes, "by which we construct our own masks of selfhood in the world … all language works as a form of prosopopeia." (2001: 78). Prosopopeia implies a close relationship between voice and face and consequently, giving voice is understood in the poem, typically for Harrison, as a means of (re)constructing identity.

279 "frightening mask", "dumb mask" (A Cold Coming 14: 156).

280 "and made a face you see today/an armature half-patched with clay." (A Cold Coming 107–108)

Another feature of the trope is that it functions at a border between the world of the living and the world of the dead, bringing them closer together: it brings the dead back to life but at the same time, reminds the survivors of their mortality, "shows a necessary inadequacy of our relation to death" (Critchley 2000: 86). By association with Greek tragedy—the charred face of the Iraqi soldier becomes a mask which the poet "puts on"—he is the one who finds the accurate words to unfold the soldier's story, and so he must occupy the "impossible subject position" of someone who speaks "for/as the dead," a position for which as it seems "there could be no authentic or 'true' voice" (Whitehead 2005: 366), as the complete witness is the one who looked at the gorgon directly and became speechless. De Man describes the threat evoked by prosopopeia as follows:

> By making the death speak, the symmetrical structure of the trope implies, by the same token, that the living are stuck dumb, frozen in their own death. To surmise of the 'Pause, Traveller!' thus acquires a sinister connotation that it is not only the prefiguration of one's own mortality but our actual entry into the frozen world of the dead. (1984: 78)

The shadow of silence and potential impossibility of fulfilling the task (i.e. finding words for the frightening mask) loom over the final line of the poem, which ends with a colon:

> I've met you though, and had my say
> which you've got taped. Now go away'
> I gazed at him and he gazed back
> staring right through me to Iraq.
> ....
> I went. I pressed REWIND and PLAY
> and I heard the charred man say: (A Cold Coming 163–166, 183–184)

The empty space that follows may suggest, as Whitehead writes, that Harrison "calls into question the authenticity of the supposed recorded interview: the poet does pretend and there is no mistaking his words for the real thing" (2005: 362). Within the scope of this interpretation, silence serves as an expression of doubt in the power of language, which ceases to possess a regenerative force in the face of the ultimate horror of death. But what should be taken into consideration at this point of the analysis is the fact that silence and absence (usually absence of voice) are precisely those entities which Harrison's poetry tries to represent; more, they are in some poems described as triggers of poetic eloquence (see: "Heredity"). Even if the poem ends with a silence that is the silence of death, it can hardly be treated as a sudden breakdown of a narrative, after all, it has always been a paradoxical "representation of an absence" (Critchley 2000: 85) that Harrison's poems operate on. It is not an abrupt movement from speech to silence the poet tries to convey at this point, but rather a momentary unveiling of what lies beneath the whole enterprise of this poetic attempt, a glimpse at what essentially the task of finding the "words for the frightening mask," (A Cold Coming 14) speaking for/ as the dead, is all about. Critchley states:

> The only relation the living can maintain with death is through representation. And yet we immediately confront a paradox: namely that the representation of death is not a representation of a presence, an object of perception or intuition.... Thus, representations of death are *misrepresentations*, or rather they are representations of an absence. The paradox at the heart of the representation of death is perhaps best conveyed by the figure of prosopopeia, that is the rhetorical trope by which an absent or imaginary person is presented as speaking and acting ... prosopopeia means to make a face; in this sense we may think of a death mask, a form which indicates the failure of presence, a face which withdraws behind the form which presents it. (2000: 85)

As the task of finding the voice, and thus a face for the dead, cannot be concluded, it can only be performed as continuity, as an ongoing labour, as work in process. The face of the Iraqi soldier exists and can be seen by others as long as the poet continues to speak, as long as he gazes unflinchingly at the horror and responds to it. The ending of the poem may be then read differently, not as the abandoning of language but as a suggestion of a forthcoming, continuous repetition of the story since the colon replaces a full stop and gives an impression that the poem is unfinished, still under construction.

The question of whether it is the Iraqi's voice the reader is about to hear or the poet's voice becomes of secondary importance, since the Iraqi soldier can be seen as one of Harrison's alter egos who populate his poetry—one of the Others within the Self. The idea is already being forged at the beginning of the poem by the association between the way the body of the Iraqi is positioned in the charred vehicle and the position of a man writing at a table, with a windscreen wiper becoming a pen with which he is to put down the story of warfare atrocities, the story of the encounter with the Gorgon.

> I saw the charred Iraqi lean
> towards me from bomb-blasted screen,
>
> his windscreen wiper like a pen
> ready to write down thoughts for men,
>
> his windscreen wiper like a quill
> he's reaching for to make his will. (A Cold Coming 1–6)

As Susan Sontag writes in *On Photography*, "some photographs right from the start refer us to other images as well as to life ... what is compelling about the photograph partly derives from what it shares" (Sontag 2008: 106–107). Harrison creates a very concrete net of possible references for the photograph in the opening lines of "A Cold Coming" by putting the encounter between the two protagonists in the context of writing and heritage: first of all a typical soldier's attribute, a gun, is replaced by a pen, secondly, the Iraqi's voice is produced by "scorched vocal cords" (A Cold Coming 16). An image that sends the reader back to an earlier poem by Harrison entitled "Fire-Eater" in which the poet/conjuror swallows tongues of fire—a painful legacy of his ancestors—and announces "constant singing from the flames" (Fire-Eater 16) despite the fact that the obligation he took upon himself turned his "vocal chords … scorched and black" (Fire-Eater 15). Associations with written and oral literary tradition bring the Other closer to the poet/journalist persona, mainly because the main constituents of the opening image of the charred Iraqi soldier are badges of the poetic profession: a pen (a quill) and vocal chords. And so, the Other becomes endowed with the features which lie in the very core of the identity of the Self.

"Cornet and Cartridge," one of the poems thematically akin to the "poetry reportage" (Herron, at al. 2011: 72) from post-war Bosnia, which Harrison wrote for the *Guardian* in 1995, describes a parallel situation: the poet meets his war-torn double, a headless and consequently faceless reflection of his own person in the broken window pane of the Shell Hotel in Sarajevo, bullet-riddled during the war. While he himself will rest his head peacefully on a pillow in a new, war-free Swell hotel, his shadow-like, ghostly companion will remain in the ruins, watchful and sleepless. The poetic persona Tony Harrison and his headless double both hold in their hands a cartridge, which in the poem is first of all understood as a pen refill but which is equally poignant as a symbol of destruction: a live cartridge for a gun. An image of armed conflict is again inscribed within the context of writing: a shadow; ghost-like creature which haunts the abandoned ruins is at the same time an incarnation of the poet. What is most interesting, however, is that the reflection actually becomes de-faced, just like the victims of war, whose features are destroyed, literally by gunfire, and metaphorically, since their identity cannot be recognized and will remain forever caught in the remains of the past. The continuity between armed conflict and writing inspired by war is additionally established by an image of a pen constructed out of what once was a part of a gun and which becomes in the post-war reality a tool the speaker of the poem uses to put down his words on paper. The poem suggests that although the war may have ended its flame has not been extinguished just yet, it still flickers and can be spotted by a watchful eye in the broken landscape, in the shreds of former glory, since the shadow of the war looms upon the land which is struggling to shore up its every-day reality against the ruins.

Clearly the war is also the force which drives the speaker towards poetry, it is the source of inspiration, it becomes the main topic of the poem just as a cartridge becomes a writing tool: images of destruction are skilfully transformed into poetic images, metaphorically speaking post-war landscape of Sarajevo is the building material for Harrison's poetry. Look, the poet is saying, this is what my poems are made of: the remains of the Shell hotel, pieces of weapons, reflections of human experience in the city deconstructed by war. "Odd limbs and corpses," "shell bursts" "glass shreds," "windowless sills," they all constitute the countenance of the suffering Other who in the poem takes up the form of a de-faced and fingerless reflection but at the same time acquires the face of the speaker himself. The poetic persona Tony Harrison identifies with his disjoined, numb and mouth-less alter-ego, one of numerous voiceless protagonists populating Harrison's poetry.[281] The ghost of war is Tony Harrison's own reflection and it wears, if only by association, Harrison's face:

> The sparrows take shelter in their windowsill shell-bursts.
> My headless reflection stares out of the *Shell*,
> no mouth to eat bread with, no tongue to speak
> or to lick on a cornet of juice-sloshed *sladoled*.
> He weighs, my reflection, on a fingerless palm
> a cartridge he could, with some effort, scratch words with
> on a floury surface where pitta dough 's kneaded
> till the next mortar thud turned his message to mote clouds.
> His cartridge isn't quite equipped for creation. Mine
> needs constant bulling up to keep its brass shiny,
> while it waits on my desk for the summons to action.
>
> We both watch the sun set behind sniperless hills. (Cornet and Cartridge 49–60)

---

281 As Carol Rutter puts it:

> He puts inarticulate on record: His uncle Harry, a deaf-mute, the stammerer, Uncle Joe; his father, who was kept down by 'a tongue that weight like lead'; a nameless convict who, to settle the toffs' wager, was winched into a bottomless pit and brought back 'flayed, grey, mad, dumb'; the skinhead dole-wallah who defaces tombstones with 'V' and himself with tattoos; the Iraqi soldier immolated in his tank, his charred lips half open; Iphigeneia Agamemnon's daughter, 'hoisted like a goat to the god-stone, a gag in her mouth' so she cannot curse as her throat is cut and the sacrifice made so the Greek ships can sail for Troy. (1995: 15)

A motif of a transformed object, which like the cartridge from the above-quoted poem, carries in itself a reminiscence of war is used by Harrison in "Shrapnel," a poem published for the first time on 21 August 2005 on the pages of *The Independent on Sunday* in the aftermath of the terrorist attack on the London Underground. "Shrapnel" opens with the scene from the speaker's study where on a summer day he is looking for a paperweight to introduce some order into the pile of sheets blown away by a "storm-presaging breeze" (Shrapnel 2). As the reader is informed, "scribbled papers" (Shrapnel 3) sliding to the floor contain the lines of the verse he/she is reading this very moment. The sudden shift from the immediate present, "here and now" (Herron et al. 2011: 72) takes place at the end of the first stanza when the speaker finds among several paperweights—all of them keepsakes or souvenirs of different journeys—the one whose origin has "all to do with the war" (Harrison, The Inkwell of Dr Agrippa, 1991: 32), a piece of shrapnel.

The action of the poem, which started as a serene observation of a fleeting moment, slides into the past to evoke an air-raid the speaker lived through as a child hiding in a cellar with his mother and sister. The shrapnel the young poet found with other lads (Shrapnel 42) after the raid does not undergo any physical metamorphoses in the poem. Unlike the cartridge, which becomes a pen in the hands of a craftsman, the shrapnel becomes something else merely through the change of its function: inscribed in Harrison's personal history and simultaneously "endowed with a historical narrative" (Herron et al. 2011: 72) of the community, it becomes for years an element of the writer's habitat, the thing which "stops the flapping poem being blown away" (Shrapnel 64). The shrapnel grounds Harrison's verse in a literal and metaphorical sense, as, besides being a useful object, it pertains in the re/creation of wartime images, which as the poet himself writes "drove ... [him] to poetry" (Harrison, The Inkwell of Dr Agrippa, 1991: 32).

> [I]t is this particular object that evokes in the poet one among the tableau of scenes familiar to readers of his poetry: memories of war-time air-raid in Leeds. On more than one occasion Harrison has cited this event as a type of primal scene: a moment in which horror, fear and excitement intersect in recurring sense of trauma. So from the beginning of a poem a tension is in operation as the bomb fragment is deployed—paradoxically enough bearing in mind its usual function of destroying, damaging, inflicting injury—to maintain order, to avoid fragmenting of a sheaf of papers. At the same time, the fragment works to unhouse the poet from the quotidian fussings to a time/space from which traumatic memories proliferate. (Herron et al. 2011: 72)

The thoughts of the speaker slip into the past suddenly, and there is no doubt that memories are evoked by the sudden emergence of the piece of shrapnel which works as a "catalyst to remembrance" (Whitehead 2009: 107). The image of the shrapnel is a synecdoche of war and a bridging device in the construction of the poem: When the time plane changes again and the reader is brought back to the present moment the paperweight is still in the hands of the speaker: "I *stroke my shrapnel* and I celebrate, /.... / A flicker of faith in man grew from that raid / where *this shrapnel that I'm stroking now*[282] comes from." (Shrapnel 61, 65–66).

The method of describing the workings of memory employed by Harrison in "Shrapnel" and elsewhere[283] calls to mind the idea of *involuntary memory*[284] developed in Proust's most famous novel (i.e. *In Search of Lost Time*) whose narrator's childhood memories are awakened by taste of a madeleine dunked in lime-blossom tea. The unexpected and spontaneous recollection is followed by meticulous reconstruction of the past, "the prolonged struggle to locate the past experience" (Whitehead 2009: 104) which is inevitable since the initial illumination is momentary and cannot be sustained without effort. The search for the time lost is essentially an investigation of one's own psyche: Proust asserts that "the truth I am seeking lies not in the cup but in myself" (ISLT[285] I: 52, 55), but he simultaneously suggests that "the past is invested in external objects .... and can be unlocked by the sensation which [an] object gives us" (Whitehead 2009: 108). In Harrison's poem, the object comes from the past and so constitutes a link between now and then, introduces an idea of continuity and forces the reader to consider possible relations between past and present time planes. The poem stresses the importance of the origin of the shrapnel; it comes from the raid, and it is a fragment of a bomb which missed the houses on Tempest Road, where the family of the speaker lived. In the course of the poem, the event which is first ascribed to mere chance is later mythologized (Herron et al. 2011: 74) and becomes the story of the humanitarian act of a German bomber who decides not to obey his orders and spares the civilian houses. "In fact there is not a slightest shred of evidence

---

282 Emphasis added by the author of this book.

283 See for example "Timer" and "Currents" The latter poem openly claims affinity to the Proustian treatment of memory, the opening line introducing an idea that the taste of a traditional northern cake brings back recollections from the childhood: "An Eccles cake's my *petite madeleine*!" (Currents I, 1).

284 "Throughout *In Search of Lost Time*, a physical sensation ... acts as the catalyst for involuntary memory: the taste of the Madeleine dipped in tea, the sensation of imbalance on unevenly laid cobblestones, the sounds of a spoon striking a plate or of water running through pipes, the touch of a heavily starched napkin brushing the lips" (Whitehead 2009: 104). Proust stresses the importance of the body and its sensations in evoking recollections and privileges, the senses of taste and smell as most powerful triggers of the process. In Harrison's poem, the sense of touch is being stressed as the speaker holds the paperweight in his hand and strokes it.

285 ISLT stands for *In Search of Lost Time*.

for such a deduction" (Herron et al. 2011: 74) says Tom Herron, referring to the account presented by Owen A. Hartley in "The Second World War and After." The heart-warming assertion about the human bomber which the speaker recalls as a part of the whole experience and which he repeats as an adult man as if he still believed in it may sound like proof of his "fundamental intellectual insufficiency" (Herron et al. 2011: 74) or of disillusion with the consolatory power of poetry (Herron et al. 2011: 74), but it can be also read as an ironic comment on the nature of community bound together by the myths it creates.

In the poem, a myth which is born out of the conversation between the young boys examining "the craters the bombs made" (Shrapnel 41) and the policemen guarding the streets gives a face to the "unseen foe" (Shrapnel 58), which due to the nature of warfare remains unknown literally (his potential victims don't know his face) and figuratively (he is a stranger, an enemy, the Other). His relation to the community can be then easily established; he is the outsider and so the gap created by the fact of his utter otherness can be easily filled with a myth. The image of the "humane bombardier" (Shrapnel 70) is juxtaposed with the counter image of three terrorists responsible for killing fifty-two people and injuring seven hundred and seventy others in the attack on London underground (Herron et al. 2011: 70).

> The naming of the men (their foreignness fore-grounded against the unremittingly British street and place names ...) and their incorporation into the final moments of the poem—almost as an afterthought, a postscriptum, a supplement—renders unnecessary, on the part of the poet, any elaboration, less still any explanation ... [the names] function as a type of *foreign body*, the effect of which is to contaminate the overwhelmingly reassuring narrative of faith formalized ... throughout the course of the poem .... such a reiteration—without qualification, without explanation—produces effects which are almost hysterical: how to negotiate this aporia? It doesn't seem adequate to leave it uncrossed. (Herron et al. 2011: 75)

Apart from its meaning i.e. *corpus alienum*, "an intruding object," the usage of the expression "foreign body" resonates with other connotations since, as Rutter suggests, words have physical quality for Harrison, they are like "objects. They have their weight and shape and density" (Rutter 1995: 23). The names indeed seem to weigh heavily at the end of the poem but they follow one another evenly, neatly, in order, as if stopped from being blown away (Shrapnel 64) by the poem's rhythmical pattern which, stands in contrast to the possible havoc and confusion which according to Herron their sound evokes. Although their names are listed at the end of the poem without, as Herron notices, any "description of their relation to the violence they perpetrate" (Herron et al. 2011: 77), it can be claimed that the fact that they are positioned in immediate proximity of the expression "humane bombardier" (Shrapnel 70) evokes in the contemporary mind an explicit association with a "human bomb."[286] The act of terrorism is implied in the poem by an "oxymoronic" expression (Herron et al. 2011: 74) suggesting a supposed act of humanity, the evoked image of violence acquires its explicitly horrific character precisely due to the stark contrast between two abovementioned terms: one given ("humane bombardier") and one evoked in the mind of the reader ("human bomb").

This sudden transition from the seemingly "reassuring narrative of faith" (Herron et al. 2011: 75) to the vision of a terrorist attack is another example of Harrison's method of setting aside the familiar, and commonplace with the alien, the potentially dangerous. However, this time, the opposition of *familiar vs. unfamiliar* is not clear cut: the identity of the attackers escapes unambiguous definition since, unlike the German bomber, they cannot be marked as outsiders. Perhaps the term "unseen foe" does not lose its relevance in the case of Tanweer, Khan and Hussain but it bears a different meaning; their faces were definitely seen and recognized by their "fellow Leodiensians" (Herron et al. 2011: 74) since they belonged to the same seemingly "unremittingly British" (Herron et al. 2011: 75) setting they are foregrounded against in Harrison's poem.

Indiscriminate acts of violence "moved out of the battlefield and into every corner of civilian life" (Winter 1995: 6) a long time ago and are coming today "not in the form of an attack from beyond the national boundaries, but from within them," they are committed "not by foreign assailants, but by our fellow citizens" (Herron et al. 2011: 75). Although remaining, as was earlier stated, in opposition, the two terms discussed above remain in a very close relation[287] just as the community which created the myth of an ethical bomber contains within itself "home-grown terrorists." (Herron et al. 2011: 75). Acknowledging "the close cultural proximity of the 'Beeston Bombers' to … himself" (Herron et al. 2011: 75) or rather to the autobiographical "I" of the poem, Harrison creates a context

---

286 The term "human bomb" is used interchangeably with the term "suicide bomber" and sometimes preferred to the latter as a more accurate one. As Nicole Argo states: Human bombs are a product of structural, social, and individual interactions. Rather than evince suicidal tendencies—as the term "suicide bombers" connotes—psychological autopsies of past and would-be bombers show many of these individuals to be wholly, even altruistically invested in life. As a result, it is more apt—and less misleading—to refer to these individuals as "human bombs" rather than "suicide bombers." (2006: 1–2)

287 Not only are the terms related etymologically but also visually, one "contains" the other: "*human*e *bomb*ardier".

in which the face of the Other is almost inseparable from the face of the Self. The "Self"[288] is represented in "Shrapnel" by a story from the past, by a memory from the war. This past, however, is being shared with people whose faces, the faces of citizens of Leeds, of the "lads," (Shrapnel 42) of Loiners, are simultaneously portraits of modern warfare.

288 The notion of the self can be understood in the poem as an individual "self" of the speaker and/or as the self of a community (it should be stated that the actual existence of a community or consistent national identity are being questioned in the poem, communal and national fragmentation is being envisaged by the foregrounding of the origin of 'Beeston bombers').

Conclusion

"How have you been useful for the polis?"

This book has been an attempt to analyze the theme of identity in Harrison's poems, to identify its most important dimensions and to trace the lines of its development from *The Loiners*, through *The School of Eloquence* and *v.*, up to the more recent works concerned with contemporary military conflicts and modern warfare. One of the tasks which inscribes itself into the context of this analysis and which was set at the beginning of the book was to determine the poetic identity of Tony Harrison, an engaged poet who pays as much attention to the private as to the public sphere of human experience. Labelled political, sentimental, misogynist, dangerous, unforgiving, insulting and militant, his work escapes easy, unambiguous definitions. To answer the question about his poetic identity is by no means easy if one considers the unquestionable richness of his verse, the controversy he can and at times undeniably wants to provoke, and the fact that he has always understood identity as an dynamic process which takes place in the context of history, never free from the political and social aspect of life.

In this book, Harrison's work is analysed in the context of numerous theoretical backgrounds, all of them relevant for understanding how the problem of identity has been perceived in twentieth century Sociology, Psychology and Cultural Studies, but also in the light of those authors who concentrated mainly upon the problems concerning working-class identity and culture. The analysis reveals a strong correspondence between Harrison's treatment of the subject and the most important questions asked by the scholars in different fields concerned with the problem of identity. The first reason for this is that Harrison's poetry remains sensitive to the current social context, to constant changes in the public sphere of life which influence the condition of the contemporary man. The second reason is Harrison's focus on the role of history in both individual and communal life, and his constant remembrance of a past which exerts pressure on the present and the future. Continuity, otherness and revolt, read by Bokszański as different concepts in whose frame identity can be understood, constitute simultaneously important focal points in Harrison's poetry and form elaborate and multidimensional themes in all the texts discussed in the book. It is true that the themes of continuity, otherness and revolt often overlap and entwine, but they always remain vital elements of the wider context of identity construction central to Harrison's verse. Today Harrison divides his life between Great Britain (still faithful to the

North, residing in Newcastle) and America. Although much has changed and his interest has shifted more to theatre, he has not stopped writing verse, remaining a close observer of a changing reality. When asked about his plans for the future, he repeats that "poetry is all he writes" and despite the fact that this is no easy enterprise, he will not cease to work for the audiences willing to listen (Private Conversation, 12 July 2013, London). "Listen" is a key word here, poetry for Harrison was always meant first for reading aloud. His new reading of *v.* (18 February 2013), the first public reading of the elegy since its broadcast by Channel 4 in 1987, shows that he will not dissociate himself from his past voice but that he is always trying to set it against a contemporary background, as if checking how it resonates here and now and whether it stands the test of time. And so it seems to be the case with Harrison that answering a question about the core of his poetic identity in the present can never be done without taking a look into his past.

One poetic project which foreshadowed the poet Harrison was to become is his 1975 translation of the works of Palladas, who lived in the forth century in Alexandria and was "generally regarded as the last poet of Paganism" (Harrison, Preface to Palladas, 1991: 134). The choice to translate selected epigrams of "one of those marginal and late poets of antiquity" (Levi 1991: 136) corresponds with Harrison's tendency to look for inspiration in peripheral, overshadowed places: ambiguous and potentially revolutionary zones whose mere existence seems to constantly threaten the order and stability maintained by the centre. Palladas is after all, one of the last recognized pagan voices in the times of an upcoming Christian hegemony and it is a very cynical voice indeed, often unforgiving and always deeply critical of human nature. Spencer describes Harrison's interest in Palladas's verse as "fascination with the power of pure negativity" (1994: 43) and recognizes lines of reference which can be traced between the tone of the Alexandrian cynic and the tone assumed by a character from Harrison's earlier collection:

> The 'nihilistic scorn' … with which Palladas surveyed the terminal decline of paganism in the face of the onslaught of militant Christianity has a great deal in common with White Queen's view of colonial Africa sixteen hundred years later; and it is thus in a direct line of development from … *The Loiners* …. Behind the masks of his adopted personae, Harrison can give free rein to the sort of sentiments that would be utterly inconsistent with the dominant … compassion of the "School of Eloquence" sonnets or the balancing of positive and negative forces attempted in "A Kumquat for John Keats," … Even the foul-mouthed skinhead in *v.* voices a critique of social injustice the scorching anger of which is a long way from the triple-distilled *Weltschmerz* of Palladas. (Spencer 1994: 44)

The first point that should be made about Spencer's criticism is that the poetic I of *The School of Eloquence*, although undeniably very close to the author himself, cannot be read otherwise than as the poetic persona Tony Harrison, a creation of the poet's mind. Spencer's suggestion that there is a clear opposition between the "true" face of the poet presented in *The School of Eloquence* and the masks he creates for himself in *The Loiners* and in *Palladas* remains unjustified. The second point is that despite obvious differences, the voice of Palladas and the voice of the skinhead have something in common. They both represent cultures on the verge of extinction and they are both perceived as barbarian: the Alexandrian voice of the pagan poet by the Christians and the working-class voice of the skin by privileged speakers of RP. To develop Spencer's line of thought, they are also both Harrison's alter egos, he is both a working-class vandal and the poet who chooses to represent a culture which rests on the "crumbled past" (Harrison 1991: 134) and has no future. The following lines of Palladas express the feeling of alienation, and divisions between "us" and "them," which in the following years recur in Harrison's working-class poetry:

> We non-Christians are dead, and only seem
> alive; the life we're living's bad dream
> or so THEY say. My version of it's this:
> we're alive but wonder if life is[289]!

As in the first movement of T. S. Eliot's *The Waste Land*, the difference between life and death depends here on the point of view of the observer.[290] In Eliot's poem, "little life" (The Waste Land 7) is precious only for the speakers remaining in a hallucinatory half-dream, whose limited world-view is presented by Eliot as existence without passion, hope or faith. In Harrison's adaptation of Palladas, the stress is put on the "Pagan hopelessness and Christian barbarity" (Harrison 1991: 134). What Christians see as a mere "bad dream," an equivalent of Eliot's "little life," (The Waste Land 7) has been a real life of the poetic "I" until the moment of extinction. "We're alive but we wonder if life is!" says the speaker of the poem, simultaneously confirming his existence and declaring its end. In the preface to the

---

289 This poems appears in *The Greek Anthology* edited by Peter Jay (Allen Lane: 1972) for which Harrison translated Palladas for the first time, only later did he produce more translations which were published in *Palladas: Poems* (1975) in Penguin *Selected Poems* (without a Preface and prefatory poem) and in *Collected Poems* (2007).

290 April is the cruelest month, breeding
Lilacs out of the dead land, mixing
Memory and desire, stirring
Dull roots with spring rain.
Winter kept us warm, covering
Earth in forgetful snow, feeding
A little life with dried tubers. (The Waste Land 1–7)

translations, Harrison explains what drew him to Palladas besides "fascination with the power of pure negativity" (1994: 43) mentioned by Spencer:

> His bitterness is compound of historical pessimism … and a bad marriage which seems to have led to general misogyny[291] …. He is one of those embarrassing but heroic figures who are not dignified in despair, refusing to be noble on the gallows or to make peace with their maker. It is perhaps this aspect of his tone, his "raging against the dying of the light," that makes commemorators like Mackail refer to his "harsh thought and half barbarous language" … certainly not elegant … but the authentic snarl of a man trapped physically in poverty and persecution, and metaphorically in deep sense of the futile. (Harrison, Preface to Palladas, 1991: 135)

Reading adaptations of Palladas, one realizes that the Alexandrian poet bears a resemblance to numerous ambiguous heroes populating Harrison's verse. He is not a likeable character, but not someone who can be easily ignored either, despite the fact that some of his writing, due to its hateful tone,[292] triggers in the contemporary reader an antagonistic reaction and prompts strong critique. And as far as his anger is concerned, it is perhaps not "triple-distilled" (Spencer 1994: 44) after all. There is an edge to it; in the grudge he nurses against those who betray him, like his own wife (Harrison, Preface to Palladas, 1991: 134), and in his abhorrence of the Christian blast which extinguishes the light of the Hellenistic world. This is precisely what Harrison wanted to convey in the translation: exhausted anger which replaces hope and flickers until the end. Palladas knows there will be no resurrection, "there is no sense of joy in his few poems on the carpe diem theme," (Harrison, Preface to Palladas, 1991: 135) but he remains "bitterly forceful" (Levi 1991: 137) and consequent in his "singing from the flames" (Fire-Eater 16). If he

---

291 His enthusiastic eulogy on Hypatia, a Greek Alexandrine thinker and teacher counterbalances to a certain extent the misogynic tone present in some of his verse. Although as Spencer notices she seems to be the "only woman about whom Palladas speaks with anything but dislike" (Spencer 1994: 45).

292 Peter Levi comments upon the introduction of classical literature into the English cultural context as follows:

"Most good translation of the Classics into English has happened because it permitted the expression of what we were unable or not permitted to express for ourselves. Marlowe's Ovid touches on an amoral sexuality he could not express in his own person. Dryden found in Lucretius almost the two last forbidden subjects, the consolation of a godless death and the sexual behavior of women. In the 1900s Classical expressions of homosexuality were privileged. What Tony Harrison pinpoints, consciously or not, includes some savage anti-feminism and some plainer speaking about Christians than is usual even today. If he were a modern writer, Palladas would not be considered a nice man" (Levi 1991: 136).

were a bard, his accompanying instrument of choice would most probably be a wooden rattle which sounds like a metronome, counting the rhythm by which a whole culture turns into dust. "There is a strong sense of form in Palladas," Harrison writes, "as if the formal endeavour and metrical tension were all that stood between … [him] and choking silence" (Harrison, Preface to Palladas, 1991: 135). Harrison could say the same thing about his own poetry where the form, as was mentioned in one of the previous chapters, plays the role of a "life support system," due to which the poet can "go closer to the fire" and "deeper into the darkness" (Harrison interviewed by Hoggart 43) though in the case of Palladas, the verses he constructs are nothing more than the last bastion which eventually has to surrender to the "cataclysm of Christianity" (Harrison, Preface to Palladas, 1991: 135). In "The Murderer & Sarapis":

> [A] murderer is warned in a dream that a wall will fall on him, and he escapes death. The next night his dream-visitor tells him that he has been saved from a quick death for the slower one of crucifixion. It is a Beckettian world without escape, and without innocence. Palladas' advice to his reader is a vicious carpe diem: to live for "wine and company and all night bars". His vision of the self is of cynical facetiousness: "Life's a performance. Either join in/light-heartedly, or toil the pain". (Rylance 1997: 157–158)

But it would be wrong to believe that there are no obligations for a poet to fulfil in this time of misery, even at the stage of "epochal death-throes of the transition from Hellenism to Christianity," (Rylance 1997: 157) a rather critical and distinctive context for creating poetry, which requires special measures to be taken. And this is the point where Palladas' and Harrison's views are closest to each other, as the former's "assault on another poet" (Hall 2007: 111) conveys the question Harrison poses from the seventies onwards.

> Where's the public good in what you write,
> raking in from all that shameless shite,
> Hawking iambics like so much *Betterbrite*?[293] (Palladas: Poems 43 1–3)

Harrison's persistent question and Palladas' deliberations are deeply rooted in the history of literature:

> In Palladas' Greek, as Harrison will have been aware, the question "where's the public good?" …. harks all the way back to the earliest extended discussion of the role of poetry

293 "The Poet whom Palladas is attacking is compared with someone selling lamp oil, and it seems that Harrison has here invented a new product, inspired by the famous British 'direct sales' company Betterware, whose inexpensive range of cleaning and other household products was (and still is) sold by door-to-door salesmen" (Hall 2007: 111–112).

in society, Aeschylus' debate with Euripides in Aristophanes' *Frogs*. But the phrase "useful for the polis" resonates most profoundly with the passage in Plato's *Republic* where Socrates declares that the poets will be turned away from the city until someone can prove to him that what they compose is useful to the community as well as pleasurable. (Hall 2007: 112)

The fact that Harrison takes up this issue in the twentieth century and carries it into the twenty-first reveals his belief in its relevance in the face of constant social changes, changes which the poet must confront with a vigilant revolutionary eye.[294]

The analysis of the body of Harrison's texts clearly shows that a continuous feature of his poetic identity is faith in writing public poetry, a task that remains central in his plays, film-poems and poems[295]. The public poet is a role Harrison has never relinquished, despite his doubt in the power of figurative language and uncertainty about the ability of verse to foster actual social change. A long time after the Palladas project, in his 2005 collection *Under the Clock*, Harrison writes about this very issue in relation to Charles Turner Thackrah (1799–1833), a surgeon from Leeds and an expert in occupational disease, who during his training at Guy's Hospital, dissected corpses side by side with John Keats.

Dissecting corpses with Keats at Guy's
Leeds-born Thackrah shared the poet's TB.
Cadavers that made Keats poeticize
made Thackrah scorn the call of poetry. (The Ode Not Taken 1–5)

Keats chose poetry whereas Thackrah gave up the chance of a career as a clergyman and, instead of scribbling sonnets (The Ode Not Taken 7), chose a more "hard-core" (Hall 2007: 115) path of "flax-hecklers' fluxes with their 'gruelly' stools" and "the shit of Yorkshire operatives" (The Ode Not Taken 11,12). His scorn of the call of poetry is in Harrison's verse a scorn directed against withdrawal in the face of death. His answer to illness and human misery is a continual engagement even if it means getting dirty and dealing directly with those areas of human experience

294 See Harrison's 2009 PEN/Pinter Prize Lecture (p. 20).

295 The book is concerned only with the last of the three areas of Harrison's writing due to the exceptional richness of his artistic oeuvre. Harrison's plays and film-poems, equally interesting from the point of view of the problem of identity construction, deserve a separate analysis in their own right. Since Harrison himself suggests that poetry is all he writes encompassing the whole body of his work under the poetry banner, it seems justifiable to follow the division into poetry, film-poetry and theatre plays and to begin the discussion on identity in Harrison's art with poetry (as he has begun his artistic quest) leaving the film-poems and plays for further studies. However, this does not mean they should be seen as any less salient.

which cannot be called poetic in the traditional sense of the word. Although the poem may be read as an expression of doubt in the force of poetry, which seems helpless in the face of suffering, it also points paradoxically to what poetry must be if it is to lift the burden of history with its "crop of terror" (A Kumquat for John Keats 62) and withstand social injustice. For Harrison, writing verse must never cease being a revolutionary undertaking, an ongoing project which at its greatest moments "harnesses the word at its most eloquent … and embeds that inspired/ inspiring eloquence in the strained and difficult diction which makes each poem an act of labour" (Byrne 1998: 232).

Bibliography

Primary Sources

1. Harrison, T. *Earthworks.* Leeds: Northern House. 1964.
2. Harrison, T. *Newcastle is Peru*. Newcastle: Eagle Press, 1969.
3. Harrison, T. *The Loiners*. London: London Magazine Editions, 1970.
4. Harrison, T. *Palladas: Poems*. London: Anvil Press Poetry, 1975.
5. Harrison, T. *From The School of Eloquence and Other Poems*. London: Rex Collins, 1978.
6. Harrison, T. *Continuous: 50 Sonnets from The School of Eloquence*. London: Rex Collings, 1978.
7. Harrison, T. *A Kumquat for John Keats*. Newcastle upon Tyne: Bloodaxe Books, 1981.
8. Harrison, T. *Selected Poems*. London: Penguin Books. 1984.
9. Harrison, T. *Selected Poems*. Second Edition. London: Penguin Books, 1987.
10. Harrison, T. *v.* Newcastle upon Tyne: Bloodaxe Books, 1985.
11. Harrison, T. *Ten Sonnets from The School of Eloquence*. Anvil Press Poetry, 1987.
12. Harrison, T. *The Gaze of the Gorgon*. Newcastle upon Tyne: Bloodaxe Books, 1992.
13. Harrison, T. *A Cold Coming*. Newcastle upon Tyne: Bloodaxe Books, 1992.
14. Harrison, T. *Laureate's Block*. Penguin Books, 2000.
15. Harrison, T. *Under the Clock*. London: Penguin Books, 2005.
16. Harrison, T. *Collected film Poetry*. London: Faber and Faber, 2007.
17. Harrison, T. *Collected Poems*. London: Viking Penguin Books Ltd, 2007.

Secondary Sources

1. Abraham, N. and Maria Torok, "Introjection-Incorporation: Mourning and Melancholia." *Psychoanalysis in France*. Ed. S. Lebovici and D. Widlocher. New York: International University Press, 1980.
2. Agamben, G. *Homo Sacer: Sovereign Power and Bare Life*. Stanford: Stanford University Press, 1998.
3. "Aimé Césaire: Martinican Author and Politician." *Encyclopedia Brytannica*. http://www.britannica.com/biography/Aime-Cesaire2013 (Accessed 14.06. 2015)

4. Akhtar, S., ed. *Three Faces of Mourning: Melancholia, Manic Defence, and Moving On*. New Jersey and London: Jason Aronson Inc., 2001.
5. Alexiou, M. *The Ritual Lament in Greek Tradition*. Cambridge: Cambridge University Press, 1974.
6. Argo, N. "Human Bombs: Rethinking Religion and Terror." *The Audit of Conventional Wisdom Series*. Massachusetts Institute of Technology, April 2006. 1–5. http://web.mit.edu/cis/pdf/argo_audit_4.06.pdf (accessed 10.06.2014)
7. Armitage, S. *The Dead Sea Poems*. London: Faber and Faber, 1995. 16–17.
8. Arnold, M. *Poems*. London: M.J. Dent, 1959.
9. Arnold, M. *The Poems of Matthew Arnold, 1840–1867*. London, New York: Oxford University Press, 2011.
10. Astley, N. "The Wizard of [Uz]: Preface." *Bloodaxe Critical Anthologies: Tony Harrison*. Ed. Neil Astley. Newscastle: Bloodaxe Books, 1991. 10–14.
11. Bakhtin, M. M. *The Dialogic Imagination*. Ed. Michael Holquist. Trans. Caryl Emerson and Michael Holquist. University of Texas Press, 1981.
12. Barker, J. "Peru, Leeds, Florida and Keats." *Bloodaxe Critical Anthologies I: Tony Harrison*. Ed. Neil Astley. Newcastle upon Tyne: Bloodaxe Books, 1991. 46–54.
13. Barker, C. *Cultural Studies: Theory and Practice*. London: Sage Publications, 2008.
14. Baudrillard, J. *The Gulf War Did Not Take Place*. Trans. Paul Patton. Bloomington and Indianapolis: Indiana University Press, 1995.
15. Bauman, Z. "Tourists and Vagabonds: Heroes and Victims of Postmodernity." *Reihe Politikwissenschaft/Political Science Series*. Institute for Advanced Studies, Vienna, no. 30 (1996): 1–15.
16. Bauman, Z. *Identity: Conversations with Benedetto Vecchi*. Cambridge: Polity Press, 2007.
17. Bauman, Z. "Ponowoczesne wzory osobowe." *Studia socjologiczne*. Nr 2 (1993): 7–31.
18. Bauman, Z. *Modernity and Ambivalence*. Ithaca, New York: Cornell University Press, 1991.
19. Bell, D. *Kulturowe sprzeczności kapitalizmu*. Trans. S. Amsterdamski. Warszawa: PWN, 1998.
20. Benney, M. "The Legacy of Mining." *Mining and Social Change*. London: Croom Helm, 1978.
21. Berger, J. *About Looking*. London, Berlin, New York, Sidney: Bloomsbury, 2009.

22. Berger, J. "Photographs of Agony." *The Photography Reader*. Ed. Liz Wells. London and New York: Routledge, 2003. 288–290.
23. Bokszański, Z. *Tożsamości zbiorowe*. Warszawa: Wydawnictwo Naukowe PWN, 2007.
24. Bourke, J. *Working-Class Cultures in Britain 1890–1960: Gender, Class and Ethnicity*. London and New York: Routledge, 1994.
25. Bracewell, M. *England is Mine*. London: Harper Collins, 1997.
26. Bragg, M. "*V.* by Tony Harrison or Production No. 73095, LWT Arts." *Tony Harrison: Loiner*. Ed. Sandie Byrne. Oxford: Clarendon Press, 1997. 49–57.
27. Brecht, B. "Bad Time for Poetry." *Bad Time for Poetry: 152 Poems and Songs*. Ed. John Willet. Methuen, 1995.
28. Brooks, C. *The Well Wrought Urn: Studies in the Structure of Poetry*. London: Dennis Dobson, 1949.
29. Bulmer, M. "Social Structure and Social Change in the Twentieth Century." *Mining and Social Change: Durham County in the Twentieth Century*. London: Croom Helm, 1978, 15–48.
30. Bulmer, M. "Sociological Models of the Mining Community." *The Sociological Review*. Vol. 23, no. 1 (1975): 61–92.
31. Burton, R. "Tony Harrison: An Introduction." *Bloodaxe Critical Anthologies: Tony Harrison*. Ed. Neil Astley. Newscastle: Bloodaxe Books, 1991, 14–32.
32. Burzyńska, A. and M. P. Markowski, eds. *Teorie literatury XX wieku: Podręcznik*. Kraków: Wydawnictwo Znak, 2007.
33. Burzyńska, A., M. P. Markowski, eds. *Teorie literatury XX wieku: Antologia*. Kraków: Wydawnictwo Znak, 2006.
34. Butler, J. *Precarious Life and Obligations of Cohabitation*. Stockholm, Nobel Museum, May 2011. http://www.nobelmuseum.se/sites/nobelmuseet.se/files/page_file/Judith_Butler_NWW2011.pdf (accessed 2.01.2016).
35. Butler, J. *Precarious Life: The Powers of Mourning and Violence*. London and New York: Verso, 2004.
36. Butler, J. *Bodies that Matter*. London: Routledge, 1993.
37. Byrne, S. *H, v., & O. The Poetry of Tony Harrison*. Manchester: Manchester University Press, 1998. Byrne. Oxford: Clarendon Press, 1998. 137–161.
38. Byrne, S. "Introduction: Tony Harrison's Public Poetry." *Tony Harrison: Loiner*. Ed. Sandie Byrne. Oxford: Clarendon Press, 1997. 1–29.
39. Byrne, S. "On Not Being Milton, Marvell, or Gray." *Tony Harrison: Loiner*. Ed. Sandie Byrne. Oxford: Clarendon Press, 1997. 57–85.
40. Cabrita, J. *Mozambique: The Tortuous Road to Democracy*. New York: Macmillan, 2001.

41. Calhoun, C. "Social Theory and the Politics of Identity." *Social Theory and the Politics of Identity*. Ed. Craig Calhoun. Wiley Blackwell, 1994. 9–37.
42. Cameron, D. *Verbal Hygiene*. London: Routledge, 1995.
43. Campbell, B. *Wigan Pier Revisited: Poverty and Politics in the Eighties*. London: Virago, 1984.
44. Castells, M. *The Power of Identity*. Oxford: Blackwell Publishers, 2000.
45. Césaire, A. *Notebook of Return to the Native Land.* Trans. Mireille Rosello and Annie Pritchard. Newcastle upon Tyne: Bloodaxe Books, 1995.
46. Church, R., et al. "The 'Isolated Mass' Revisited: Strikes in British Coal Mining." *The Sociological Review*. Vol. 39, no.1 (1991): 55–87.
47. Clewell, T. "Mourning beyond melancholia: Freud's psychoanalysis of loss." *Journal of the American Psychoanalitic Association*. 52(1), (2004): 46–67.
48. Cote, J. E. and Charles G. Levine. *Identity, Formation, Agency and Culture: A Social Psychological Synthesis.* Mawhah, New Yersey, London: Lawrence Erlbaum Associates Publishers, 2002.
49. Craig, R. "Memory in Literature." *Memory an Anthology*. Eds Harriet Marvey and A. S. Byatt. Vintage Books: London, 2009. 28–40.
50. Cristopher, D. P. *British Culture: An Introduction.* London: Routledge, 2010.
51. Critchley, S. *Very Little ... Almost Nothing: Death, Philosophy and Literature.* London: Routledge, 2000.
52. Crowley, T. *Proper English: Readings in Language, History and Cultural Identity*. London: Routledge, 1991.
53. Crowley, T. *The Politics of Discourse: The Standard Language Question in British Cultural Debates*. London: Macmillan, 1989.
54. Crucefix, M. "The Drunken Porter Does Poetry: Meter and Voice in the Poems of Tony Harrison." *Tony Harrison: Loiner*. Ed. Sandie Byrne, Oxford: Clarendon Press, 1997. 161–167.
55. Davidson, P. *The Idea of North*. London: Reaktion Books, 2005.
56. De Man, P. "Autobiography as De-facement." *The Rhetoric of Romanticism*. New York: Columbia University Press, 1984. 68–81.
57. Defoe, D. *A Tour Through the Whole Island of Great Britain.* 3 vols. London: Peter Davis, 1927.
58. Derrida, J. *Memoirs of the Blind: The Self Portrait and Other Ruins.* Trans. Anne Brault and Michael Naas. Chicago, IL and London: University of Chicago Press, 1993.
59. Derrida, J. *Positions.* Chicago: University of Chicago Press, 1981.
60. Doniphan, L. *The Poetry of John Donne: A Study in Explication.* New York: Bookman Associates, 1951.

61. Donne, J. *The Complete English Poems.* Harmondsworth: Penguin Books, 1973.
62. Duffy, M. "The Progress of Love." *Bloodaxe Critical Anthologies: Tony Harrison.* Ed. Neil Astley. Newscastle: Bloodaxe Books, 1991. 338–346.
63. Dumitrescu, M. "2001: 11 Modernism, Postmodernism, and the Question of Identity." *Dialogos* 3/2001, 1–13.
64. Easthope, A. *Poetry as Discourse.* Methuen: 1983.
65. Edkins, J. *Trauma and the Memory of Politics.* Cambridge: Cambridge University Press, 2003.
66. Edwards, J. *Language and Identity: Key Topics in Sociolinguistic.* Cambridge: Cambridge University Press, 2009.
67. Eliot, T. S. "Journey of the Magi." *Collected Poems 1909–1962.* London: Faber, 1994.
68. Eliot, T. S. "The Waste Land." *Collected Poems 1909–1962.* London: Faber, 1994.
69. Empson, W. *Some Versions of a Pastoral.* UK, U.S.A.: Penguin Books, 1995.
70. Enfield, W. *A Familiar Treatise on Rhetoric.* London, 1809.
71. Erikson, E. *Identity: Youth and Crisis.* New York: Norton, 1968.
72. Eyre, R. "Such Men are Dangerous." *Bloodaxe Critical Anthologies I: Tony Harrison.* Ed. Neil Astley. Newcastle upon Tyne: Bloodaxe Books, 1991. 362–367.
73. Fanon, F. *Black Skin, White Masks.* Trans. Charles Lam Markmann. London: Pluto, 1993.
74. Fanon, F. *The Wretched of The Earth.* Harmondsworth: Penguin, 1965.
75. Foote, N. N. "Identification as a Basis for the Theory of Motivation." *American Sociological Review* 16, (1951): 14–21.
76. Forbes, P. "In the Canon's Mouth: Tony Harrison and Twentieth-Century Poetry." *Tony Harrison: Loiner.* Ed. Sandie Byrne. Oxford: Clarendon Press, 1997. 189–201.
77. Forbes, Peter. "The Bald Figures of Canaveral." *Bloodaxe Critical Anthologies I: Tony Harrison.* Ed. Neil Astley. Newcastle upon Tyne: Bloodaxe Books, 1991. 486–496.
78. Francis, H. "The Law, Oral Tradition and the Mining Community." *Journal of Law and Society.* Vol. 12, no. 3, (1985): 267–271.
79. Freud, S. "The Ego and the Id." *The Standard Edition of the Complete Psychological Works.* XIX. London: Hogarth Press, 1954.
80. Freud, S. "Mourning and Melancholia." *A General Selection from the Works of Sigmund Freud.* London: Hogarth Press, 1937.

81. Garofalakis, M. "One Continuous Us." *Bloodaxe Critical Anthologies I: Tony Harrison*. Ed. Neil Astley. Newcastle upon Tyne: Bloodaxe Books, 1991. 202–210.
82. Gaventa, J. *Power and Powerlessness*. Urbana, Chicago, London: University of Illinois Press, 1980.
83. Gecas V. and P. J. Burke. *Self and Identity Sociological Perspectives on Social Psychology*. Eds. K S. Cook, et al. Boston: Allyn and Becon, 1995. 41–67.
84. Geyer-Ryan, H. "Heteroglossia in the Poetry of Bertold Brecht and Tony Harrison". *The Taming of the Text*. Ed. Wille Van Peer. London: Routledge, 1988. 193–221.
85. Giddens, A. *Modernity and Self Identity*. Cambridge: Polity Press, 1991.
86. Gleason, P. "Identifying Identity: A Semantic History." *The Journal of American History*. 69.4 (1983): 910–931.
87. Gorer, G. *Death, Grief and Mourning*. Garden City: Doubleday, 1965.
88. Grant, D. "Poetry Versus History: Voices Off." *Bloodaxe Critical Anthologies I: Tony Harrison*. Ed. Neil Astley. Newcastle upon Tyne: Bloodaxe Books, 1991. 104–114.
89. Gray, T. "Elegy Written in a Country Churchyard." *The Norton Anthology of English Literature*. London: Norton and Company, 1993.
90. Gunn, T. *Boss Cupid*. London: Faber and Faber, 2000.
91. Habib, M. A. R. *A History of Literary Criticism and Theory*. Oxford: Blackwell Publishing, 2008.
92. Hacking, I. "Memoro-politics, Trauma and the Soul." *History of the Human Sciences* 7, 2, (1994): 29–52.
93. Hacking, I. *Rewriting the Soul: Multiple Personality and the Science of Memory*. Princeton, NJ.: Princeton University Press, 1995.
94. Haffenden, J. "Interview with Tony Harrison." *Bloodaxe Critical Anthologies: Tony Harrison*. Ed. Neil Astley. Newcastle upon Tyne: Bloodaxe Books, 1991. 227–247.
95. Hagberg, G. L. Ed. *Art and Ethical Criticism*. Oxford: Blackwell Publishing, 2008.
96. Hairsine, N. *I is the Other: Conflicts and Continuities of Identity in Tony Harrison's The Loiners, Continuous and v*. Newcastle upon Tyne: University of Newcastle upon Tyne, 1997.
97. Hall, E. "Classics, Class, and Cloaca: Harrison's Humane Coprology". *ARION* 15.2 Fall 2007. 113–135.
98. Hall, S. "Who Needs Identity?"*Cultural Identity*. Eds. Stuart Hall and Paul du Guy. Los Angeles and London: Sage Publications, 2008. 1–18.

99. Hall, S. "The Question of Cultural Identity." *Modernity and Its Futures*. Eds. S. Hall, D. Held and T. McGrew. Cambridge: Polity Press, 1992. 274–316.
100. Hargreaves, R. "Tony Harrison and the Poetry of Leeds." *Poetry in The British Isles: Non-Metropolitan Perspectives*. Ed. Hans Werner Ludwig, Cardiff: University of Wale Press, 1995. 23–151.
101. Harrison, T. "Cornet and Cartridge." *London Review of Books*. Vol. 33, no. 4 (2011): 11.
102. Harrison, T. *The Inky Digit of Defiance: The PEN/Pinter Prize Lecture*. Privately Printed for Faber and Faber, 2009.
103. Harrison, T. "Facing Up to the Muses." *Bloodaxe Critical Anthologies I: Tony Harrison*. Ed. Neil Astley. Newcastle upon Tyne: Bloodaxe Books, 1991. 429–455.
104. Harrison, T. "Preface to Palladas." *Bloodaxe Critical Anthologies I: Tony Harrison*. Ed. Neil Astley. Newcastle upon Tyne: Bloodaxe Books, 1991. 133–136.
105. Harrison, T. "The Inkwell of Dr Agrippa." *Bloodaxe Critical Anthologies I: Tony Harrison*. Ed. Neil Astley. Newcastle upon Tyne: Bloodaxe Books, 1991. 32–36.
106. Harrison, T. "The Memory of Troy." BBC Radio 4. 24 August 1988. Radio.
107. Harrison, T. "Black and white and red all over: The Fiction of Empire." *London Magazine*, N.S. 12 (3) Aug./Sept. 1972. 91–103.
108. Hartley, O. A. "The Second World War and After." *A History of Modern Leeds*. Ed. D. Fraser. Manchester: Manchester University Press, 1980. 437–461.
109. Helie, C. "Private Voice and Public Discourse: A Poetics of Northern Dialect." *Intimate Exposure: Essays on Public—Private Divide in British Poetry since 1950*. Eds. Emily Taylor Merriman and Adrian Grafe. North Caroline and London: McFarland and Company Inc., Publishers Jefferson, 2000.
110. Herron, T. et al. "Dislocations of Culture in Tony Harrison's 'Shrapnel.'" *Literature and History* 20(2) (2011): 68–82.
111. Hewitt, M. and R. Poole, "Samuel Bamford and Northern Identity." *Northern Idenities: Historical Interpretations of 'the North' and 'Northerness.'* Ed. Neville Kirk pp. 11–31. Aldershot: Ashgate, 2000.
112. Hirsch, E. and E. Bolan, eds. *The Making of a Sonnet: A Norton Anthology*. W.W. Norton & Company, 2008.
113. Hoggart, R. *The Uses of Literacy: Aspects of Working-class Life, with Special References to Publications and Entertainments*. New Brunswick and London: Transaction Publishers, 2005.

114. Hoggart, R. "In Conversation with Tony Harrison" *Bloodaxe Critical Anthologies I: Tony Harrison*. Ed. Neil Astley. Newcastle upon Tyne: Bloodaxe Books, 1991, 36–46.
115. Honey, J. *Does Accent Matter? The Pygmalion Factor.* London: Faber, 1989.
116. Hughes, T. "The Hughes and Crow, Interview with Ted Hughes." *Ted Hughes: The Unaccommodated Universe.* Ed. Ekbert Faas. Santa Barbara: Black Sparrow Press, 1980.
117. Huk, R. "Poetry of the Committed Individual: Jon Silkin, Tony Harrison. Geoffrey Hill and the Poets of Postwar Leeds." *Contemporary British Poetry: Essays in Theory and Criticism.* Ed. James Acheson and Romana Huk. New York: State University of New York Press, 1996.
118. Huk, R. "Tony Harrison and the 'Leeds Renaissance.'" *Bloodaxe Critical Anthologies I: Tony Harrison*. Ed. Neil Astley. Newcastle upon Tyne: Bloodaxe Books, 1991. 75–84.
119. Hyam, R. *Empire and Sexuality: The British Experience.* Manchester: Manchester University Press, 1990.
120. Jacobson-Widding, A. *Identity: Personal and Socio-Cultural; A Symposium.* Acta Universitatis Upsaliensis: Humanities Press, 1983.
121. Jackson, B. and Dennis Marsden. *Education and the Working Class.* Revival Books Ltd, 1986.
122. Jarniewicz, J. *Heaney: Wiersze pod dotyk.* Kraków: Wydawnictwo Znak, 2011.
123. Jarniewicz, J. *W brzuchu wieloryba: Szkice o dwudziestowiecznej poezji brytyjskiej i irlandzkiej.* Warszawa: Dom Wydawniczy Rebis, 2001.
124. Jarniewicz, J. *The Uses of the Commonplace in Contemporary British Poetry: Larkin, Dunn and Raine.* Łódź: Wydawnictwo Uniwersytetu Łódzkiego, 1994.
125. Jawłowska, A. „Tożsamość na Sprzedaż" *Wokół Problemów Tożsamości.* Ed. by A. Jawłowska. Warszawa: 2001. 51–79.
126. Jennings, Ch. *Up North: Travels Beyond the Watford Gap.* London: Abacus, 1995.
127. Jewell, H. *The North-South Divide: The Origins of Northern Consciousness in England.* Manchester: Manchester University Press, 1994.
128. Johnson, S. *The Lives of the Poets.* Oxford: Oxford University Press, 2009.
129. Kay, D. *Melodious Tears: The English Funeral Elegy from Spenser to Milton.* Oxford: Clarendon Press, 1990.
130. Keats, J. "Ode to the Grecian Urn". *The Oxford Book of English Verse: 1250–1900.* Ed. Arthur Quiller-Couch. Oxford: Clarendon, 1919.

131. Kelleher, J. *Tony Harrison*. UK: Northcote House, 1996.
132. Kennedy, D. *New Relations: The Refashioning of British Poetry 1980–94*. Bridgend, Mid Glamorgan: Poetry Wales Ltd., 1996.
133. Kennedy, D. *The New Critical Idiom: Elegy*. London and New York: Routledge, 2007.
134. Kerr, C. and A. Siegel, "The Interindustry Propensity to Strike – An International Comparison." *Industrial Conflict*. Eds A. Kornhauser et al. New York, Toronto, London: McGraw-Hill Book Compan, Inc., 1954.
135. Knightley, P., S. Jackson, & A. Merullo, eds. *The Eye of War: Words and Photographs from the Front Line*. Washington, DC: Smithsonian Books, 2003.
136. Kirk, N., ed. *Northern Identities: Historical Interpretations of 'the North' and Northerness'*. Aldershot: Ashgate, 2000.
137. Kracauer, S. *Ornament der Masse*. Frankfurt am Main: Suhrkamp, 1963.
138. Kristeva, J. *Intimate Revolt: The Powers and Limits of Psychoanalysis*. Vol. 2. New York: Columbia University Press, 2002.
139. Kristeva, J. *The Sense and Non-Sense of Revolt*. New York: Columbia University Press, 2000.
140. Kristeva, J. *Strangers to Ourselves*. London: Harvester Wheatsheaf, 1991.
141. Kuhn, A. *Family Secrets: Acts of Memory and Imagination*. London—New York: Verso, 1995.
142. Kundera, M. *Ignorance*. Trans. Lidia Aster. London: Faber and Faber, 2002.
143. Laclau, E. *New Reflections on the Revolution of Your Time*. London: Verso, 1990.
144. Lamb, C. "Tony Harrison." *Dictionary of Literary Biography: Poets of Great Britain and Ireland Since 1960*. Ed. Vincent B. Sherry, Jr, vol. 40, part 1, Columbia, SC: Bruccoli Clark BC Research (1985): 158–159.
145. Langbaum, R. *The Mysteries of Identity: A Theme in Modern Literature*. New York: Oxford University Press, 1977.
146. Lawler, S. *Identity: Sociological Perspectives*. Cambridge: Polity Press, 2010.
147. Lefevre, A. *Translation, Rewriting and the Manipulation of Literary Fame*. London: Routledge, 1992.
148. Levi, Peter. "Pagan Idioms." *Bloodaxe Critical Anthologies: Tony Harrison*. Ed. Neil Astley. Newscastle: Bloodaxe Books, 1991. 158–167.
149. Levi, Primo. *The Drowned and the Saved*. Trans. Raymond Rosenthal. London: Abacus, 1988. 63–64.
150. Levinas, E. "Peace and Proximity." *Basic Philosophical Writings*. Eds. T. Peperzak, et al. Bloomington: Indiana University Press, 1996. 161–171.

151. Levinas, E. *Ethics and Infinity*. Trans. Richard A. Cohen. Pittsburgh: Duquesne University Press, 1985.
152. Levinas, E. and R. Kearney. “Dialogue with Emmanuel Levinas.” *Face to Face with Levinas*. Albany: SUNY Press, 1986. 13–35.
153. Levine, G. C. *Identity Formation, Agency and Culture: A Social Psychological Synthesis*. Mahwah, NJ: Lawrence Erlbaum Associates, 2002.
154. Lilley, K. *To Dy in Writinge: Figure and Narrative in Masculine Elegy*. Unpublished PhD Thesis University of London, 1988.
155. Lim, M. “The Ethics of Alterity and the Teaching of Otherness.” *Business Ethics: A European Review* 16 (3) (2007): 251–263.
156. Lockwood, D. “Sources of Variation in Working-Class Images of Society.” *Working Class Images of Society*. Ed. M. Bulmer. London and Boston: Routledge and Kegan Paul, 1975.
157. Luhmann, N. *Love as Passion: The Codification of Intimacy*. Trans. Jeremy Gaines and Doris L. Jones. Cambridge, Mass.: Harvard University Press, 1986.
158. Lutz, T. *Crying: The Natural and Cultural History of Tears*. New York and London: W.W. Norton and Company, 1999.
159. MacNeice, L. “Epilogue for W.H. Auden.” *Letters from Iceland*. London: Faber & Faber, 1937.
160. Man, Paul de. “Autobiography As De-Facement.” *The Rhetoric of Romanticism*. New York: Columbia University Press, 1984. 67–83.
161. Marshall, C. “‘Inwardness’ and the ‘Quest for a Public Poetry’ in the Works of Tony Harrison.” *Intimate Exposure: Essays on Public—Private Divide in British Poetry since 1950*. Eds. Emily Taylor Merriman and Adrian Grafe. North Caroline and London: McFarland and Company, Inc., Publishers Jefferson, 2010.
162. Marshall, P. “Following the Fight to the Finish.” *Marxism Today*. Vol. 28, no. 12 (1984): 38–40.
163. Masefield, J. “Cargoes” http://allpoetry.com/Cargoes (accessed 01.12.2015).
164. Mcafee, N. *Routledge Critical Thinking: Julia Kristeva*. New York and London: Routledge, Taylor and Francis Group, 2007.
165. Mcquillan, M. *Routledge Critical Thinkers: Paul de Man*. London: Routledge, 2001.
166. Medhurst, A. *If Anywhere: Class Identifications and Cultural Studies Academics. Cultural Studies and the Working Class: Subject to Change*. Ed. Sally R. Munt. London and New York: Cassel, 2000. 19–35.

167. Merton, R. K. *Social Theory and Social Structure.* New York: The Free Press, A Division of Macmillan Publishing. 1968.
168. Milroy, J. and Milroy, L. *Authority in Language: Investigating Standard English.* London and New York: Routledge, 2005.
169. Milton, J. "To My Father" *Milton's Latin Poems.* Trans. David R. Slavitt. Baltymore, Meryland: John Hopkins University Press, 2011.
170. Misztal, B. A. *Theories of Social Remebering.* Maidenhead: Open University Press, 2003.
171. Misztal, B. *Globalizacja, ryzyko i tożsamość, Teoria socjologiczna a praktyka społeczna.* Kraków: Universitas, 2000.
172. Morrison, B. "The Filial Art." *Bloodaxe Critical Anthologies: Tony Harrison.* Ed. Neil Astley. Newcastle upon Tyne: Bloodaxe Books, 1991. 54–61.
173. Motion, A. "Poetry can speak decisively to power" http: // www.guardian.co.uk/ books/2007/oct/04/poetry.andrewmotion/ (accessed 01.01.2009).
174. Mugglestone, L. *Talking Proper: The Rise of Accent as Social Symbol.* Oxford: Oxford University Press, 2007.
175. Mulvey, L. (1975) "Visual Pleasure and Narrative Cinema" *Screen* 16.3, Autumn: 6–18.
176. Myers, A. 2004. *Myers Literary Guide.* http://www.seaham.i12.com/myers/mcleveland. html (accessed September 15, 2008).
177. Neruda, P. "Childhood and Poetry."*The Book of Virtues.* Ed. William J. Bennet. New York: Simon and Schuster, 1993. 339–340.
178. Nicholson, C. "Reciprocal Recognitions: Race, Class and Subjectivity in Tony Harrison's *The Loiners.*" *Sage Journals: Race and Class.* Vol. 51, no. 4 (2010): 59–78.
179. O'Brien, S. *The Deregulated Muse.* Newcastle upon Tyne: Bloodaxe Books, 1998.
180. Ovid. *Metamorphoses.* Trans. Frank Justus Miller. London: Heinemann, 1960.
181. Parkinson, W. E. "Poetry in the North East." *British Poetry Since 1960.* Eds. Schmidt, et al. Carcanet Press, 1972. 90–122.
182. Pascal, B. *Pensees.* Trans. Martin Turnell. London: Harvill Press, 1962.
183. Paxman, J. *The English: A Portrait of People.* London: Michael Joseph, 1998.
184. Poster, J. "Open to Experience: Structure and Exploration in Tony Harrison's Poetry." *Loiner.* Ed. Sandie Byrne. Oxford: Clarendon Press, 1997. 85–93.
185. Potts, A. F. *The Elegiac Mode: Poetic Form in Wordsworth and Other Elegists.* Ithaca: Cornell University Press, 1967.

186. Prager, J. "Melancholic Identity: Post-traumatic Loss Memory and Identity Formation." *Identity in Question*. Ed. Anthony Elliott and Paul du Gay. London: Sage Publication LTD, 2009. 138–157.
187. Proust, M. *In Search of Lost Time*. Trans. H. E. Butler, Cambridge, MA and London: Harvard University Press and William Heinemann, 2002.
188. Puttenham, G. *The Arte of English Poesie*. Ed. Edward Arber. London: Constable Facsimile, 1589/1909.
189. Raine, C. *Memories in Literature Memory. An Anthology*. Eds. Harriet Harvey Wood and A.S. Byatt. London: Vintage Books, 2009.
190. Ramazani, J. *Poetry of Mourning: The Modern Elegy from Hardy to Heaney*. Chicago and London: The University of Chicago Press, 1994.
191. Richards, A. J. *Miners in Strike: Class Solidarity and Division in Britain*. Oxford: Berg, 1996.
192. Ricœur, P. "Narrative and Time." *Critical Inquiry*. 7(1) (1980): 169–190.
193. Roberts, N. "Poetry and class: Tony Harrison, Peter Reading, Ken Smith, Sean O'Brien". *The Cambridge Companion to Twentieth-Century English Poetry*. Ed. N. Corcoran. Cambridge: Cambridge University Press, 2007. 215–229.
194. Roberts, N. *Narrative and Voice in Postwar Poetry*. London and New York: Longman, 1999.
195. Rose, J. *Intellectual Life of the British Working Classes*. New Haven: Yale University, 2002.
196. Ross, Ch. "The 'Body' in Fragments: Anxieties, Fascination and the Ideal of 'Wholeness.'" *Thinking in Fragments: Romanticism and Beyond*. University of Birmingham (UK), December 2010. Unpublished conference proceedings.
197. Rowland, A. "Mourning and Annihilation in Tony Harrison's The School of Eloquence." *Working Papers in Literary and Cultural Studies*. No. 27 (1998): 1–15.
198. Rowland, A. *Tony Harrison and the Holocaust* Liverpool: Liverpool University Press, 2001.
199. Royle, E. "Introduction: Region and Identities". *Issues Of Regional Identity*. Ed. Edward Royle. Manchester: Manchester University Press, 1998. 1–13.
200. Rusbridger, A. "Tony Harrison and The Guardian." *Tony Harrison: Loiner*. Ed. Sandy Byrne. Oxford: Clarendon Press, 1997. 133–136.
201. Russel, D. *Looking North: Northern English and the National Imagination*. Manchester: Manchester University Press, 2004.

202. Rutter, C. "Introduction." *Permanently Bard: Selected Poetry.* By Tony Harrison. Ed. Carol Rutter. Newcastle upon Tyne: Bloodaxe Books, 1995. 9–30.
203. Rylance, R. "On Not Being Milton." In: *Bloodaxe Critical Anthologies I: Tony Harrison*, Ed. Neil Astley. Newscastle: Bloodaxe Books, 1991.
204. Rylance, R. "Doomsongs: Tony Harrison and War". *Tony Harrison: Loiner.* Ed. Sandie Byrne. Oxford: Clarendon Press, 1997. 135–161.
205. Rylance, R. "On Not Being Milton." *Bloodaxe Critical Anthologies I: Tony Harrison.* Ed. Neil Astley. Newcastle upon Tyne: Bloodaxe Books, 1991. 10–14.
206. Sacks, P. M. *The English Elegy: Studies in the Genre from Spencer to Yeats.* Baltimore and London: The John Hopkins University Press, 1985.
207. Said, E. *Culture and Imperialism.* London: Chatto & Windus, 1993.
208. Samuel, R. *Theatres of Memory: Past and Present in Contemporary Culture.* London: Verso, 1994.
209. Savage, M., et al. "Local Habitus and Working-Class Culture." *Rethinking Class: Culture, Identities and Lifestyles.* Eds. F. Devine, et al. New York: Palgrave Macmillan, 2005. 95–122.
210. Schenck, C. M. "Feminism and Deconstruction: Re-Constructing the Elegy." *Tulsa Studies in Women's Literature.* Vol. 5, no. 1 (1986): 13–27.
211. Schenck, C. M. "When the Moderns Write Elegy: Crane, Kinsella, and Nemerov." *Classical and Modern Literature*, 1986. 97–108.
212. Schneider, D. M. *American Kinship: A Cultural Account.* Eaglewood Cliffs, NJ: Prentice Hall: 1968.
213. Scruton, R. "Photography and Representation." *The Aesthetic Understanding.* London: Methuen, 1983.
214. Shaw, W. D. "Elegy and Theory: Is Historical and Critical Knowledge Possible?" *Modern Language Quarterly.* Vol. 55, no. 1 (1994b): 1–16.
215. Shaw, W. D. *Elegy and Paradox: Testing the Conventions.* Baltimore and London: The John Hopkins University Press, 1994a.
216. Short, J. R. *Imagined Country: Environment, Culture and Society.* London: Routledge, 1991.
217. Silkin, J. Ed. *Poetry of the Committed Individual: A Stand Anthology of Poetry*. London: Victor Gollancz Ltd, 1973.
218. Skarga, B. *Tożsamość i różnica. Eseje metafizyczne.* Kraków: Wydawnictwo Literackie, 1997.
219. Skeggs, B. *Class, Self, Culture*. London: Routledge, 2004.

220. Smith, E. ed. *By Mourning Tongues: Studies in English Elegy.* Boyden Press, Rowman and Littlefield, 1977.
221. Sontag, S. *On Photography*. London: Penguin Books, 2008.
222. Sontag, S. *Regarding the Pain of Others.* London: Penguin Books, 2004.
223. Spencer, L. *The Poetry of Tony Harrison.* London: Harvester Wheatsheaf, 1994.
224. Stanley, L. *The Auto/biographical I.* Manchester: Manchester University Press, 1992.
225. Stantner, E. L. *Stranded Objects: Mourning, Memory, and Film in Postwar Germany.* Ithaca, N.Y: Cornell University Press, 1990.
226. Steedman, C. *Landscape for Good Women: A Story of Two Lives.* London: Virago, 1986.
227. Sturken, M. and Cartwright, L. *Practices of Looking: An Introduction to Visual Culture.* Oxford: Oxford University Press, 2001.
228. Sweet, H. *The Sounds of English.* Oxford: 1908.
229. Taylor, P. M. "The Meaning of the North: England's 'Foreign Country' Within". *Political Geography 12.* 1993. 136–155.
230. Taylor, P. M. *War and Media: Propaganda and Persuasion in the Gulf War.* Manchester and New York: Manchester University Press, 1998.
231. Thébia-Melsan, A., ed. *Aimé Césaire, pour regarder le siècle en face.* Paris: Maisonneuve & Larose, 2000.
232. Thomas, L. "Variation in English Grammar." *English: History, Diversity and Change.* Eds David Graddol, et al. London: Routledge, 1996.
233. Thompson, E. P. *The Making of the English Working Class.* London: Victor Gollancz Ltd, 1963.
234. Thompson, N. S. "Book Ends: Public and Private in Tony Harrison's Poetry." *Tony Harrison: Loiner.* Ed. Sandie Byrne. Oxford: Clarendon Press, 1997. 115–133.
235. Thornborrow, J. "Language and Identity". *Language, Society and Power.* Eds. Linda Thomas, et al. London and New York: Routledge, 2005. 157–172.
236. Tonkin, E. *Narrating Our Pasts: The Social Construction of Oral History.* Cambridge: CUP, 1992.
237. Turner, R. H. (1976). "The Real Self: From Institution to Impulse." *American Journal of Sociology.* No. 81: 989–1016.
238. Tusa, J. "Interview with Tony Harrison." *The John Tusa Interviews* BBC Radio 3 4 Nov. 2001. http://www.bbc.co.uk/programmes/p00nc89r broadcast (accessed 14.06.2014)

239. Valbuena, O. L. "The Dyer's Hand: the Reproduction of Coercion and Blot in Shakespeare Sonnets." *Shakespeare's Sonnets: Critical Essays*. Ed. James Schiffer. New York: Garland Publishing Inc., 2000. 325–347.
240. Van Wolputte, S. "Hang on to Your Self: Of Bodies, Embodiment, and Selves." *The Annual Review of Anthropology*. Vol. 33 (2004): 251–269.
241. Waldenfels, B. "Levinas and The Face of the Other." *The Cambridge Companion to Levinas*. Eds. Simon Critchley and Robert Bernasconi. Cambridge: Cambridge University Press, 2004. 64–81.
242. Wales, K. *Northern English: A Social and Cultural History*. Cambridge: Cambridge University Press, 2008.
243. Watkin, W. *On Mourning: Theories of Loss in Modern Literature*. Edinburgh: Edinburgh University Press, 2004.
244. Watts, R. "From Polite Language to Educated Language: The Re-Emergence of Ideaology." *Alternative Histories of English*. Eds R. Watts and T. Trudgill, London: Routledge, 2002. 155–172.
245. Weigert, A. J. et al., *Society and Identity*. New York: Cambridge University Press, 1986.
246. Whitehead, A. "Tony Harrison, The Gulf War and the Poetry of Protest". *Textual Practice* 19(2) (2005): 349–372.
247. Whitehead, A. *The New Critical Idiom: Memory*. London and New York: Routledge, 2009.
248. Widdowson, H. G. "Person to Person: Relationships in the Poetry of Tony Harrison." *Twentieth-Century Poetry: From Text to Context*. Ed. Peter Verdonk. Routledge: London and New York, 1993.
249. Winter, J. *Sites of Memory, Sites of Mourning*. Cambridge: Cambridge University Press, 1995.
250. Wordsworth, W. *The Prelude—The 1805 Text*. Oxford: Oxford University Press, 1986.
251. Worpole, K. "Scholarship Boy." *Bloodaxe Critical Anthologies I: Tony Harrison*. Ed. by Neil Astley. Newscastle: Bloodaxe Books, 1991. 61–75.
252. Zadura, B. *Zamiast Wstępu*. http://www.swistak.pl/aukcje/3.608134/Kumkwat-dla-Johna-Keatsa-Tony -Harrison.html/ (accessed January 1, 2009).
253. Zandy, J. *Liberating Memory: Our Work and Our Working-Class Consciousness*. New Brunswick, NJ: Rutgers University Press, 1994.
254. Zeiger, M. F. *Beyond Consolation: Death, Sexuality, and the Changing Shapes of Elegy*. Ithaca and London: Cornell University Press, 1997.
255. Žižek, S. "Melancholy and the Act" *Critical Inquiry*. Vol. 26, no. 4 (2000): 657–68.

Gdańsk Transatlantic Studies in British and North American Culture

Edited by Marek Wilczyński

The interdisciplinary series "GdańskTransatlantic Studies in British and North American Culture" brings together literary and cultural studies concerning literatures and cultures of the English-speaking world, particularly those of Great Britain, Ireland, the United States, and Canada. The range of topics to be addressed includes literature, theater, film, and art, considered in various twenty-first-century theoretical perspectives, such as, for example (but not exclusively), New Historicism and canon formation, cognitive narratology, gender and queer studies, performance studies, memory and trauma studies, and New Art History. The editors are leaving a broad margin for the innovative and the unpredictable, hoping to attract authors whose approaches will point to new directions of research as regards both thematic areas and methods. Comparative Polish-Anglo-American proposals will be considered, too.

Vol. 1 Mirosława Modrzewska: Byron and the Baroque. 2013.

Vol. 2 Andrzej Ceynowa / Marek Wilczyński (eds.): American Experience – The Experience of America. 2013.

Vol. 3 Marta Koval: "We search the Past...for Our Own Lost Selves." Representations of Historical Experience in Recent American Fiction. 2013.

Vol. 4 Tomasz Basiuk: Exposures. American Gay Men´s Life Writing since Stonewall. 2013.

Vol. 5 Klara Naszkowska: The Living Mirror. The Representation of Doubling Identities in the British and Polish Women's Literature (1846–1938). 2014.

Vol. 6 Urszula Elias / Agnieszka Sienkiewicz-Charlish (eds.): Crime Scenes. Modern Crime Fiction in an International Context. 2014.

Vol. 7 Justyna Kociatkiewicz / Laura Suchostawska/Dominika Ferens (eds.): Eating America. Crisis, Sustenance, Sustainability. 2014.

Vol. 8 Agnieszka Pantuchowicz / Sławomir Masłoń (eds.): Affinities. Essays in Honour of Professor Tadeusz Rachwał. 2014.

Vol. 9 Janusz Semrau / Marek Wilczyński (eds.): Image in Modern(ist) Verse. 2015.

Transatlantic Studies in British and North American Culture

Edited by Marek Wilczyński

Vol. 10 Małgorzata Grzegorzewska / Jean Ward / Mark Burrows (eds.): Breaking the Silence. Poetry and the Kenotic Word. 2015.

Vol. 11 Dominika Oramus: Charles Darwin's Looking Glass. The Theory of Evolution and the Life of its Author in Contemporary British Fiction and Non-Fiction. 2015.

Vol. 12 Miłosz Wojtyna: The Ordinary and the Short Story. Short Fiction of T.F. Powys and V.S. Pritchett. 2015.

Vol. 13 Bartosz Wójcik: Afro-Caribbean Poetry in English. Cultural Traditions (1970s-2000s). 2015.

Vol. 14 Izabela Morska: Glorious Outlaws: Debt as a Tool in Contemporary Postcolonial Fiction. 2016.

Vol. 15 Edyta Frelik: Painter's Word. Thomas Hart Benton, Marsden Hartley and Ad Reinhardt as Writers. 2016.

Vol. 16 Małgorzata Grzegorzewska: George Herbert and Post-phenomenology. A Gift for Our Times. 2016.

Vol. 17 Anna Cholewa-Purgał: Therapy Through Faërie. Therapeutic Properties of Fantasy Literature by the Inklings and by U. K. Le Guin. 2016.

Vol. 18 Agata Handley: Constructing Identity. Continuity, Otherness and Revolt in the Poetry of Tony Harrison. 2016.

Vol. 19 Dominika Oramus: Ways of Pleasure. Angela Carter's 'Discourse of Delight' in her Fiction and Non-Fiction. 2016.

Vol. 20 Aneta Dybska: Regeneration, Citizenship, and Justice in the American City since the 1970s. 2016.

Vol. 21 Maciej Reda: The Apology for Catholicism in Selected Writings by G. K. Chesterton. 2016.

Vol. 22 Przemysław Uściński: Parody, Scriblerian Wit and the Rise of the Novel. Parodic Textuality from Pope to Sterne. 2016.

www.peterlang.com

www.ingramcontent.com/pod-product-compliance
Ingram Content Group UK Ltd.
Pitfield, Milton Keynes, MK11 3LW, UK
UKHW041414270426
12127UKWH00002B/7

9 783631 658819